Help

Saint Germain

Stop Poverty

Spiritualizing the World, vol 4

Help

Saint Germain

Stop Poverty

KIM MICHAELS

Copyright © 2016 Kim Michaels. All rights reserved. No part of this book may be used, reproduced, translated, electronically stored or transmitted by any means except by written permission from the publisher. A reviewer may quote brief passages in a review.

MORE TO LIFE PUBLISHING

www.morepublish.com

For foreign and translation rights,

contact info@ morepublish.com

ISBN: 978-87-93297-33-3

The information and insights in this book should not be considered as a form of therapy, advice, direction, diagnosis, and/or treatment of any kind. This information is not a substitute for medical, psychological, or other professional advice, counseling and care. All matters pertaining to your individual health should be supervised by a physician or appropriate health-care practitioner. No guarantee is made by the author or the publisher that the practices described in this book will yield successful results for anyone at any time. They are presented for informational purposes only, as the practice and proof rests with the individual.

For more information: *www.ascendedmasterlight.com and www.transcendencetoolbox.com*

CONTENTS

Introduction 7

Introduction to Saint Germain 11

1 | Poverty Is not the Will of God 15

2 | Invoking the Will to Overcome Poverty 37

3 | Overcoming Poverty through God Wisdom 73

4 | Invoking the Wisdom to Overcome Poverty 95

5 | Reconnect to Your Highest Love 133

6 | Invoking the Love to Overcome Poverty 153

7 | Poverty Is Hatred of the Mother 189

8 | Invoking Purity to Consume Hatred of the Mother 211

9 | With Pure Vision You Manifest a Golden Age 249

10 | Invoking Vision to Overcome Poverty 271

11 | True Service Means Acceleration into Unity 307

12 | Invoking an Acceleration of Service 321

13 | Freedom Means Surrender into Oneness 357

14 | Invoking Freedom from the Fear of Making Choices 389

15 | Protecting Yourself from the Fallen Beings 425

16 | Protection from Dark Forces 433

INTRODUCTION

This book belongs to the series *Spiritualizing the World*. The books in this series are given by the ascended masters as workbooks that provide the knowledge and practical tools we need in order to make a contribution to solving concrete world problems. This book obviously contains the knowledge and the tools we need in order to deal with the problem of poverty. These books do not contain foundational knowledge about ascended masters and their teachings. In order to make the most efficient use of this book, you need to have a general knowledge of the following topics:

- You need to know who the ascended masters are, how they give their teachings and how you can make the best use of them on a personal and planetary level. You can find extensive teachings on this in the books: *How You Can Help Change the World* and *The Power of Self*.

- You need to know how the earth functions as a cosmic schoolroom. You need to know your own role and the authority you have as a spiritual being in embodiment. You need to know the role of the ascended masters and how only we who are in embodiment can give them the authority to use their unlimited power to affect change on earth. You can find more on these topics in the first book in this series: *How You Can Help Change the World.*

- You need to know how to use the practical tools given by the ascended masters. You can find more on this topic in: *How You Can Help Change the World* and on the website: *www.transcendencetoolbox.com.*

- You need to know about the existence and methods of the dark forces who are ultimately responsible for creating poverty and war on earth. You can find foundational teachings on this in: *Cosmology of Evil.*

How to use this book

There is no one way of using the teachings and tools in this book. However, if you want to make a significant contribution to stopping poverty, it is suggested that you start by following this program:

- You read one of the chapters in the book completely in order to increase your understanding of the topic.

- You give the invocation associated with that chapter once a day for nine days while studying the same chapter again.

The reasoning behind this program is that the chapters in the book form a progression. As you give an invocation for one chapter, you are also clearing your own consciousness from certain energies and illusions. This makes it easier for you to absorb and apply the teachings from the next chapter.

You can, of course, also read the book all the way through and then select one or more invocation(s) that you give several times. It is always more powerful to give an invocation once a day for nine or 33 days.

If you feel burdened

The purpose of this book is not to merely give you intellectual knowledge. The real purpose is that you give the invocations, whereby you give the ascended masters the authority to remove the dark forces and energies that promote poverty. These forces will not be happy that you contribute to the process of removing them from the earth. They may therefore seek to direct energy at you that can make you feel burdened in various ways. Their purpose is to make you stop your efforts (or prevent you from starting).

If you feel burdened, please read the last chapter in the book and use the invocation associated with that chapter to make the calls for the protection of yourself and all people around you. As stated in that chapter, most people can quickly come to a point where they are no longer vulnerable to the attacks from the forces of darkness.

The dark forces will always seek to inflate any condition in our personal lives that makes us vulnerable. If you have particular issues, it may be helpful to use other tools that address those issues in a more direct manner. The ascended masters have given many invocations and decrees that can help you deal with specific topics, and you can find most of them on *www.transcendencetoolbox.com*. Some tools are found in the other books by Kim Michaels, and you can see them on *www.morepublish.com*.

It is important that a certain number of people give the invocations and transcend the consciousness behind poverty. It is highly recommended that you talk to other people about this book, including using social media. If enough people use this book and its invocations, it will be possible for the ascended masters to remove poverty from earth within the foreseeable future. *Isn't that a message worth spreading?*

INTRODUCTION TO SAINT GERMAIN

Saint Germain is the hierarch or overseer of the Aquarian Age who holds the Flame of Freedom for the earth. For the next 2,000 years, Saint Germain will be the primary architect for humankind's spiritual and material development. He has a vision of making this time period a golden age with tremendous progress in all areas of society. This plan is, as everything else, subject to the free will of people in embodiment. It is up to us to open ourselves to receive Saint Germain's vision and to bring it into physical manifestation through our calls and actions.

During the 1500's and 1600's Saint Germain worked with many of the kings of Europe, seeking to establish a United Nations of Europe. He was known as the Wonderman of Europe because he performed various miraculous feats, such as removing flaws from diamonds, appearing out of nowhere and maintaining a youthful appearance for over a century.

During the 1930's Saint Germain released a number of violet flame decrees and affirmations. Up until then, the violet flame had been known only to initiates of secret societies and orders. Saint Germain received a special dispensation to release the knowledge of the violet flame to the general public.

Saint Germain has said about himself: I, as the Being known on earth as Saint Germain, chose to embody the quality of God Freedom, for this seemed to me to be the most desirable quality. I recognize that there are other God qualities that are equally valuable, but I chose to embody Freedom as my individual choice. I AM a spiritual Being who is holding what we might call a spiritual flame for the earth, the Flame of Freedom, my beloved.

Everything on earth, as your scientists have already discovered, is made from energy. Energy is a form of vibration. Your scientists have not yet fully understood energy, for energy truly is an expression of a finer quality. Physical energy is an expression of what we might call spiritual energy. But spiritual energy does not take the form of a physical something that can drive your electrical motors or have other effects.

Spiritual energy will appear to you as a fire, as a flame. When Moses, on the mountain, encountered this spiritual energy, you saw the bush burning without being consumed. Thus, the saying: "Our God is a consuming fire" that consumes all unlike itself, all that would trap you in a lesser sense of identity. The Flame of Freedom is indeed a form of spiritual energy that has the potential to burn away all limitations that trap you in a limited sense of identity.

Yet my beloved, you need to recognize that, on planet earth, everything revolves around free will. I am a spiritual Being, and I have become one with the Flame of Freedom. That flame is an expression of the infinite God. It has infinite potential. It can consume anything and everything that is limiting you.

Introduction to Saint Germain

I, Saint Germain, will not consume your limitations unless you use your free will to give up those limitations, which not only involves simply saying: "Saint Germain, take away my limitations." It involves you recognizing that you have created those limitations by accepting imperfect beliefs and images about yourself, God and the world.

Before you can actually let go of those limitations, you must take ownership of your limitations by recognizing that you have created them by accepting imperfect beliefs and images. You must then see through those imperfect beliefs and images, see through the reasoning and the consciousness behind it, and then replace those limiting choices with better choices that set you free from your current limitations. When you have been willing to make that shift in consciousness, then you have the potential to make the choice to let go of what limits you, my beloved. Until you have seen through the limitations and why they limit you, then you simply cannot let go of them.

Only when you let go, can I then step in and through my Flame of Freedom burn away the imperfect energies so that you are now free to walk higher on your personal path toward freedom. My purpose is to set you free individually, to give you teachings and tools that can set you free. More than that, I want to set humanity free so that this earth can rise to what I call my Golden Age—that I envision for the earth.

This is an age in which, I can assure you, you do not find the limitations in human society that you see all around you, and which I am sure you have experienced up until this point in your life. My purpose here is to give you, not simply a hope, but to give you teachings and tools that will allow you to come to the point of an inner knowing where you know that this planet has the potential to rise into a Golden Age.

You personally have the potential to rise, not only to a Golden Age but to rise above any limitations in the material realm and win your freedom as an immortal spiritual Being. The basic message is that, I, Saint Germain, have risen above the limitations on Earth and the motto of the ascended masters is: "What one has done, all can do." Learn from me, learn from other members of the ascended masters and see that you too can be free!

1 | POVERTY IS NOT THE WILL OF GOD

Saint Germain I AM, and I am grateful to be given a platform on this continent of South America, to bring forth a teaching that will be essential and instrumental for bringing about the Golden Age—both here in South America and elsewhere. You might recall that some time ago the Great Divine Director, my own guru, gave a dictation through this messenger at Machu Picchu where he talked about the potential for bringing about a Golden Age in South America. He gave a somewhat sober and somber assessment of that potential.

This was partly because we wanted an expression of the difficulty that we face in bringing about a Golden Age on a continent like South America, and other continents in the world. Because we want the people to understand, that bringing about a Golden Age is not an easy thing, nor is it a sure thing. There can be no absolute guarantee that a Golden Age will come about for everything is up to the free will of the inhabitants of this planet.

A new dispensation from the Great Central sun

We of the ascended masters have the Victory Consciousness and never, ever accept defeat or that anything is impossible. What has happened in the meantime is that so many people in South America, especially here in Colombia, and in many other parts of the world have been more willing to come up higher in consciousness—partly through the teachings given, partly through the invocations and partly simply because they are flowing with the River of Life. Even though many have never heard of the ascended masters, they realize that the winds of change, the winds of the Holy Spirit, have started blowing on a planetary scale. They have stood up more straight and looked up higher to their own higher being – however they conceive of it – for new ideas and new ways of thinking of how to solve society's problems.

Because of this response from the people – both in and out of the teachings of the ascended masters – I have decided to travel from the earth to the Great Central sun and plead before Alpha and Omega for a new dispensation, a very important release of light, that can bring about one of the changes that are necessary for the Golden Age to be manifest. This is a specific dispensation of light, that has the effect of illuminating one of the major problems that blocks the Golden Age.

My beloved, going before the throne of Alpha and Omega and asking for a dispensation for planet earth is no straight-forward matter. This planet is a very, very small planet in a very, very large physical universe. You understand that Alpha and Omega are the highest manifestations of God known in this material universe. They hold the vision and the spiritual balance for the immensity of the entire material universe with all of the many lifestreams and lifewaves that are evolving in this platform. Their role is to always hold the vision of the whole.

They cannot ever allow the needs of one particular part of that whole to jeopardize or hold back the forward movement of the whole itself.

That is why the ascended masters, who work with planet earth, sometimes – in our eagerness to help humankind, in our eagerness to see this planet have a breakthrough to a higher level – can become a little bit focused on this planet, thinking that if only we could help this planet grow, we could surely help the entire universe. Not that this is necessarily wrong. But I can tell you – as one who has traveled to the Great Central sun on several occasions on behalf of planet earth – that being in the Presence of Alpha and Omega – and suddenly seeing that overall perspective – can be very sobering, even for an ascended master.

When you stand in that Court of the Sacred Fire and see the immensity of the flames of Alpha and Omega, the figure-eight flow between them and the white cube between their thrones, suddenly you are jolted out of any lesser manifestation. You see that before a dispensation can be granted to planet earth, one must first look at the whole and carefully weigh the balances of the whole versus the needs of one little planet.

A cosmic perspective on the earth

I am not trying to make you think that earth is insignificant. I am simply trying to give you a realistic perspective of what it feels like, even for an ascended master, to stand before the throne of Alpha and Omega and ask for a dispensation for this planet. I want you to realize that such a dispensation is not given lightly and is not something that is granted automatically because some ascended master – whom you might think is very important – suddenly shows up at Alpha and Omega's doorstep and asks for it. It is important for you, as the spiritual people, to realize that while planet earth is important in the cosmic perspective, it is still only one part of a very large whole. As I have said before, we have yet other worlds to conquer. In fact, we have many other worlds to conquer. I can assure you that it is very healthy for the spiritual people on earth to once in a while be jolted out of the mental box that is of necessity focused on this planet, and realize that there is a very vast universe and that this entire universe is connected as one whole. The needs of one planet, such as earth, must be seen in connection with the whole and with all aspects of that whole who are evolving and who are tied to earth. Therefore, everything must evolve harmoniously and together. If you have the Body of God and suddenly one foot starts lagging behind, or one hand starts moving beyond the rest of the body, well then what have you? You do not have harmony. You do not have coherence.

Having given you this realistic assessment, I can with great joy tell you that I have been granted this dispensation of an extraordinary release of light to planet earth. This release of light will do one very specific thing. It will focus attention on the one problem that right now is a major block to the manifestation of the Golden Age. It will literally illumine that problem to the point where it will become more and more difficult for humankind to ignore that problem.

People will, so to speak, be "forced" by the light to look at that problem, to examine its cause. They need to make the choice of whether they will move out of the consciousness that has caused the problem or whether they will choose to stay in that consciousness. If they stay, they will be judged by the light so that they will eventually be removed from this planet and go to some other system where this particular manifestation can still be tolerated. Within a very short time span, this manifestation will no longer be tolerated on earth. The light will simply make it impossible that this manifestation can continue. That is, if the light is accepted and multiplied by those in embodiment, such as yourselves, but also by many other people who are in position in society worldwide to do something about this particular problem.

The problem of poverty

What is the problem that I am talking about? What is the one problem that right now is the greatest block to the manifestation of a Golden Age? Well, my beloved, it is the problem of poverty. That is precisely why I am giving this dictation and the following dictations on this continent of South America where there is indeed great poverty.

Obviously, this is not the only continent that has this manifestation. It is indeed a continent where there is a potential that the people can be awakened and can move away from poverty without falling into the trap of materialism, of what you see going on right now in certain nations in South East Asia and in China herself. The people are awakened to the potential to overcome poverty, but they are becoming sucked into the vortex, the beast, of materialism. This beast has taken over the West and has reigned the West and the thinking of the West for a long time now, far longer than it was necessary.

I will in this and the following discourses give you some teachings on poverty and the cause of poverty and the consciousness behind it. Let me make one thing perfectly clear: We of the ascended masters are committed to completely and utterly eradicating poverty on planet earth!

You do not seriously believe that you can have a Golden Age and still have a majority of the world's population living below the poverty level, not knowing where their next meal will come from, not knowing where they are going to find safe drinking water that will not make them sick, not knowing how to have a way to provide an income for themselves or their family, not knowing how to have a sustainable growth in their material wealth, in their spiritual wealth, in their free time? Seriously, you cannot believe that it would be possible to have a Golden Age and still have these manifestations of poverty that you see, not only on this continent, but several other places You even see it in some of the so-called rich nations where you see a small percentage of the population living in abject poverty with absolutely no hope and no viable physical path for overcoming that condition.

The ascended masters are NOT elitists

Let it be made absolutely clear that we of the ascended masters are not elitists! I am making this statement specifically because those of you who know of our history on this planet will know that in the past we have worked with those who were in power, those who formed the elite. This was done out of a realistic assessment of who had the potential to bring about positive changes in society. It was also done because in the Piscean age one of the challenges facing humankind was precisely the concept of elitism. The question was whether a small elite should rule the people or whether the people would free themselves from elitism and the consciousness of elitism and acknowledge the power of God within them. This was what Jesus demonstrated to humankind 2,000 years ago by acknowledging the power of God within himself.

We have in the past – when necessity called for it – worked with certain people who belonged to an elite. What has shifted in the meantime is two things. Number one: we are moving rapidly into the Aquarian age and the Aquarian age consciousness. We have moved into the Aquarian age, but we have not yet made the shift, the shift in the collective consciousness, where most people on this planet can tune in to the Aquarian age consciousness and leave behind the Piscean consciousness. That is why I say we are moving into the Aquarian age.

The other major thing that has happened is that – due in no small part to my own dispensations of working with science and bringing forth communications technology – we now have the communications technology that makes it possible to spread knowledge very quickly to the people independently of the elite. People all over this planet – the little people, so to speak, those who are not members of the elite – can communicate with each other in a way that is unprecedented and has not been seen before on this planet, unless you go very far back to past Golden Ages.

This is a major opportunity for the creation of a dramatic shift in the collective consciousness by people who are connected all over the world. They can suddenly become aware of new ideas and gain a new understanding of an old problem, a new way to look at that problem and its potential solutions. Do you see what an incredible opportunity it is through the internet and other ways of communication? Yes I know that you can look at the internet and see how it is certainly also being misused, as new technology has always been misused. You can look at it being used to spread pornography. You can look at how many people are into social networking that really has no direct effect on raising people's consciousness.

You might look deeper and see that just by the mere fact that people all over the world are beginning to communicate – even if they do so in seemingly mundane ways – it is still providing the potential for a shift in the collective consciousness that is unprecedented in known history. The collective consciousness has the potential to actually be reborn into a higher awareness. What is now social networking and seemingly superficial can quickly become a way to really spread new ideas and new understandings that transcend all national borders, transcend race, religion, ethnicity, transcends continents. Suddenly, this shifts the collective consciousness to a new awareness that a certain particular problem is no longer acceptable and that it has an actual viable solution. People no longer need to accept it as something that cannot be solved.

Poverty is a form of energy

This is precisely the major problem with poverty. Poverty is, as everything else in the material universe, a very specific form of energy, a very specific vibration. Poverty has been around now for quite some time. You can go back in history, and you will see that there have been many societies, even in known history, where there was not the extreme form of poverty that you see in today's world. There have been many societies where – even though people were by no means rich according to today's standards – there were very few people who did not have food on the table and a viable way to provide that food through farming or through working for society.

The modern world has in many ways made poverty worse. It has also made it possible that some people in some nations have become very rich, much richer than you have seen in known history. This has created the greater contrast between those who are rich and those who are poor. This has created a vortex of the energy of poverty that has actually increased on a

1 | Poverty Is not the Will of God

planetary level over the last several hundred years, going back to the beginning of what is called the Dark Ages in Europe. There you saw for the first time – with the advent of the feudal societies – some people who were living at extreme levels of poverty that were rarely seen, even in previous societies where they also had something rather similar to the feudal system that you saw in Europe. You have seen in medieval Europe greater poverty, greater misery than you have seen in many past societies.

From the Middle Ages forward, the planetary vortex of poverty, of the energy of poverty, has increased in strength. It has also been balanced by a positive – at least partially positive – building of a momentum of a vortex of victory, of the abundance consciousness. As so often happens when things are polarized, you have certain areas of the planet where the vortex, the spiral, of abundance is quite strong.

Then you have others where the vortex of poverty has grown very strong and very powerful, to the point where it overpowers most of the people who live in those areas. It overpowers them to the point where they simply cannot see and cannot believe how they could possibly escape the extreme poverty in which they were born, in which they have grown up, in which they have grown old, and in which they think they are destined to die.

This, my beloved, is clearly what you see in South America. Even here in Colombia you see a percentage of the population who live in a state of consciousness where they can never even conceive of overcoming their current level of abundance, or rather lack of it. You see other nations, such as Peru, where it is even more pronounced and where the vortex of poverty is even stronger.

Poverty and the First Ray of God's Will

What is the effect of this vortex, other than overpowering and pacifying the people who are affected by it? How exactly does it overpower them? How does it affect them? Why not begin at the very beginning, with the first of the seven rays, which is the Ray of the Will of God. The First Ray is the Will of God because the first act of creation was God's will to create, God's will to be *more. That,* my beloved, is why the Chohan of the first ray is the master El Morya, who is now the Master MORE, to fully embody even in his name that quality of becoming more.

You cannot separate the will of God from the will to be more. They are one and the same. This is one of the fundamental shifts that needs to happen, especially among the top 10 percent of the most spiritual people. We have talked before of the need to overcome your sense that there is a remote God up in heaven who has a will for you that he is trying to force upon you. We have given the magnificent Invocation of the Will of God specifically to help you with this. I am asking you to even make a higher shift in consciousness where you realize that will is not something static, will is not something that says: "This is the way things should be, now and forever."

If everything on this planet in an instant was brought into alignment with the will of God, do you think growth would stop on this planet? Nay, for what is the will of God? It is that everything becomes more by transcending itself until everything becomes the fullness of what God is. Of course, as those who are extensions of God's Being become more, then God's Being becomes more. Therefore, the fullness of what God is, is becoming more all the time. This is a wondrous, never-ending process of alchemy where the baser – that which is here now – can always be transcended into the gold of that which is more. You need to make that shift in consciousness because only by doing that will you overcome the programming – the subtle lies that have been programmed into the collective consciousness on this planet for centuries and beyond – about the will of God and poverty. Those who are the brothers of darkness, those who are the forces of anti-christ, have spread their lies into the collective consciousness that poverty is somehow inevitable because it is either the will of God or an expression of the laws of nature.

Religion and poverty

Many religions on this earth have been elitist in nature and in practice. They have brought forth an elitist doctrine that has maintained a status quo that allowed a small elite to have an ungodly control over the majority of the population. They have been able to have privileges for themselves – such as great wealth – because they took the wealth and the abundance from the people, keeping the people at an artificial level of poverty.

This is no more clearly demonstrated in recent history than by the Catholic Church during the Middle Ages. I must tell you that without the Catholic Church and its doctrines, the feudal system would not have spread in Europe, would not have been able to survive for as long as it did. The Catholic doctrines were a total perversion of Jesus' true teachings where he said: "Inasmuch as you have done it onto the least of these, my little ones, you have done it onto me." Had the Catholic Church been faithful to that teaching, it would not have supported the elitist system. Because it perverted the teachings of Christ in many ways, it did indeed support an elitist system that allowed the feudal lords and the kings to remain in control of the population, keeping the population as virtual slaves for centuries.

What was the core of the Catholic doctrines that supported poverty? It was that certain conditions on earth were the result of the will of God, including the condition that a small elite would rule, even that a small elite of clergy and the Pope were controlling whether the people could have their sins remitted and enter the Kingdom of Heaven. Again, a total perversion of the teachings of Christ who said: "The Kingdom of God is within you," meaning that you do not need an institution and its clergy in order to enter that inner kingdom.

How could the Pope take you by the hand and lead you to the kingdom that is within *you?* This, of course, is ridiculous. It was not ridiculous to the people of the Middle Ages who had grown up being indoctrinated and programmed that this was the absolute truth and that they would go to hell if they dared question the authority of the Pope and the Catholic Church and its doctrines. What was it that set the condition for the physical manifestation of poverty? It was the spiritual poverty that was brought on by the Catholic Church perverting the teachings of Christ!

You might look to South America, where the Catholic Church is still strong in many nations, and realize that for poverty to be overcome in South America, the people must dare to question the Catholic Church and its doctrines, especially those that are out of alignment with the true teachings of Christ. Why do you think it is important for us to get the translation of our books out to the people? This is precisely why. Otherwise, how shall they learn that there is a difference between the true teachings of Christ and the outer doctrines of the Catholic Church?

Throughout the Dark Ages, going into the modern age, there has been this subtle programming by the forces of antichrist – even using the religion that claims to represent Christ on earth – to hammer into the collective consciousness that poverty is the will of God. It is the will of God that some people are more powerful and more rich than others. The majority of the population should simply accept their lot and not try to rock the boat and not try to demand something.

After all, what is the will of God—according to the Catholic Church? Well, it is that all people ascend to heaven after this lifetime, and so people have been programmed to not look at the now and not look at the situation on earth and say: "This is not right! This is not acceptable. We want change!" No, they have been programmed to be passive about conditions on earth and say: "Oh we will just be good Christians, and not rock the boat so that we can be resurrected and be raised to heaven after we leave this physical octave."

Can you see that this is a very subtle and very effective way to pacify the people so that they will not work for changes in the physical octave? They believe that they just need to be good Christians and wait for the changes in the next world. Thereby, they leave this world to the forces of anti-christ who have set themselves up to be the undisputed rulers of this world. Can you see that as long as that programming is allowed to continue unquestioned, then there cannot be a dramatic shift in the collective consciousness?

It has been the goal of the forces of anti-christ to use a perversion of the teachings of Christ to deprive the people of their will, their willpower to stand up and say: "Enough is enough! We demand that this planet earth should be an outpicturing of the truth of God so that the Kingdom of God can be manifest here below as it is already manifest above. We demand that this society of ours be an outpicturing of the true teachings of Christ who said: 'I am come that all might have life and that they may have it more abundantly.'" Religion is the one factor, the perversion of the Father aspect, that has programmed the people to sap their will, to take away their willpower so they will not stand up to the elite and demand that poverty be eradicated.

Science and poverty

As there is always two sides to the coin, there is of course the other side—the perversion of the Mother aspect. That perversion has come through science and the philosophy of natural selection. This is the philosophy that everything in life is an outpicturing of the struggle for limited resources, thereby causing some to be more fit than others. Again, this has been used by those among the power elite, those among the forces of anti-christ, who would not accept and would not submit to the authority of the Catholic Church. They were the aspiring power elite who wanted to take power away from the established power elite—who had been in an unholy alliance with the Catholic Church for centuries.

The aspiring power elite saw that the emerging philosophy of materialism, especially boosted by the theory of evolution, was their vehicle for setting themselves up as the unquestioned rulers of this world through their philosophy that there is nothing beyond this world. Again, elitism and the fact that some people are rich and that many people are poor is simply an outpicturing of the laws of nature. Those who are more fit have a right to rule, have a right to take onto themselves privileges, such as abundance, and keep the majority of the population in poverty.

Not only is this a complete fabrication, it is actually a perversion of the reality and the laws of nature. I dare you to carefully analyze history on this planet, even by using the knowledge that has already been brought forth through science itself, including the science of physics and the science of biology. If you were to perform such an analysis and read between the lines – look beyond the official doctrines of science and refuse to listen to the priesthood of science – you would find that the theory of evolution is based on an utterly and completely false premise.

First of all, it is based on the consciousness of lack, the concept that this is a planet with limited resources. This is, as I have spoken about before, a complete lie. The only real resource is the knowledge of people in embodiment, combined with the will to let God's light flow through them, thereby bringing forth more abundance than is in existence today. This is the will to become more.

It is not true that this planet has limited resources. As Jesus said, with men this is impossible, meaning that when you are in the human consciousness and you deny the power of God within you, then this planet *does* have limited resources. It is not possible to bring forth greater resources through the power and the wisdom of man. Those who have become completely identified with the consciousness of anti-christ and their identity of separation, they are indeed cut off from that power. To them, it seems as if this planet *has* limited resources.

The reality is that when you exercise the potential (that all people have) to find the Kingdom of God within you, then it *is* possible to increase the amount of abundance on this planet. In fact this is, despite what science says currently, precisely the force that is driving evolution on a planetary historical scale. The drive to be more, the drive to grow, that is built into life is what causes species and the entire planet to transcend itself and come to higher and higher levels, greater and greater levels of complexity. More complex life forms are, of course, an expression of abundance.

Historically, if it had only been the consciousness of lack and the competition for limited resources, then this planet would not have been in an upward evolutionary spiral. It would have been in a downward evolutionary spiral and would long ago have disintegrated under the weight of that spiral. The reality is that it is indeed possible to bring forth greater and greater resources, thereby overcoming poverty and giving the abundant life to all people. This is perfectly possible within the laws of nature. What has been programmed into the collective consciousness through the philosophy of science and materialism is precisely that this is not possible, causing millions, if not billions, of people around the world to accept that this is simply their lot in life and there is nothing they can do about it. After all, resources are limited so how could all people be rich? How could all people have a certain standard of living?

The illusion of inequality is the basis for poverty

This is a very subtle and very insidious state of consciousness, but what is the real purpose for it? What is the real mechanism behind it? It is that there are those lifestreams on this planet [See the book *Cosmology of Evil*] who have cut themselves off from God and therefore cannot use God's power to bring forth greater abundance. Why did they cut themselves off from God? It was precisely because they could not accept the reality that because all self-conscious beings are expressions of God's Being, then all have the same value. In fact, it is meaningless to attach value and to perform a value judgment and a comparison between individualizations of God. Each individualization of God is unique and how can there be comparisons in uniqueness?

What these lifestreams wanted was a world where there was not uniqueness, not true equality of uniqueness, where they could set themselves up as being better and more important than other people. Do you see that for some to be better than others, there must be distance, inequality? It is now possible for some people to take resources away from others so that they have more and the others have less. What is it that makes such a world possible? It is that the world is, at least to some degree, cut off from the abundance, the power, the love of God that forms the River of Life where everything is constantly becoming more. When everything is becoming more, it is not possible to have a situation where some have more and others have less, for all are constantly becoming more.

Those who left off from oneness with God used their free will to demand, based on the Law of Free Will, to be given a world in which they could experience that inequality. They demanded to be cut of from the abundance of God so that they could set themselves up as being the haves and thereby condemn other people to being the have-nots. Because of the Law of Free Will, they were granted such a world – planet earth among others – where they could exercise that desire. The purpose was that eventually they would tire of it and its limitations by realizing that what you have done to others, you have already done to yourself. By putting other people in the box of being the have-nots, they have actually put themselves in a box that is just as limited, although they have more in the physical. They are just as limited spiritually and thus have as great, if not greater, poverty than those who are the have-nots materially.

It was the hope that these lifestreams would eventually tire of playing this dualistic game and therefore desire to once again get back into the River of Life and take the entire planet back into it. Many have indeed transcended that need to feel better than others, have simply left it behind. Some of them are still in embodiment, and you see them now as people who are honestly working to raise up the All. Some of them have even become social reformers who have worked to raise up the conditions of the people. There is still a core of these lifestreams who have remained on the planet and who have not budged, who have not changed their consciousness.

The judgment of those who uphold inequality

As the Law of Free Will gives people the right to separate themselves from the River of Life, it does not give them the right to do so forever. We have now come to the point where we have reached a critical mass, and those lifestreams who will not let go of this consciousness of the haves and the have-nots must face the final initiation. Either they change their consciousness or they are judged and thereby sent to a lower level than planet earth.

The dispensation I have been granted by the Great Central sun will – by the release of light – accelerate that process of the judgment of those who will not let go of the dualistic consciousness. They are keeping the majority of the population on this planet in poverty, and it prevents them from having the abundant life that it is indeed God's will that they have.

It is indeed the purpose of the laws of nature to give them the abundant life. Those laws of nature were not designed by materialistic scientists. They were designed by the Creator and those who are working in oneness with the Creator to define the parameters for life on planet earth. They have defined those laws of nature so that this planet naturally is designed to bring forth greater and greater states of abundance for all inhabitants on it. It is both the will of God and the laws of nature that there should be greater abundance so that all people are raised above poverty. They all have the abundant life, both materially and spiritually. When you come to this realization, you see that there is much work to be done in terms of changing the collective consciousness. What I am telling you is that those of you who are willing to tune in to the dispensation and the light released from Alpha and Omega themselves – flowing through the heart of myself as the God of Freedom for the earth – you can become the forerunners. You can feel that energy flowing through you, and you can be the open doors for it to flow into the physical octave.

Many of you might indeed be impelled by that light to speak out against poverty and the consciousness of poverty. Even if you do not have the opportunity to speak out physically, I can assure you that you can hold the balance spiritually. Thereby, many other people who have never heard of the ascended masters – and who do not need to hear of the ascended masters in this lifetime – will be awakened to the fact that they came to this earth for a purpose and that purpose was to assist me, Saint Germain – even if they do not know me by name – to bring forth the Golden Age. Part of that Golden Age is to eradicate poverty and bring the abundant life to all people.

Do you see that it starts with the will of God—the will to change, the will to question whether it is really true that God has mandated poverty or that the laws of nature have mandated poverty? Is this reality? This is what needs to be questioned first. For that to be questioned, there must be the will to question these very subtle beliefs that have been programmed into the collective consciousness and the individual consciousness for so long.

The will of God always overcomes the anti-will

It takes courage, it takes will, it takes determination to stand up against the mass consciousness and the elite. They will use whatever power they have in society to ridicule and put down those who question their basic paradigms. Nevertheless, if you have the will, you will succeed. You will stand up and the power of God working through you will turn back the opposition from those who also have will, but it is the anti-will that can never be as strong as the will of God. Why is that, my beloved? The anti-will is based on the consciousness of separation, and the consciousness of separation has built into it fear. When you separate yourself from oneness with the Infinite, then it is inevitable that you become vulnerable to fear. Only in oneness with God do you escape fear.

The power elite on earth might appear mighty because they have the outer weapons of power. They seem to have great determination, even to use those weapons to destroy anyone who opposes them. You need to look beyond it and say: "Why do they hide in their palaces? Why do they hide in their fortresses? Why do they hide behind their weapons?" It is because they have fear, and the greater the weapons, the greater the fear. It is the only way they can keep it at bay so they can continue to exist without disintegrating into insanity because of the fear.

Look at them and see that their willpower is hollow. It goes only to a certain point. When you overcome the consciousness of fear and lock in to the will of God – the will of God that is not based on fear but is based on love, the unconditional love of God – you will know that their willpower, their determination and their weapons of power are simply conditions in the material universe. They are not as powerful as the unconditional River of Life where there are no conditions.

1 | Poverty Is not the Will of God

When you have that unconditional love, you will not accept any conditions on earth as causing you to hold back the power of God from flowing through you. When you allow that unconditional love to flow through you, you will seek to raise up all life, even those who are trapped and who are forming a power elite. You will not seek to destroy them, as some have done in the past. They became the aspiring power elite, seeking to destroy the established power elite because they wanted the position of the power elite. Nay, it will not be so. You will walk the middle way where you will not seek the power. You will seek to bring that power to the people by bringing the abundance to the people. First of all, by giving them spiritual abundance of ideas and awakening, and then also material abundance.

True willpower is not based on fear but is based on love. That love is God's Love, which is unconditional. It is able to sweep aside and consume any conditions on this earth that would hold back the changes that are mandated by the will of God, mandated by the laws of nature. God's will is that this planet transcends poverty and manifests the abundant life for all of the 10 billion souls that are meant to find a home on this planet and find the abundant life on this planet. Earth has the potential to sustain 10 billion people in a state of abundance, spiritually and materially. If they have the spiritual abundance, then the planet will gratefully and lovingly outpicture the material abundance as well.

My beloved, I thank you for providing me this platform, and I shall continue to speak about poverty on the other rays. I will explain how each ray has a role to play in the eradication of poverty. The perversion of each ray has been used to create the vortex and the illusions that uphold the beast of poverty and keep it alive, and keep it eating the abundance and the lifeblood of the people themselves. I thank you and I seal you in the unconquerable and unstoppable flame of the will of God, infused with the freedom flame that I AM. I say: "I release an extraordinary measure of light on this planet—the will to BE FREE!"

2 | INVOKING THE WILL TO OVERCOME POVERTY

In the name of the I AM THAT I AM, Jesus Christ, I call upon Saint Germain and Archangel Michael for the transformation of the consciousness of poverty on earth. Awaken people to the reality that we are spiritual beings and that we can co-create a new future by working with the ascended masters. I especially call for …

[Make your own calls here.]

Part 1

1. Saint Germain, I invoke the dispensation you have been granted from the Great Central Sun. I call forth an extraordinary release of light to illuminate the problem of poverty.

O Saint Germain, you do inspire,
my vision raised forever higher,
with you I form a figure-eight,
your Golden Age I co-create.

**O Saint Germain, what love you bring,
it truly makes all matter sing,
your violet flame does all restore,
with you we are becoming more.**

2. Saint Germain, I call forth the light that will get people to look at the problem of poverty and examine its cause.

O Saint Germain, what Freedom Flame,
released when we recite your name,
acceleration is your gift,
our planet it will surely lift.

**O Saint Germain, what love you bring,
it truly makes all matter sing,
your violet flame does all restore,
with you we are becoming more.**

3. Saint Germain, I call forth the light that will make people see the need to make the choice of whether they will move out of the consciousness that caused poverty, or whether they will stay in that consciousness.

O Saint Germain, in love we claim,
our right to bring your violet flame,
from you Above, to us below,
it is an all-transforming flow.

> O Saint Germain, what love you bring,
> it truly makes all matter sing,
> your violet flame does all restore,
> with you we are becoming more.

4. Saint Germain, I call forth the judgment of Christ upon those who stay in the consciousness behind poverty, and I demand that they be removed from this planet.

> O Saint Germain, I love you so,
> my aura filled with violet glow,
> my chakras filled with violet fire,
> I am your cosmic amplifier.

> **O Saint Germain, what love you bring,**
> **it truly makes all matter sing,**
> **your violet flame does all restore,**
> **with you we are becoming more.**

5. Saint Germain, I affirm with you that the manifestation of poverty will no longer be tolerated on earth. I invoke the light that is making it impossible that poverty can continue to manifest.

> O Saint Germain, I am now free,
> your violet flame is therapy,
> transform all hang-ups in my mind,
> as inner peace I surely find.

> **O Saint Germain, what love you bring,**
> **it truly makes all matter sing,**
> **your violet flame does all restore,**
> **with you we are becoming more.**

6. Saint Germain, I accept and multiply the release of light from the Great Central Sun on behalf of myself and the people who are in positions in society to do something about poverty.

> O Saint Germain, my body pure,
> your violet flame for all is cure,
> consume the cause of all disease,
> and therefore I am all at ease.

> **O Saint Germain, what love you bring,**
> **it truly makes all matter sing,**
> **your violet flame does all restore,**
> **with you we are becoming more.**

7. Saint Germain, I call for the people to be awakened so they can move away from poverty without falling into the trap of materialism. I call for them to be awakened to the potential to overcome poverty without becoming sucked into the vortex of materialism.

> O Saint Germain, I'm karma-free,
> the past no longer burdens me,
> a brand new opportunity,
> I am in Christic unity.

> **O Saint Germain, what love you bring,**
> **it truly makes all matter sing,**
> **your violet flame does all restore,**
> **with you we are becoming more.**

8. Saint Germain, I call forth the judgment of Christ upon the beast of materialism that has taken over the West and has dominated the thinking of the West for too long.

O Saint Germain, we are now one,
I am for you a violet sun,
as we transform this planet earth,
your Golden Age is given birth.

**O Saint Germain, what love you bring,
it truly makes all matter sing,
your violet flame does all restore,
with you we are becoming more.**

9. Saint Germain, I say with you and all ascended masters that I am committed to completely and utterly eradicating poverty on planet earth!

O Saint Germain, the earth is free,
from burden of duality,
in oneness we bring what is best,
your Golden Age is manifest.

**O Saint Germain, what love you bring,
it truly makes all matter sing,
your violet flame does all restore,
with you we are becoming more.**

Part 2

1. Saint Germain, awaken people to the reality that the ascended masters are not elitists.

Archangel Michael, light so blue,
my heart has room for only you.
My mind is one, no longer two,
your love for me is ever true.

**Archangel Michael, you are here,
your light consumes all doubt and fear.
Your Presence is forever near,
you are to me so very dear.**

2. Saint Germain, awaken people to the reality that in the Piscean age, humankind faced the question of whether a small elite should rule the people or whether the people would free themselves from the consciousness of elitism and acknowledge the power of God within them.

Archangel Michael, I will be,
all one with your reality.
No fear can hold me as I see,
this world no power has o'er me.

**Archangel Michael, you are here,
your light consumes all doubt and fear.
Your Presence is forever near,
you are to me so very dear.**

3. Saint Germain, awaken the spiritual people to the need to tune in to the Aquarian consciousness and leave behind the Piscean consciousness.

> Archangel Michael, hold me tight,
> shatter now the darkest night.
> Clear my chakras with your light,
> restore to me my inner sight.
>
> **Archangel Michael, you are here,
> your light consumes all doubt and fear.
> Your Presence is forever near,
> you are to me so very dear.**

4. Saint Germain, awaken people to the need for people from all over the world to communicate with each other and spread new ideas and a new awareness.

> Archangel Michael, now I stand,
> with you the light I do command.
> My heart I ever will expand,
> till highest truth I understand.
>
> **Archangel Michael, you are here,
> your light consumes all doubt and fear.
> Your Presence is forever near,
> you are to me so very dear.**

5. Saint Germain, awaken people to the reality that even seemingly mundane communication between people has the potential to bring about a shift in the collective consciousness by spreading new ideas that transcend nationality, race, religion or ethnicity.

Archangel Michael, in my heart,
from me you never will depart.
Of hierarchy I am a part,
I now accept a fresh new start.

**Archangel Michael, you are here,
your light consumes all doubt and fear.
Your Presence is forever near,
you are to me so very dear.**

6. Saint Germain, awaken people to the reality that poverty is a specific form of energy, a specific vibration.

Archangel Michael, sword of blue,
all darkness you are cutting through.
My Christhood I do now pursue,
discernment shows me what is true.

**Archangel Michael, you are here,
your light consumes all doubt and fear.
Your Presence is forever near,
you are to me so very dear.**

7. Saint Germain, awaken people to the reality that the modern world has in many ways made poverty worse. It has made it possible that some people have become richer than seen in known history.

Archangel Michael, in your wings,
I now let go of lesser things.
God's homing call in my heart rings,
my heart with yours forever sings.

> Archangel Michael, you are here,
> your light consumes all doubt and fear.
> Your Presence is forever near,
> you are to me so very dear.

8. Saint Germain, awaken people to the reality that the modern world has created greater contrast between those who are rich and those who are poor.

> Archangel Michael, take me home,
> in higher spheres I want to roam.
> I am reborn from cosmic foam,
> my life is now a sacred poem.

> Archangel Michael, you are here,
> your light consumes all doubt and fear.
> Your Presence is forever near,
> you are to me so very dear.

9. Saint Germain, awaken people to the reality that this has created a vortex of the energy of poverty that has increased on a planetary level over several centuries.

> Archangel Michael, light you are,
> shining like the bluest star.
> You are a cosmic avatar,
> with you I will go very far.

> Archangel Michael, you are here,
> your light consumes all doubt and fear.
> Your Presence is forever near,
> you are to me so very dear.

Part 3

1. Saint Germain, awaken people to the reality that from the feudal societies and forward, the planetary vortex of the energy of poverty has increased in strength.

> O Saint Germain, you do inspire,
> my vision raised forever higher,
> with you I form a figure-eight,
> your Golden Age I co-create.
>
> **O Saint Germain, what love you bring,**
> **it truly makes all matter sing,**
> **your violet flame does all restore,**
> **with you we are becoming more.**

2. Saint Germain, awaken people to the reality that this has been partially balanced by the building of a momentum of victory, of the abundance consciousness.

> O Saint Germain, what Freedom Flame,
> released when we recite your name,
> acceleration is your gift,
> our planet it will surely lift.
>
> **O Saint Germain, what love you bring,**
> **it truly makes all matter sing,**
> **your violet flame does all restore,**
> **with you we are becoming more.**

3. Saint Germain, awaken people to the reality that in certain areas of the planet the vortex of poverty has grown very powerful, to the point where it overpowers most of the people who live in those areas.

> O Saint Germain, in love we claim,
> our right to bring your violet flame,
> from you Above, to us below,
> it is an all-transforming flow.

> **O Saint Germain, what love you bring,**
> **it truly makes all matter sing,**
> **your violet flame does all restore,**
> **with you we are becoming more.**

4. Saint Germain, awaken the people who are overpowered by poverty to see how they can escape the extreme poverty in which they were born, in which they have grown up, in which they have grown old, and in which they think they are destined to die.

> O Saint Germain, I love you so,
> my aura filled with violet glow,
> my chakras filled with violet fire,
> I am your cosmic amplifier.

> **O Saint Germain, what love you bring,**
> **it truly makes all matter sing,**
> **your violet flame does all restore,**
> **with you we are becoming more.**

5. Saint Germain, awaken the spiritual people from the sense that there is a remote God up in heaven who has a will for us that he is trying to force upon us.

> O Saint Germain, I am now free,
> your violet flame is therapy,
> transform all hang-ups in my mind,
> as inner peace I surely find.

> **O Saint Germain, what love you bring,**
> **it truly makes all matter sing,**
> **your violet flame does all restore,**
> **with you we are becoming more.**

6. Saint Germain, awaken people to the reality that will is not something static. The will of God is that everything becomes more by transcending itself until everything becomes the fullness of what God is.

> O Saint Germain, my body pure,
> your violet flame for all is cure,
> consume the cause of all disease,
> and therefore I am all at ease.

> **O Saint Germain, what love you bring,**
> **it truly makes all matter sing,**
> **your violet flame does all restore,**
> **with you we are becoming more.**

7. Saint Germain, awaken people to the reality that life is a wondrous, never-ending process of alchemy where that which is here now can always be transcended into the gold of that which is more.

O Saint Germain, I'm karma-free,
the past no longer burdens me,
a brand new opportunity,
I am in Christic unity.

**O Saint Germain, what love you bring,
it truly makes all matter sing,
your violet flame does all restore,
with you we are becoming more.**

8. Saint Germain, awaken people from the subtle lies that have been programmed into the collective consciousness on this planet, saying that poverty is the will of God.

O Saint Germain, we are now one,
I am for you a violet sun,
as we transform this planet earth,
your Golden Age is given birth.

**O Saint Germain, what love you bring,
it truly makes all matter sing,
your violet flame does all restore,
with you we are becoming more.**

9. Saint Germain, I call forth the judgment of Christ upon the brothers of darkness, the forces of anti-christ, who have spread their lies into the collective consciousness that poverty is inevitable because it is either the will of God or an expression of the laws of nature.

> O Saint Germain, the earth is free,
> from burden of duality,
> in oneness we bring what is best,
> your Golden Age is manifest.
>
> **O Saint Germain, what love you bring,**
> **it truly makes all matter sing,**
> **your violet flame does all restore,**
> **with you we are becoming more.**

Part 4

1. Saint Germain, awaken people to the reality that many religions on this earth have been elitist in nature and in practice. They have brought forth an elitist doctrine that has maintained a status quo that allowed a small elite to have an ungodly control over the majority of the population.

> Archangel Michael, light so blue,
> my heart has room for only you.
> My mind is one, no longer two,
> your love for me is ever true.
>
> **Archangel Michael, you are here,**
> **your light consumes all doubt and fear.**
> **Your Presence is forever near,**
> **you are to me so very dear.**

2. Saint Germain, awaken people to the reality that members of the elite have been able to take privileges for themselves because they took the wealth and the abundance from the people, keeping the people at an artificial level of poverty.

> Archangel Michael, I will be,
> all one with your reality.
> No fear can hold me as I see,
> this world no power has o'er me.
>
> **Archangel Michael, you are here,**
> **your light consumes all doubt and fear.**
> **Your Presence is forever near,**
> **you are to me so very dear.**

3. Saint Germain, awaken people to the reality that without the Catholic Church and its doctrines, the feudal system would not have spread in Europe, and it would not have been able to survive for as long as it did.

> Archangel Michael, hold me tight,
> shatter now the darkest night.
> Clear my chakras with your light,
> restore to me my inner sight.
>
> **Archangel Michael, you are here,**
> **your light consumes all doubt and fear.**
> **Your Presence is forever near,**
> **you are to me so very dear.**

4. Saint Germain, awaken people to the reality that the Catholic doctrines are a total perversion of Jesus' true teachings about the oneness of all life.

Archangel Michael, now I stand,
with you the light I do command.
My heart I ever will expand,
till highest truth I understand.

**Archangel Michael, you are here,
your light consumes all doubt and fear.
Your Presence is forever near,
you are to me so very dear.**

5. Saint Germain, awaken people to the reality that because the Catholic Church perverted the teachings of Christ, it supported an elitist system that allowed the feudal lords and the kings to remain in control of the population, keeping the population as virtual slaves for centuries.

Archangel Michael, in my heart,
from me you never will depart.
Of hierarchy I am a part,
I now accept a fresh new start.

**Archangel Michael, you are here,
your light consumes all doubt and fear.
Your Presence is forever near,
you are to me so very dear.**

6. Saint Germain, awaken people to the reality that the core of the Catholic doctrines that supported poverty is that certain conditions on earth are the result of the will of God, including the condition that a small elite would rule, even that a small elite of clergy and the Pope were controlling whether the people could have their sins remitted and enter the Kingdom of Heaven.

> Archangel Michael, sword of blue,
> all darkness you are cutting through.
> My Christhood I do now pursue,
> discernment shows me what is true.
>
> **Archangel Michael, you are here,
> your light consumes all doubt and fear.
> Your Presence is forever near,
> you are to me so very dear.**

7. Saint Germain, awaken people to the reality that what set the condition for the physical manifestation of poverty was the spiritual poverty that was brought on by the Catholic Church perverting the teachings of Christ.

> Archangel Michael, in your wings,
> I now let go of lesser things.
> God's homing call in my heart rings,
> my heart with yours forever sings.
>
> **Archangel Michael, you are here,
> your light consumes all doubt and fear.
> Your Presence is forever near,
> you are to me so very dear.**

8. Saint Germain, awaken people to the reality that for poverty to be overcome in many nations, the people must dare to question the Catholic Church and its doctrines, especially those that are out of alignment with the true teachings of Christ.

> Archangel Michael, take me home,
> in higher spheres I want to roam.
> I am reborn from cosmic foam,
> my life is now a sacred poem.
>
> **Archangel Michael, you are here,**
> **your light consumes all doubt and fear.**
> **Your Presence is forever near,**
> **you are to me so very dear.**

9. Saint Germain, I call forth the judgment of Christ upon the forces of anti-christ who have been using religion to program into the collective consciousness that poverty is the will of God and that it is the will of God that some people are more powerful and more rich than others.

> Archangel Michael, light you are,
> shining like the bluest star.
> You are a cosmic avatar,
> with you I will go very far.
>
> **Archangel Michael, you are here,**
> **your light consumes all doubt and fear.**
> **Your Presence is forever near,**
> **you are to me so very dear.**

Part 5

1. Saint Germain, awaken people to the reality that the Catholic Church has programmed people to be passive about conditions on earth and focus on going to heaven after this life.

O Saint Germain, you do inspire,
my vision raised forever higher,
with you I form a figure-eight,
your Golden Age I co-create.

**O Saint Germain, what love you bring,
it truly makes all matter sing,
your violet flame does all restore,
with you we are becoming more.**

2. Saint Germain, awaken people to the reality that this is a very subtle and effective way to pacify the people so that they will not work for changes in the physical octave. Thereby, they leave this world to the forces of anti-christ who have set themselves up to be the undisputed rulers of this world.

O Saint Germain, what Freedom Flame,
released when we recite your name,
acceleration is your gift,
our planet it will surely lift.

**O Saint Germain, what love you bring,
it truly makes all matter sing,
your violet flame does all restore,
with you we are becoming more.**

3. Saint Germain, awaken people to the reality that as long as this programming is allowed to continue unquestioned, there cannot be a dramatic shift in the collective consciousness.

> O Saint Germain, in love we claim,
> our right to bring your violet flame,
> from you Above, to us below,
> it is an all-transforming flow.
>
> **O Saint Germain, what love you bring,
> it truly makes all matter sing,
> your violet flame does all restore,
> with you we are becoming more.**

4. Saint Germain, awaken people to the reality that it has been the goal of the forces of anti-christ to use a perversion of the teachings of Christ to deprive the people of their will to stand up and demand change.

> O Saint Germain, I love you so,
> my aura filled with violet glow,
> my chakras filled with violet fire,
> I am your cosmic amplifier.
>
> **O Saint Germain, what love you bring,
> it truly makes all matter sing,
> your violet flame does all restore,
> with you we are becoming more.**

5. Saint Germain, by the authority of the Christ within me, I say on behalf of all people: "Enough is enough! We demand that this planet will be an outpicturing of the truth of God. We demand that our society be an outpicturing of the true teachings of Christ who said: 'I am come that all might have life and that they may have it more abundantly.'"

> O Saint Germain, I am now free,
> your violet flame is therapy,
> transform all hang-ups in my mind,
> as inner peace I surely find.
>
> **O Saint Germain, what love you bring,**
> **it truly makes all matter sing,**
> **your violet flame does all restore,**
> **with you we are becoming more.**

6. Saint Germain, awaken people to the reality that religion is the perversion of the Father aspect, and that scientific materialism is the perversion of the Mother aspect.

> O Saint Germain, my body pure,
> your violet flame for all is cure,
> consume the cause of all disease,
> and therefore I am all at ease.
>
> **O Saint Germain, what love you bring,**
> **it truly makes all matter sing,**
> **your violet flame does all restore,**
> **with you we are becoming more.**

7. Saint Germain, awaken people to the reality that the philosophy of natural selection has been used by those among the power elite who would not accept and would not submit to the authority of the Catholic Church.

> O Saint Germain, I'm karma-free,
> the past no longer burdens me,
> a brand new opportunity,
> I am in Christic unity.

> O Saint Germain, what love you bring,
> it truly makes all matter sing,
> your violet flame does all restore,
> with you we are becoming more.

8. Saint Germain, awaken people to the reality that there is always an aspiring power elite who wants to take power away from the established power elite.

O Saint Germain, we are now one,
I am for you a violet sun,
as we transform this planet earth,
your Golden Age is given birth.

> O Saint Germain, what love you bring,
> it truly makes all matter sing,
> your violet flame does all restore,
> with you we are becoming more.

9. Saint Germain, awaken people to the reality that the aspiring power elite saw that the emerging philosophy of materialism, especially boosted by the theory of evolution, was their vehicle for setting themselves up as the unquestioned rulers of this world through their philosophy that there is nothing beyond this world.

O Saint Germain, the earth is free,
from burden of duality,
in oneness we bring what is best,
your Golden Age is manifest.

> O Saint Germain, what love you bring,
> it truly makes all matter sing,
> your violet flame does all restore,
> with you we are becoming more.

Part 6

1. Saint Germain, awaken people to see the lie saying that elitism, and the fact that some people are rich and that many people are poor, is an outpicturing of the laws of nature. Those who are more fit have a right to rule, have a right to take privileges and keep the majority of the population in poverty.

> Archangel Michael, light so blue,
> my heart has room for only you.
> My mind is one, no longer two,
> your love for me is ever true.

> **Archangel Michael, you are here,**
> **your light consumes all doubt and fear.**
> **Your Presence is forever near,**
> **you are to me so very dear.**

2. Saint Germain, awaken people to the reality that this is a perversion of the laws of nature. The theory of evolution is based on a completely false premise.

> Archangel Michael, I will be,
> all one with your reality.
> No fear can hold me as I see,
> this world no power has o'er me.

> Archangel Michael, you are here,
> your light consumes all doubt and fear.
> Your Presence is forever near,
> you are to me so very dear.

3. Saint Germain, awaken people to the reality that this planet does not have limited resources. The only real resource is the knowledge of people in embodiment, combined with the will to let God's light flow through them, thereby bringing forth more abundance than is in existence today.

> Archangel Michael, hold me tight,
> shatter now the darkest night.
> Clear my chakras with your light,
> restore to me my inner sight.

> **Archangel Michael, you are here,**
> **your light consumes all doubt and fear.**
> **Your Presence is forever near,**
> **you are to me so very dear.**

4. Saint Germain, awaken people to the reality that when we exercise our potential to find the Kingdom of God within us, it is possible to increase the amount of abundance on this planet.

> Archangel Michael, now I stand,
> with you the light I do command.
> My heart I ever will expand,
> till highest truth I understand.

**Archangel Michael, you are here,
your light consumes all doubt and fear.
Your Presence is forever near,
you are to me so very dear.**

5. Saint Germain, awaken people to the reality that the force that is driving evolution on a planetary scale is the drive to be more, the drive to grow. This is built into life and causes the entire world to transcend itself and come to higher and higher levels of complexity.

Archangel Michael, in my heart,
from me you never will depart.
Of hierarchy I am a part,
I now accept a fresh new start.

**Archangel Michael, you are here,
your light consumes all doubt and fear.
Your Presence is forever near,
you are to me so very dear.**

6. Saint Germain, awaken people to the reality that it is possible to bring forth greater and greater resources, thereby overcoming poverty and giving the abundant life to all people. This is perfectly possible within the laws of nature.

Archangel Michael, sword of blue,
all darkness you are cutting through.
My Christhood I do now pursue,
discernment shows me what is true.

> Archangel Michael, you are here,
> your light consumes all doubt and fear.
> Your Presence is forever near,
> you are to me so very dear.

7. Saint Germain, I call forth the judgment of Christ upon those who have used the philosophy of scientific materialism to program into the collective consciousness that it is not possible to increase abundance, causing billions of people to accept that because resources are limited, all people cannot be rich.

> Archangel Michael, in your wings,
> I now let go of lesser things.
> God's homing call in my heart rings,
> my heart with yours forever sings.

> Archangel Michael, you are here,
> your light consumes all doubt and fear.
> Your Presence is forever near,
> you are to me so very dear.

8. Saint Germain, I call forth the judgment of Christ upon those lifestreams who have cut themselves off from God and therefore cannot use God's power to bring forth greater abundance.

> Archangel Michael, take me home,
> in higher spheres I want to roam.
> I am reborn from cosmic foam,
> my life is now a sacred poem.

2 | *Invoking the Will to Overcome Poverty*

> **Archangel Michael, you are here,**
> **your light consumes all doubt and fear.**
> **Your Presence is forever near,**
> **you are to me so very dear.**

9. Saint Germain, I call forth the judgment of Christ upon the lifestreams who wanted a world where there was no equality of uniqueness. Therefore, they could set themselves up as being better and more important than other people.

> Archangel Michael, light you are,
> shining like the bluest star.
> You are a cosmic avatar,
> with you I will go very far.

> **Archangel Michael, you are here,**
> **your light consumes all doubt and fear.**
> **Your Presence is forever near,**
> **you are to me so very dear.**

Part 7

1. Saint Germain, I call forth the judgment of Christ upon those beings who wanted inequality so they could take resources away from others and thereby have more and the others have less.

> O Saint Germain, you do inspire,
> my vision raised forever higher,
> with you I form a figure-eight,
> your Golden Age I co-create.

**O Saint Germain, what love you bring,
it truly makes all matter sing,
your violet flame does all restore,
with you we are becoming more.**

2. Saint Germain, I call forth the judgment of Christ upon those who left off from oneness and demanded to be given a world in which they could experience inequality. They demanded to be cut off from the abundance of God so that they could set themselves up as being the haves and thereby condemn other people to being the have-nots.

O Saint Germain, what Freedom Flame,
released when we recite your name,
acceleration is your gift,
our planet it will surely lift.

**O Saint Germain, what love you bring,
it truly makes all matter sing,
your violet flame does all restore,
with you we are becoming more.**

3. Saint Germain, awaken people to the reality that as the Law of Free Will gives people the right to separate themselves from the River of Life, it does not give them the right to do so forever.

O Saint Germain, in love we claim,
our right to bring your violet flame,
from you Above, to us below,
it is an all-transforming flow.

> **O Saint Germain, what love you bring,**
> **it truly makes all matter sing,**
> **your violet flame does all restore,**
> **with you we are becoming more.**

4. Saint Germain, awaken people to the reality that earth has now reached a critical mass, and those lifestreams who will not let go of this consciousness of the haves and the have-nots must face the final initiation. Either they change their consciousness or they are judged and thereby sent to a lower level than planet earth.

> O Saint Germain, I love you so,
> my aura filled with violet glow,
> my chakras filled with violet fire,
> I am your cosmic amplifier.

> **O Saint Germain, what love you bring,**
> **it truly makes all matter sing,**
> **your violet flame does all restore,**
> **with you we are becoming more.**

5. Saint Germain, I call forth your dispensation from the Great Central sun to accelerate the process of the judgment of those who will not let go of the dualistic consciousness.

> O Saint Germain, I am now free,
> your violet flame is therapy,
> transform all hang-ups in my mind,
> as inner peace I surely find.

> O Saint Germain, what love you bring,
> it truly makes all matter sing,
> your violet flame does all restore,
> with you we are becoming more.

6. Saint Germain, awaken people to the reality that a few fallen beings are keeping the majority of the population on this planet in poverty. This prevents people from having the abundant life that it is God's will that they have.

> O Saint Germain, my body pure,
> your violet flame for all is cure,
> consume the cause of all disease,
> and therefore I am all at ease.

> O Saint Germain, what love you bring,
> it truly makes all matter sing,
> your violet flame does all restore,
> with you we are becoming more.

7. Saint Germain, awaken people to the reality that the Elohim defined the laws of nature so that this planet is designed to bring forth greater and greater states of abundance for all inhabitants.

> O Saint Germain, I'm karma-free,
> the past no longer burdens me,
> a brand new opportunity,
> I am in Christic unity.

**O Saint Germain, what love you bring,
it truly makes all matter sing,
your violet flame does all restore,
with you we are becoming more.**

8. Saint Germain, awaken people to the reality that it is both the will of God and the laws of nature that there should be greater abundance so that all people are raised above poverty. They all have the abundant life, both materially and spiritually.

O Saint Germain, we are now one,
I am for you a violet sun,
as we transform this planet earth,
your Golden Age is given birth.

**O Saint Germain, what love you bring,
it truly makes all matter sing,
your violet flame does all restore,
with you we are becoming more.**

9. Saint Germain, awaken the spiritual people to the reality that those who are willing to tune in to the dispensation and the light released from Alpha and Omega can become the forerunners for a shift in the collective consciousness.

O Saint Germain, the earth is free,
from burden of duality,
in oneness we bring what is best,
your Golden Age is manifest.

**O Saint Germain, what love you bring,
it truly makes all matter sing,
your violet flame does all restore,
with you we are becoming more.**

Part 8

1. Saint Germain, awaken all people who can be impelled by the light to speak out against poverty and the consciousness of poverty.

> Archangel Michael, light so blue,
> my heart has room for only you.
> My mind is one, no longer two,
> your love for me is ever true.

> **Archangel Michael, you are here,
> your light consumes all doubt and fear.
> Your Presence is forever near,
> you are to me so very dear.**

2. Saint Germain, awaken all people who can hold the balance spiritually so that other people, who have never heard of the ascended masters, will remember that they came to earth for the purpose of assisting to bring forth the Golden Age.

> Archangel Michael, I will be,
> all one with your reality.
> No fear can hold me as I see,
> this world no power has o'er me.

> Archangel Michael, you are here,
> your light consumes all doubt and fear.
> Your Presence is forever near,
> you are to me so very dear.

3. Saint Germain, awaken all people who have the will to question whether God has mandated poverty or that the laws of nature have mandated poverty. Awaken those who can question the very subtle beliefs that have been programmed into the collective consciousness.

> Archangel Michael, hold me tight,
> shatter now the darkest night.
> Clear my chakras with your light,
> restore to me my inner sight.

> Archangel Michael, you are here,
> your light consumes all doubt and fear.
> Your Presence is forever near,
> you are to me so very dear.

4. Saint Germain, awaken all people who have the inner courage, the will, the determination to stand up against the mass consciousness and the elite that will use their power to ridicule and put down those who question their paradigms.

> Archangel Michael, now I stand,
> with you the light I do command.
> My heart I ever will expand,
> till highest truth I understand.

> **Archangel Michael, you are here,**
> **your light consumes all doubt and fear.**
> **Your Presence is forever near,**
> **you are to me so very dear.**

5. Saint Germain, awaken all people who can stand up to the power elite by letting the power of God work through us. Help us turn back the opposition from those who have the anti-will that can never be as strong as the will of God.

> Archangel Michael, in my heart,
> from me you never will depart.
> Of hierarchy I am a part,
> I now accept a fresh new start.

> **Archangel Michael, you are here,**
> **your light consumes all doubt and fear.**
> **Your Presence is forever near,**
> **you are to me so very dear.**

6. Saint Germain, awaken all people to see that the power elite might appear mighty because they have the outer weapons of power. Yet they have fear, and the greater the weapons, the greater the fear.

> Archangel Michael, sword of blue,
> all darkness you are cutting through.
> My Christhood I do now pursue,
> discernment shows me what is true.

> **Archangel Michael, you are here,**
> **your light consumes all doubt and fear.**
> **Your Presence is forever near,**
> **you are to me so very dear.**

7. Saint Germain, awaken all people to see that the willpower of the elite is hollow. When we overcome the consciousness of fear and lock in to the will of God, we will know that their will is not as powerful as the unconditional River of Life where there are no conditions.

> Archangel Michael, in your wings,
> I now let go of lesser things.
> God's homing call in my heart rings,
> my heart with yours forever sings.

> **Archangel Michael, you are here,**
> **your light consumes all doubt and fear.**
> **Your Presence is forever near,**
> **you are to me so very dear.**

8. Saint Germain, awaken all people who can see that true willpower is not based on fear but is based on love. Love is able to sweep aside and consume any conditions on this earth that would hold back the changes that are mandated by the will of God and the laws of nature.

> Archangel Michael, take me home,
> in higher spheres I want to roam.
> I am reborn from cosmic foam,
> my life is now a sacred poem.

> Archangel Michael, you are here,
> your light consumes all doubt and fear.
> Your Presence is forever near,
> you are to me so very dear.

9. Saint Germain, awaken all people who can see that this planet has the potential to sustain 10 billion people in a state of abundance, spiritually and materially. If we have the spiritual abundance, then the planet will gratefully and lovingly outpicture the material abundance as well.

> Archangel Michael, light you are,
> shining like the bluest star.
> You are a cosmic avatar,
> with you I will go very far.

> Archangel Michael, you are here,
> your light consumes all doubt and fear.
> Your Presence is forever near,
> you are to me so very dear.

Sealing

In the name of the I AM THAT I AM, I accept that Archangel Michael, Astrea and Shiva form an impenetrable shield around myself and all constructive people, sealing us from all fear-based energies in all four octaves. I accept that the Light of God is consuming and transforming all fear-based energies that make up the forces behind war!

3 | OVERCOMING POVERTY THROUGH GOD WISDOM

Saint Germain I AM, and I come to discourse with you on the consciousness of poverty, especially as it relates to the Second Ray of God's Wisdom. My beloved, as the first step is to take away the will of the people, the will to change, the second step – building upon it – is to take away their knowledge of how to change by keeping them in ignorance.

The flow of God, the flow of the River of Life, starts with the will to be more, the will to create. As for you – who are co-creators with God – it starts with the will to co-create. Building upon that comes the vision of what to co-create and of how to co-create within the framework of God's law. It is, of course, the desire of God, it is the desire of the ascended masters, that all people on earth should have the correct knowledge of who they are, as co-creators with God, and how to use their own, built-in creative abilities to work within the framework of God's law, the laws of nature, in order to bring forth the abundant life on planet earth.

The forces of anti-christ have taken it upon themselves to use every effort, every lie, every illusion that springs from the consciousness of separation in order to destroy the people's ability to co-create the abundant life. It is important for you to understand that most of the people who are aligned with the consciousness of anti-christ, the consciousness of duality, are completely blinded by that consciousness. As Jesus said: "Father forgive them, for they know not what they do." They are so blinded by duality that they believe they are doing the right thing, and that what they are doing will actually bring about the abundant life, and even the Kingdom of God or some other Edenic state on planet earth.

Beings who must steal life energy to survive

It is also important for you to realize that beyond people in embodiment, there are disembodied beings who have a greater awareness than all people in embodiment. They know to some degree what they do, they know at least that they are exploiting people on earth, even those who are working for the forces of anti-christ while thinking they are working for a good cause. There are beings, especially in the emotional realm, but also in the mental realm, who are deliberately using people in embodiment in order to simply extract light from the population of earth [See *Cosmology of Evil*].

They do this for one purpose only, namely to extract the life energy from the people on earth that allows them to continue some form of existence separated from the River of Life. As we have explained, a lifestream has the right – according to the Law of Free Will – to set itself outside the River of Life, but it cannot do so indefinitely. There must come a time when that lifestream has used up its opportunity, and thus it will actually be cut off from the stream of energy, spiritual energy, from its own higher being, its own I AM Presence. After that cut-off point, such a lifestream can maintain an existence that is separate from the River of Life only by stealing life energy from those lifestreams who are still receiving it from the spiritual source. You must understand – as the spiritually aware people – that there are many activities on this earth that are designed for one purpose only. That purpose is to keep the people on earth engaged in the dualistic struggle so that they continue to misqualify their spiritual light with a lower vibration, such as fear, anger, hatred, envy, jealousy or other spiritual poisons. This qualifies the light of God with a lower vibration that allows those beings who exist in the mental and emotional realms to absorb that energy and use it to sustain themselves. This is precisely what the vast majority of the population on earth are ignorant of. They really have no defense against being used, literally as a form of cows that are milked for their spiritual light, even though they believe that they are engaged in a positive cause that will improve society in some way.

My beloved, one of the most obvious examples of this is, of course, the people who are engaged in violent conflicts. This can be seen most clearly in the Middle East where you have groups of people who for thousands of years have been engaged in fighting against each other. The outer reason why they are fighting at this particular time truly is insignificant. It is just an excuse that allows these groups of people to continue in this dualistic struggle against the other group that they have elevated to the status of being the scapegoats. One group believes that if only they can eradicate the other group, they will solve all of their own problems. They have allowed themselves to believe in the illusion that all of the problems they encounter are caused by these other people. If those people were destroyed, their problems would disappear.

Ignorance of the cosmic mirror

This is a complete denial of responsibility. It is something that can spring only from a complete ignorance of the most fundamental reality of the material universe, namely that the four levels of the universe form the cosmic mirror. Whatever you project into that cosmic mirror, will be reflected back to you in the form of physical circumstances. You co-create – through your own consciousness – your own physical circumstances. Even though it may seem as if other people are the cause of your problems, the reality is that the real cause of your problems is your own state of consciousness. The cause is found in your own physical, emotional, mental and identity minds that you project into the cosmic mirror. You are receiving the return current in the form of physical circumstances that outpicture the images you hold in your four lower bodies, the four levels of your mind.

When you are ignorant of these basic facts, then you have no defense against being pulled into this ongoing dualistic struggle against other people. You have no defense that allows you to step back and say: "The cause for which I am fighting truly cannot be the highest cause. For when I look at the scriptures of my religion [regardless of which religion that might be], then I see that this dualistic struggle of fighting against other people out of pure hatred and anger truly cannot be the cause of my God, as prescribed in my religion." No matter which religion people might follow, all major religions on earth state the same basic facts, namely that God has said once and for all: "Thou shalt not kill."

The ignorance you see on this planet is that people have been seduced into overriding the basic command of God not to kill their fellow human beings. Even if you happen to believe in scientific materialism, then once again you must say that it cannot be according to the survival of the fittest that you kill the members of your own species. That cannot in the long run ensure the survival of the species as a whole. Even the theory of evolution actually states that killing other human beings jeopardizes the survival of the entire race. Those who are the most fit cannot be the ones who are most aggressive and most willing to kill their fellow human beings. Those who are the most fit – in terms of long-term survival – must be those who are not willing to kill, but who are willing to work for the survival of the entire species.

Inconsistencies in the theory of evolution

The problem in the theory of evolution is that it, of course, cannot explain how there can be such an overall consciousness that is able to consider what is best for the entire species. This enables human beings who have self-awareness to consciously and willingly override their own narrow, short-term self-interest in order to work for the survival of the race as a whole. Those scientists who promote the theory of evolution have an inconsistency in their own logic.

The very fact that they are seeking to promote the theory of evolution as a way to create peace on earth and overcome the fighting caused by religion, demonstrates that they have a greater awareness, an awareness that cannot be explained simply through the survival of the fittest, as the theory of evolution currently explains this mechanism. Even in the materialistic paradigm there is a logical flaw, and the scientists themselves demonstrate that flaw by arguing that materialism would create peace where religion has created war. The very fact that they argue this shows that there must be some state of consciousness that can allow human beings to look beyond their own narrow self-interest, to tune in to what is best for the race as a whole.

Where in the current materialistic paradigm is there room for an overall state of consciousness that goes beyond the individual and the individual genes? It simply is not there. It is not there because scientists themselves, the scientists in the field of biology, have not been willing to look at the philosophical consequences of the science of quantum physics, which has proven that the consciousness of the scientist has a fundamental influence on the experiment itself. There must be a deeper reality, namely that consciousness is part of everything that happens on planet earth. It is not logical that the evolutionary process is guided only by chance and the adaptation to the environment. There must be a greater consciousness behind the evolutionary process.

This demonstrates to you that scientific materialism is not – as it claims – a philosophy designed to set people free by giving them a greater understanding of the reality of life than what was found in medieval Catholic doctrine. Nay, my beloved, scientific materialism is not aimed at setting people free from the illusions that keep them trapped in a lesser state of abundance and keep them trapped in poverty. It is simply – as I explained yesterday – a philosophy created by the aspiring power elite who want to take over the position of the established power elite that was based on the medieval church.

The war between religion and science

Dogmatic religion in any form and scientific materialism are simply the outplaying of the age-old power struggle between two dualistic opposites. This is what you see very obviously in the Middle East where you have groups of people that fight against each other and have been doing so for generations. For outsiders it is very easy to see that they are fighting over nothing, for there is no real reason for them to be fighting other than the fact that they hate each other.

It should be possible for people in the West, who see this nonsense going on in the Middle East, to step back and look at their own society and see that the mechanism, the dualistic struggle that they see in the Middle East, is also present in their own Western societies, only in a more subtle form that is not expressed in physical violence but is expressed in a form of mental and spiritual violence. There are two forces that are fighting, both claiming to be fighting to liberate the people in some ultimate way, whether it be through the Catholic doctrine of salvation or through the scientific doctrine of freeing people's minds from the illusions of religion.

In reality neither of those two systems will free the people's minds to know the reality of what is happening on this planet. None of the two systems, neither dogmatic religion nor scientific materialism, will educate people to the basic reality that I started this discourse explaining. The reality is that people are being used by forces beyond this planet who are seeking to steal their light and energy by causing them to engage in the dualistic struggle.

How do they do this? By causing people to engage in the dualistic consciousness whereby they project a dualistic image into the cosmic mirror and therefore inevitably receive back from the cosmic mirror physical circumstances where it seems as if there is another group of people or another belief system that is opposing their progress. It seems that if they only fight those people or fight that belief system, then that will solve all their problems and bring forth some greater state of abundance on this planet. The people in the Middle East, or in other areas of the world, really do believe that if they kill all of the members of the opposing group, paradise will come to earth. There are people in the West who believe that if only they can make their religion the only established religion, or if they can just eradicate all religion and make scientific materialism the only established belief system, then they will solve all of humankind's problems and bring paradise to earth.

In Western societies you have many people who are truly very intelligent people and very well-meaning people. They truly believe that they are fighting for a good cause by fighting for this or that belief system, even political belief systems or economic philosophies. They do not see that they have simply been seduced into engaging in the dualistic struggle, and all of their well-meant efforts do nothing to actually free humankind to step up to a higher level. It only keeps humankind engaged in the dualistic struggle.

Their efforts are simply reinforcing and continuing that struggle, serving to keep the people trapped in a state of poverty that begins as a state of spiritual poverty. As long as people do not know who they are – as spiritual beings who are designed to be co-creators with God – how can those people use their co-creative abilities to actively and personally co-create the abundant life on earth?

Looking for an external savior

When the people are ignorant of who they are as co-creators with God, they cannot use their own built-in abilities to co-create the abundant life. This means that they go into a passive state of mind where they look for some force outside of themselves to give them that abundance. In past ages, such as the dark ages, many people believed that God was the only force that could give them the abundant life. If they did not have the abundant life, it must be God's will that they do not have the abundant life, at least at the present moment. This caused them, as I said, to look beyond this world for some state of abundance in the next life, in the life after this world.

Even today, many people throughout the world have been lured into the modern non-religious version of this pacifying paradigm. They believe that they have no ability to create wealth and abundance beyond what is already manifest in this world. They have come to believe in the philosophy of lack, which says that this earth is a limited place with limited resources, and therefore there is only a certain amount of abundance that can be brought forth.

Many people passively wait for some external force, such as the government, to bring forth some kind of law or program that will magically transform their society and bring about the abundant life for the common people. Do you not see that for decades the people in Russia, Eastern Europe and elsewhere believed that through the philosophy of socialism, Marxism and communism, one day they would magically have a society that gave the abundant life to all people.

My beloved, did that society ever come to pass? No it did not; and why not? Because it is a philosophy that is based on the consciousness of lack. It is based on the denial of the Christ in every human being, thus denying that the people have the ability to co-create the abundant life. This makes them passive and looking for the state to do everything for them. This is cutting off the creativity of the people and systematically and gradually lowering the abundance that can be brought forth in such a society.

Today, you have people in many nations who have let go of the communist dream and who are instead looking to capitalism as the way to bring forth material abundance. You see this in South-East Asia especially. You see it even in China where they are trying to blend communism with capitalism—unrestrained capitalism, meaning unrestrained exploitation in the name of profit. They now look to some big business conglomerate, some multi-national corporation or financial institution, to come in and bring some transformation that will bring a more abundant life.

Why capitalism does not work

From a realistic perspective, you can look at the Western world and see that through capitalism there has been an increase in material wealth in many Western nations. From this, one might say that capitalism must work. The reality is that capitalism does not work, but capitalism in the West has given greater freedom to individual initiative than was given in the communist countries. Therefore, there has been more of an opening for people in the West to express their creativity—and this is what has brought forth greater abundance.

The problem with capitalism is that it has allowed a small elite to exploit the creativity of the individual people. They have used it to generate profit for big multi-national corporations instead of spreading the abundance to all people in society. If you analyze the capitalist economy, you will see that it also has built-in limitations for how much abundance can be brought forth. In fact, you will see that many of the older nations in Europe have already gone through a period where their economies started to stagnate.

The United States has started this process but has not gone as far as the European nations had gone a decade or two ago. You will still see a stagnation beginning. What has kept this from being accelerated further is only that capitalism has expanded to other areas of the world. It has therefore been able to spread the exploitation of the working people to those in other countries who – because they were living at the starvation level – have now been willing to work for wages that no sane person in the Western world would work for. This has allowed the capitalists to continue to exploit the people whereas the people in the Western world have become educated to how the economy works and how the labor situation is. They would no longer allow themselves to be exploited to the degree that these people in other parts of the world are allowing themselves to be exploited, thereby providing cheaper goods to the Western world.

What do those cheaper goods allow? They allow the people in the Western world to feel that they still have some sense of material abundance. They can buy inexpensive goods imported from China and elsewhere, which gives them the illusion that they can maintain their standard of living, perhaps even expand that standard a little bit. In reality, this only serves to maintain status quo where a small elite in the Western world are becoming increasingly wealthy. The people, the general population, in the Western world are seeing a lowering of their actual standard of living, compared to what it was a decade or two ago.

The value of your labor

What is it that determines your actual standard of living? It is the value of your labor and your ability to express your creativity in bringing forth more abundance. The value of the labor of the people in the Western world has actually deteriorated over the last few decades. It has only been offset by the import of inexpensive goods from countries where the value of the people's labor is even less. The people in the West have been duped into thinking that they have expanded or maintained their standard of living. In reality, the value of their labor and their ability to express their creativity has deteriorated.

If they were aware of this, if they knew what was happening, they would have revolted against capitalism. They would have overthrown the capitalist system that allows a small elite of international financiers to keep the people in a state that is in an economic sense almost the same as the feudal societies of the middle ages. The international power elite owns the means of production and the means of exchange, just as the feudal lords in the middle ages owned the land that back then was the only source of abundance.

Today, the source of abundance is the means of production, the means of transportation, the means of exchange, including the money system. That system is virtually owned as a monopoly by an international power elite whose members manipulate corporations, manipulate countries, manipulate currencies and the money system to their own benefit. Including, of course, what you see right now where they have manipulated the price of oil, using crude oil as a way to extract inordinate amounts of money from the people, almost as a form of artificial taxation. This taxation does not even go to the government elected by the people, but goes to the international financial institutions and the big corporations, who answer to no government elected by any people in any nation.

There was a former American president who said that if the people understood how the money system works, there would be a revolution tomorrow. I can assure you that if the people in the Western world understood how the money system truly works – and how it is set up in very subtle ways to allow the elite to maintain a monopoly on the means of production and on the money system – then they would indeed create a revolution tomorrow and demand a total reform of the money system on a planetary scale.

The Alpha and the Omega of ignorance

The only thing that prevents an overthrow of the status quo in any society, in any historical period, has been that the elite has managed to keep the people in ignorance. This ignorance has, as everything else, an Alpha and an Omega aspect. The Alpha aspect is that the people are kept in ignorance of their true identity as spiritual beings, as co-creators with God, who have the ability, not to simply create abundance through what is already in the material realm. They have the ability to draw forth spiritual light from their own higher beings and use that light to bring forth a greater amount of abundance than is currently manifest in the physical realm. Thereby, they are increasing the amount of resources and abundance available on earth to truly create the abundant life for all people.

The Omega aspect of this ignorance is that the people are kept in ignorance of how society works. They do not clearly see how they are being exploited by the power elite. Go back to the Middle Ages and see how the Catholic Church in Europe served to keep the people in ignorance in the Alpha aspect by telling them that they were miserable sinners who did not have the ability to co-create with God. They were not sons and daughters of God because Jesus was the only son of God and they were created as sinners. At the same time there was the Omega ignorance where the feudal lords would not allow the people – that they believed they owned – to be educated. They could not even learn how to read and write so they had no possibility of truly understanding how they were being exploited. Nor did they have any opportunity to organize with other people and therefore put up a united front, as I talked about yesterday.

What has changed in the modern world is that you now have the possibility of spreading knowledge and information around the world. You have an unprecedented opportunity for awakening the people to both the Alpha and the Omega aspect of how they are being deliberately kept in ignorance in order to prevent them from rising up and demanding a change in the status quo. What we of the ascended masters desire to see happen is that the people realize that physical poverty, poverty that is based on a lack of money, is only the effect of a deeper cause. Part of that cause is the spiritual poverty that comes from a poverty of knowledge, a lack of knowledge, a lack of understanding of who people are, a lack of understanding of how society works.

Hold the vision for people awakening

We desire you, who are the spiritual people, to hold the vision that a critical mass of people will be awakened to this reality so that they will escape the dualistic struggle. Instead of continuing (out of their best intentions) to promote that struggle, they will actually be enlightened to the mechanism of the struggle itself. They will even see the mechanism where those who are starting to become enlightened have been pulled into working for a cause that is not truly the cause that will set people free, but only another part of the dualistic struggle.

This is present in every society. Most certainly, also here in South America where you see so many people who are somewhat enlightened to what I have talked about, namely the dangers of capitalism. Many people in South America are very well aware of the dangers of the International Monetary Fund, the World Bank and the world financial institutions. They see that when they seek the help of those financial institutions, there is always a catch that puts their nations into a debt to this financial system, this money beast, as we might call it.

Many people in South America are very well aware of the dangers of capitalism and unrestricted exploitation. Many of these people are currently trapped because they do not see the dualistic struggle itself. Many of them have been pulled into believing that the only way to create more justice and abundance for the little people, for the population, is through some version of a socialist, Marxist philosophy. They believe that socialism can bring the abundant life to the people of South America.

Or they have been trapped into another form of intellectual philosophizing where you see many people in South America who are somewhat awakened, but they are awakened only in an intellectual sense. They are trapped into pursuing ways to use the intellect to come up with a new philosophy that will change society. What I have just told you is that there is no intellectual philosophy that will change society. The philosopher's stone, that will change the lead of the human consciousness into gold, is a spiritual recognition that all people are spiritual beings who have a Christ potential. They can co-create the abundant life—not by using the resources already available and redistributing those resources according to some man-made scheme, but by reaching beyond the physical realm, drawing forth the light of God to increase the amount of resources and wealth on this planet.

I desire you, who are the spiritual people, to hold the vision, that those people who have already started to awaken will be further awakened. Help them go beyond the traps created for them by the forces of anti-christ—who seek to prevent them from attaining full enlightenment, instead side-tracking them into fighting for one of these causes that will not set the people free. Hold that vision and do whatever you feel moved to do from within to speak the higher truth that you know, in whatever form is suited to the people you are dealing with. Say what can help enlighten them to the spiritual reality beyond the intellectual man-made doctrines. Do what you can to help them see the reality of the dualistic struggle itself.

You will find ample teachings for how to do this in the book: *The Art of Non-War*, which was written specifically for this purpose. It is designed to help those who are beginning to awaken – but who have not yet risen above the intellect – connect to their own higher beings so that they will see that there is a higher source of truth than the human intellect. There is even a higher source of truth than science or scientific research based on a materialistic paradigm, which therefore cannot ever reveal the fullness of the reality of life and the reality of people's spiritual identity.

Hold the vision for a breakthrough in science

If you understand the reality described by quantum physics, you will see that if the consciousness of the scientist has a fundamental influence on the scientific observation, then a scientist cannot see – through any scientific means – what he in his consciousness believes does not exist. You will not see reality if you put the spyglass in front of the blind eye, as Lord Nelson did at that famous battle of Trafalgar. There are so many people in the scientific community who are very, very close to breaking through, but they are still putting their scientific spyglass in front of the blind eye. They refuse to see that there could be some spiritual reality to life, that there could be something beyond the material universe. They will not acknowledge that their own science has already pointed to that something—if only they would look at it through the objectivity that they claim is the very cornerstone of science.

There are already scientists who have seen the unreality and the limitations of the materialistic paradigm. They have started to bring forth new observations and new theories, including theories about the actual intelligence of the cell. They see the fact that a human being is not exclusively the product of the DNA but that the cell itself actually has a form of intelligence. This allows it to respond to the environment and to respond to a greater state of consciousness that is beyond the DNA and what can be encoded in the DNA.

This is already there at the forefront of biology, but of course it has not been recognized by the mainstream of science. Again, you have people who have been trapped into thinking that by promoting the materialistic paradigm, they are actually working for an ultimate cause, working for some ultimate truth. They have refused to see that they are simply being used in order to keep the people pacified through that materialistic paradigm—by believing that they have no built-in ability to fundamentally change their situation in life. Therefore, the people have become slaves of forces in the material realm.

Many of those who are the scientifically-minded people clearly see that the medieval churches kept people trapped in ignorance because they had made the people believe that they were subject to a human, earthly institution, namely the Catholic Church and the Pope. Is it not irony that these people believe that they are working for the cause of setting human beings free from such slavery, but they fail to see that they have simply created another earthly institution which now defines that there is not – nor can there be – any force beyond the material universe?

What is the logical conclusion of this philosophy? If there is nothing beyond the material universe, then human beings have no possibility whatsoever of ever becoming free of the limitations of the material realm. They can never be free from those forces who form a power elite and who at any time are setting up their institutions to control the people, using whatever philosophy is prevalent in society, whether it be the medieval Catholic Church or the modern scientific establishment that is based on materialism.

What really enslaves the people

What has kept the people in ignorance for thousands of years is that a small elite has prevented the people from realizing and accepting their built-in divinity. People do not see their Christ potential to escape any limitations, to go beyond any institutions on this earth, by connecting to a reality that is beyond the material universe and therefore can never be subject to, or restricted by, any institutions in this world. The only way for the people to be truly free is to connect to something that cannot be controlled by any philosophy or institution on this earth, something that is beyond any philosophy or force that springs from the consciousness of anti-christ.

Only by reaching beyond this world can the people be truly free. They can reach beyond this world only when they discover, understand and fully accept the reality that Jesus attempted to teach humankind 2,000 years ago, namely that the Kingdom of God is within you. You might look at the people – for example in South America – who have grown up in a small village where they have lived in poverty their entire lives. You might look at those people and see the immense distance between their current standard of living, between their current outlook on life, and the standard of living found in some of the rich nations and among some of the people who are more educated and more enlightened. You might look at that distance and say: "How could they ever overcome that and manifest a more abundant life?"

It all starts in consciousness. It all starts with the top 10 percent of the most spiritually aware people, many of whom are precisely the people I have talked about. They are somewhat enlightened, but they have been trapped in intellectual philosophies and therefore are not aware that they are part of the spiritual top 10 percent. Those are the people who can bring forth a change that will start at the highest level and will spread to all levels of society. Therefore, it will inevitably pull the people up to a different outlook on life. It will also change conditions in society so that all people have an opportunity to create a more abundant life for themselves because they live in a society that rewards effort.

The people who have grown up under the most poor conditions have been programmed to believe that no matter how hard they work, they cannot get ahead, for they are boxed in by limitations over which they have no control. As I explained at the very beginning, the universe is a mirror. If you project into the cosmic mirror that you are boxed in by physical limitations over which you have no control, then, my beloved, the universe can do only one thing. It must reason that you want to experience physical conditions that box you in, and so it gives you what you want because it is forever responsive to the Law of Free Will.

How can you change status quo? Only by helping the people overcome the sense of hopelessness, the sense that nothing matters, that they can never get ahead. Once you create a shift in society where there is a change in the people's mindset – and there is a change in physical conditions and the laws of society so that people can see that by working harder, by making an effort, they can actually get ahead – you have the beginning of a fundamental change. It can very quickly shift a society away from being weighted down by the consciousness of lack into beginning to believe in the consciousness of abundance.

Creating a positive spiral

This is the only thing that will help a nation, or even a continent, overcome what I talked about yesterday, the vortex of poverty, the vortex of the consciousness of lack. People can then reverse the downward spiral so that it is no longer self-reinforcing, but so that you gradually get back to a zero point where people are not being pulled down. Now they can start building a positive momentum of the consciousness of abundance that allows them to shift their society into a state of growth that is sustainable and will accelerate gradually.

This is very significant. The people who see the fallacy of capitalism but who have not yet seen the restrictions of communism or another Marxist or intellectually based system, if they can be awakened to see the spiritual reality, then they can see the middle way between the two extremes, such as capitalism or communism or any other duality on earth. By seeing that middle way, they can create a society where a country can build a positive momentum that gives abundance to all of its people without selling their nation, the soul of their nation, to the international financial elite—and thereby making their people slaves of that financial elite through the money system.

It is not true that a nation has to either sell its soul to capitalism and international banks or become a communist nation. There is always a middle way, but that middle way cannot be found through the intellect. The intellect is an analytical faculty that always looks to two extremes, two polarities. It can be found only through a recognition of the spiritual reality that goes beyond and sees that with men it is impossible to bring forth a society that is not in this or that extreme. But with God – working through men and women, through the Christ truth – this is indeed possible and is a living reality, a living potential.

Many nations have already started this transformation process, and many nations are close to breaking through. Even Colombia and other nations in South America are much closer to breaking through than you might think by looking at outer conditions. I tell you, there are wonderful enlightened people in all nations. They are enlightened at inner levels, and it only takes a very small switch of consciousness for them to be consciously enlightened so that they know with their outer minds what they already know in their higher beings.

They are mature beings who have volunteered to come into embodiment even in some of the poorest nations of the world. They are my own, they are devoted to Saint Germain. They see my vision and they wanted to help bring forth that vision as a physical reality, and thus they volunteered to embody at this particular time. Many of them volunteered to embody in poor nations under very difficult conditions so that they might demonstrate how you can overcome those limitations and still rise to manifest a more abundant life spiritually and materially.

My beloved, I thank you again for providing me a platform. I thank you for your attention. I thank you for being willing to be the open doors whereby the words spoken by me physically can reach out through your own beings and penetrate to a much deeper level of the mass consciousness than if you had not been here and had not been willing to come into a state of oneness with me, whereby we can be One, me Above and you below. I seal you in my gratitude and in the flame of God's Wisdom, as the Flame of Freedom expressed through

Wisdom. Truly, it is only through knowing that you can be completely free.

4 | INVOKING THE WISDOM TO OVERCOME POVERTY

In the name of the I AM THAT I AM, Jesus Christ, I call upon Saint Germain and Gautama Buddha for the transformation of the consciousness of poverty on earth. Awaken people to the reality that we are spiritual beings and that we can co-create a new future by working with the ascended masters. I especially call for …

[Make your own calls here.]

Part 1

1. Saint Germain, I call forth the judgment of Christ upon the forces of anti-christ who have used every lie that springs from the consciousness of separation in order to destroy the people's ability to co-create the abundant life.

O Saint Germain, you do inspire,
my vision raised forever higher,
with you I form a figure-eight,
your Golden Age I co-create.

**O Saint Germain, what love you bring,
it truly makes all matter sing,
your violet flame does all restore,
with you we are becoming more.**

2. Saint Germain, I call forth the judgment of Christ upon the people who are aligned with the consciousness of anti-christ and believe what they are doing will bring about some Edenic state on earth.

O Saint Germain, what Freedom Flame,
released when we recite your name,
acceleration is your gift,
our planet it will surely lift.

**O Saint Germain, what love you bring,
it truly makes all matter sing,
your violet flame does all restore,
with you we are becoming more.**

3. Saint Germain, I call forth the judgment of Christ upon the disembodied beings who know that they are exploiting people on earth, especially the people who are working for the forces of anti-christ while thinking they are working for a good cause.

> O Saint Germain, in love we claim,
> our right to bring your violet flame,
> from you Above, to us below,
> it is an all-transforming flow.
>
> **O Saint Germain, what love you bring,
> it truly makes all matter sing,
> your violet flame does all restore,
> with you we are becoming more.**

4. Saint Germain, I call forth the judgment of Christ upon the beings in the emotional and mental realms who are deliberately using people in embodiment in order to extract light from the population.

> O Saint Germain, I love you so,
> my aura filled with violet glow,
> my chakras filled with violet fire,
> I am your cosmic amplifier.
>
> **O Saint Germain, what love you bring,
> it truly makes all matter sing,
> your violet flame does all restore,
> with you we are becoming more.**

5. Saint Germain, I call forth the judgment of Christ upon those beings who are cut off from the stream of spiritual energy from their higher beings so they have to steal life energy from those who are still receiving it from the source.

O Saint Germain, I am now free,
your violet flame is therapy,
transform all hang-ups in my mind,
as inner peace I surely find.

**O Saint Germain, what love you bring,
it truly makes all matter sing,
your violet flame does all restore,
with you we are becoming more.**

6. Saint Germain, awaken people to the reality that many activities are designed for the purpose of keeping people engaged in the dualistic struggle. If people are ignorant of this, they have no defence against being used as a form of cows that are milked for their spiritual light.

O Saint Germain, my body pure,
your violet flame for all is cure,
consume the cause of all disease,
and therefore I am all at ease.

**O Saint Germain, what love you bring,
it truly makes all matter sing,
your violet flame does all restore,
with you we are becoming more.**

7. Saint Germain, I call forth the judgment of Christ upon the beings who are using violent conflicts to steal people's light.

O Saint Germain, I'm karma-free,
the past no longer burdens me,
a brand new opportunity,
I am in Christic unity.

**O Saint Germain, what love you bring,
it truly makes all matter sing,
your violet flame does all restore,
with you we are becoming more.**

8. Saint Germain, I call forth the judgment of Christ upon the groups in the Middle East who have for thousands of years been engaged in fighting against each other because they will not let go of the dualistic struggle against the other group that they have elevated to the status of being the scapegoats.

O Saint Germain, we are now one,
I am for you a violet sun,
as we transform this planet earth,
your Golden Age is given birth.

**O Saint Germain, what love you bring,
it truly makes all matter sing,
your violet flame does all restore,
with you we are becoming more.**

9. Saint Germain, awaken people to the reality that the four levels of the universe form the cosmic mirror. Whatever consciousness we project into that mirror, will be reflected back to us in the form of physical circumstances.

O Saint Germain, the earth is free,
from burden of duality,
in oneness we bring what is best,
your Golden Age is manifest.

**O Saint Germain, what love you bring,
it truly makes all matter sing,
your violet flame does all restore,
with you we are becoming more.**

Part 2

1. Saint Germain, awaken people to the reality that the real cause of our problems is our own state of consciousness. We are receiving the return current in the form of physical circumstances that outpicture the images we hold in our four lower bodies.

> Gautama, show my mental state
> that does give rise to love and hate,
> your exposé I do endure,
> so my perception will be pure.

> **Gautama, Flame of Cosmic Peace,
> unruly thoughts do hereby cease,
> we radiate from you and me
> the peace to still Samsara's Sea.**

2. Saint Germain, awaken people to the need to step back and say: "The cause for which I am fighting truly cannot be the highest cause. For when I look at the scriptures of my religion, then I see that this dualistic struggle of fighting against other people cannot be the cause of God."

> Gautama, in your Flame of Peace,
> the struggling self I now release,
> the Buddha Nature I now see,
> it is the core of you and me.
>
> **Gautama, Flame of Cosmic Peace,**
> **unruly thoughts do hereby cease,**
> **we radiate from you and me**
> **the peace to still Samsara's Sea.**

3. Saint Germain, I call forth the judgment of Christ upon the fallen beings who have seduced people into overriding the basic command of God not to kill their fellow human beings.

> Gautama, I am one with thee,
> Mara's demons do now flee,
> your Presence like a soothing balm,
> my mind and senses ever calm.
>
> **Gautama, Flame of Cosmic Peace,**
> **unruly thoughts do hereby cease,**
> **we radiate from you and me**
> **the peace to still Samsara's Sea.**

4. Saint Germain, I call forth the judgment of Christ upon the fallen beings who have created an artificial conflict between religion and science. Awaken people to see that this is a war between an established and an aspiring power elite.

> Gautama, I now take the vow,
> to live in the eternal now,
> with you I do transcend all time,
> to live in present so sublime.

> Gautama, Flame of Cosmic Peace,
> unruly thoughts do hereby cease,
> we radiate from you and me
> the peace to still Samsara's Sea.

5. Saint Germain, awaken people in the West to the reality that the dualistic struggle they see in the Middle East is also present in their own Western societies, only in a more subtle form that is not expressed in physical violence but in mental and spiritual violence.

> Gautama, I have no desire,
> to nothing earthly I aspire,
> in non-attachment I now rest,
> passing Mara's subtle test.

> **Gautama, Flame of Cosmic Peace,
> unruly thoughts do hereby cease,
> we radiate from you and me
> the peace to still Samsara's Sea.**

6. Saint Germain, awaken people to the reality that neither dogmatic religion nor materialistic science will free people's minds to know that they are being used by non-material forces who are seeking to steal their light and energy by causing them to engage in the dualistic struggle.

> Gautama, I melt into you,
> my mind is one, no longer two,
> immersed in your resplendent glow,
> Nirvana is all that I know.

> Gautama, Flame of Cosmic Peace,
> unruly thoughts do hereby cease,
> we radiate from you and me
> the peace to still Samsara's Sea.

7. Saint Germain, I call forth the judgment of Christ upon the fallen beings who are causing people to engage in the dualistic consciousness by projecting a dualistic image into the cosmic mirror and therefore getting back physical circumstances where it seems another group of people is a threat.

> Gautama, in your timeless space,
> I am immersed in Cosmic Grace,
> I know the God beyond all form,
> to world I will no more conform.

> Gautama, Flame of Cosmic Peace,
> unruly thoughts do hereby cease,
> we radiate from you and me
> the peace to still Samsara's Sea.

8. Saint Germain, I call forth the judgment of Christ upon the people who believe that if they kill all of the members of the opposing group, paradise will come to earth.

> Gautama, I am now awake,
> I clearly see what is at stake,
> and thus I claim my sacred right
> to be on earth the Buddhic Light.

> Gautama, Flame of Cosmic Peace,
> unruly thoughts do hereby cease,
> we radiate from you and me
> the peace to still Samsara's Sea.

9. Saint Germain, I call forth the judgment of Christ upon the people in the West who believe that if they can make their religion the only established religion, or if they can eradicate all religion and make scientific materialism the only established belief system, then they will solve all of humankind's problems and bring peace to earth.

> Gautama, with your thunderbolt,
> we give the earth a mighty jolt,
> I know that some will understand,
> and join the Buddha's timeless band.

> Gautama, Flame of Cosmic Peace,
> unruly thoughts do hereby cease,
> we radiate from you and me
> the peace to still Samsara's Sea.

Part 3

1. Saint Germain, I call forth the judgment of Christ upon the intelligent and well-meaning people who believe they are fighting for a good cause, but they refuse to see that they have been seduced into engaging in the dualistic struggle.

> O Saint Germain, you do inspire,
> my vision raised forever higher,
> with you I form a figure-eight,
> your Golden Age I co-create.
>
> **O Saint Germain, what love you bring,**
> **it truly makes all matter sing,**
> **your violet flame does all restore,**
> **with you we are becoming more.**

2. Saint Germain, awaken people to the reality that their well-meant efforts are reinforcing and continuing the dualistic struggle, serving to keep the people trapped in a state of poverty that begins as spiritual poverty.

> O Saint Germain, what Freedom Flame,
> released when we recite your name,
> acceleration is your gift,
> our planet it will surely lift.
>
> **O Saint Germain, what love you bring,**
> **it truly makes all matter sing,**
> **your violet flame does all restore,**
> **with you we are becoming more.**

3. Saint Germain, awaken people from the illusion that God does not want them to have abundance or that the laws of nature make it impossible for them to have abundance.

> O Saint Germain, in love we claim,
> our right to bring your violet flame,
> from you Above, to us below,
> it is an all-transforming flow.

> O Saint Germain, what love you bring,
> it truly makes all matter sing,
> your violet flame does all restore,
> with you we are becoming more.

4. Saint Germain, awaken people from the pacifying paradigm, the philosophy of lack, which says that earth is a limited place with lack of resources, and therefore there is only a certain amount of abundance.

> O Saint Germain, I love you so,
> my aura filled with violet glow,
> my chakras filled with violet fire,
> I am your cosmic amplifier.

> O Saint Germain, what love you bring,
> it truly makes all matter sing,
> your violet flame does all restore,
> with you we are becoming more.

5. Saint Germain, awaken people to the reality that they cannot passively wait for some external force, such as the government, to bring forth a law or program that will magically transform their society and bring about the abundant life for the common people.

> O Saint Germain, I am now free,
> your violet flame is therapy,
> transform all hang-ups in my mind,
> as inner peace I surely find.

> **O Saint Germain, what love you bring,**
> **it truly makes all matter sing,**
> **your violet flame does all restore,**
> **with you we are becoming more.**

6. Saint Germain, awaken people from the illusion that through the philosophy of socialism, Marxism and communism, one day they will magically have a society that gives the abundant life to all people.

> O Saint Germain, my body pure,
> your violet flame for all is cure,
> consume the cause of all disease,
> and therefore I am all at ease.

> **O Saint Germain, what love you bring,**
> **it truly makes all matter sing,**
> **your violet flame does all restore,**
> **with you we are becoming more.**

7. Saint Germain, awaken people to the illusion that capitalism is the way to bring forth material abundance and that some big business conglomerate, some multi-national corporation, will come in and bring a more abundant life.

> O Saint Germain, I'm karma-free,
> the past no longer burdens me,
> a brand new opportunity,
> I am in Christic unity.

> O Saint Germain, what love you bring,
> it truly makes all matter sing,
> your violet flame does all restore,
> with you we are becoming more.

8. Saint Germain, awaken people to the reality that capitalism does not work, but capitalism in the West has given greater freedom to individual initiative and this has brought forth greater abundance.

> O Saint Germain, we are now one,
> I am for you a violet sun,
> as we transform this planet earth,
> your Golden Age is given birth.

> O Saint Germain, what love you bring,
> it truly makes all matter sing,
> your violet flame does all restore,
> with you we are becoming more.

9. Saint Germain, awaken people to the reality that capitalism has allowed a small elite to exploit the creativity of the individual people. They have used it to generate profit for multinational corporations instead of spreading the abundance to all people in society.

> O Saint Germain, the earth is free,
> from burden of duality,
> in oneness we bring what is best,
> your Golden Age is manifest.

**O Saint Germain, what love you bring,
it truly makes all matter sing,
your violet flame does all restore,
with you we are becoming more.**

Part 4

1. Saint Germain, awaken people to the reality that the capitalist economy also has built-in limitations for how much abundance can be brought forth. Many of the older nations have already seen their economies stagnate.

> Gautama, show my mental state
> that does give rise to love and hate,
> your exposé I do endure,
> so my perception will be pure.

> **Gautama, Flame of Cosmic Peace,
> unruly thoughts do hereby cease,
> we radiate from you and me
> the peace to still Samsara's Sea.**

2. Saint Germain, awaken people to the reality that capitalism has spread the exploitation of the working people to other countries. This has allowed the capitalists to continue to exploit the people.

> Gautama, in your Flame of Peace,
> the struggling self I now release,
> the Buddha Nature I now see,
> it is the core of you and me.

> Gautama, Flame of Cosmic Peace,
> unruly thoughts do hereby cease,
> we radiate from you and me
> the peace to still Samsara's Sea.

3. Saint Germain, awaken people to the reality that cheeper goods imported from other parts of the world have given people in the West the illusion that they can maintain their standard of living.

> Gautama, I am one with thee,
> Mara's demons do now flee,
> your Presence like a soothing balm,
> my mind and senses ever calm.

> Gautama, Flame of Cosmic Peace,
> unruly thoughts do hereby cease,
> we radiate from you and me
> the peace to still Samsara's Sea.

4. Saint Germain, awaken people to the reality that this only serves to maintain status quo where a small elite is becoming increasingly wealthy while the people are seeing a lowering of their standard of living.

> Gautama, I now take the vow,
> to live in the eternal now,
> with you I do transcend all time,
> to live in present so sublime.

> Gautama, Flame of Cosmic Peace,
> unruly thoughts do hereby cease,
> we radiate from you and me
> the peace to still Samsara's Sea.

5. Saint Germain, awaken people to the reality that what determines our standard of living is the value of our labor and our ability to express our creativity in bringing forth more abundance.

> Gautama, I have no desire,
> to nothing earthly I aspire,
> in non-attachment I now rest,
> passing Mara's subtle test.

> Gautama, Flame of Cosmic Peace,
> unruly thoughts do hereby cease,
> we radiate from you and me
> the peace to still Samsara's Sea.

6. Saint Germain, awaken people to the reality that the people in the West have been duped into thinking they have expanded or maintained their standard of living. In reality, the value of their labor and their ability to express their creativity has deteriorated.

> Gautama, I melt into you,
> my mind is one, no longer two,
> immersed in your resplendent glow,
> Nirvana is all that I know.

> **Gautama, Flame of Cosmic Peace,**
> **unruly thoughts do hereby cease,**
> **we radiate from you and me**
> **the peace to still Samsara's Sea.**

7. Saint Germain, I call forth the judgment of Christ upon the capitalist system that allows a small elite of international financiers to keep the people in a state that is in an economic sense almost the same as the feudal societies of the middle ages.

> Gautama, in your timeless space,
> I am immersed in Cosmic Grace,
> I know the God beyond all form,
> to world I will no more conform.

> **Gautama, Flame of Cosmic Peace,**
> **unruly thoughts do hereby cease,**
> **we radiate from you and me**
> **the peace to still Samsara's Sea.**

8. Saint Germain, I call forth the judgment of Christ upon the international power elite that owns the means of production and the means of exchange, just as the feudal lords in the middle ages owned the land.

> Gautama, I am now awake,
> I clearly see what is at stake,
> and thus I claim my sacred right
> to be on earth the Buddhic Light.

> Gautama, Flame of Cosmic Peace,
> unruly thoughts do hereby cease,
> we radiate from you and me
> the peace to still Samsara's Sea.

9. Saint Germain, I call forth the judgment of Christ upon the international power elite who own the means of production, transportation and the money system and who manipulate corporations, countries, currencies and the money system to their own benefit.

> Gautama, with your thunderbolt,
> we give the earth a mighty jolt,
> I know that some will understand,
> and join the Buddha's timeless band.

> Gautama, Flame of Cosmic Peace,
> unruly thoughts do hereby cease,
> we radiate from you and me
> the peace to still Samsara's Sea.

Part 5

1. Saint Germain, I call forth the judgment of Christ upon the international power elite who manipulate the price of oil, using crude oil as a way to extract inordinate amounts of money from the people, as a form of artificial taxation.

> O Saint Germain, you do inspire,
> my vision raised forever higher,
> with you I form a figure-eight,
> your Golden Age I co-create.
>
> **O Saint Germain, what love you bring,
> it truly makes all matter sing,
> your violet flame does all restore,
> with you we are becoming more.**

2. Saint Germain, I call forth the judgment of Christ upon the international financial institutions and the big corporations who answer to no government elected by any people, but who are still stealing the money from the people.

> O Saint Germain, what Freedom Flame,
> released when we recite your name,
> acceleration is your gift,
> our planet it will surely lift.
>
> **O Saint Germain, what love you bring,
> it truly makes all matter sing,
> your violet flame does all restore,
> with you we are becoming more.**

3. Saint Germain, I call forth the judgment of Christ upon the fallen beings who have set up the money system to allow the elite to maintain a monopoly on the means of production and on the money system.

> O Saint Germain, in love we claim,
> our right to bring your violet flame,
> from you Above, to us below,
> it is an all-transforming flow.
>
> **O Saint Germain, what love you bring,
> it truly makes all matter sing,
> your violet flame does all restore,
> with you we are becoming more.**

4. Saint Germain, I call forth the judgment of Christ upon the fallen beings who are keeping the people in ignorance about their true identity as co-creators with God. Awaken people to their ability to draw forth spiritual light and increase the amount of resources for creating the abundant life for all people.

> O Saint Germain, I love you so,
> my aura filled with violet glow,
> my chakras filled with violet fire,
> I am your cosmic amplifier.
>
> **O Saint Germain, what love you bring,
> it truly makes all matter sing,
> your violet flame does all restore,
> with you we are becoming more.**

5. Saint Germain, I call forth the judgment of Christ upon the fallen beings who are keeping people in ignorance of how society works and how they are being systematically exploited by a small elite.

O Saint Germain, I am now free,
your violet flame is therapy,
transform all hang-ups in my mind,
as inner peace I surely find.

**O Saint Germain, what love you bring,
it truly makes all matter sing,
your violet flame does all restore,
with you we are becoming more.**

6. Saint Germain, awaken people to the reality that physical poverty, poverty that is based on a lack of money, is only the effect of a deeper cause. Part of that cause is the spiritual poverty that comes from a poverty of knowledge of how society works.

O Saint Germain, my body pure,
your violet flame for all is cure,
consume the cause of all disease,
and therefore I am all at ease.

**O Saint Germain, what love you bring,
it truly makes all matter sing,
your violet flame does all restore,
with you we are becoming more.**

7. Saint Germain, awaken people so they will not be pulled into working for a cause that will not set people free, but is only another part of the dualistic struggle.

4 | Invoking the Wisdom to Overcome Poverty

> O Saint Germain, I'm karma-free,
> the past no longer burdens me,
> a brand new opportunity,
> I am in Christic unity.
>
> **O Saint Germain, what love you bring,**
> **it truly makes all matter sing,**
> **your violet flame does all restore,**
> **with you we are becoming more.**

8. Saint Germain, awaken the people who are aware of the dangers of capitalism and unrestricted exploitation, so they will not be pulled into believing that the only way to create more justice and abundance for the people is through some version of a socialist, Marxist philosophy.

> O Saint Germain, we are now one,
> I am for you a violet sun,
> as we transform this planet earth,
> your Golden Age is given birth.
>
> **O Saint Germain, what love you bring,**
> **it truly makes all matter sing,**
> **your violet flame does all restore,**
> **with you we are becoming more.**

9. Saint Germain, awaken the people who are trapped into pursuing ways to use the intellect to come up with a new philosophy that will change society.

O Saint Germain, the earth is free,
from burden of duality,
in oneness we bring what is best,
your Golden Age is manifest.

**O Saint Germain, what love you bring,
it truly makes all matter sing,
your violet flame does all restore,
with you we are becoming more.**

Part 6

1. Saint Germain, awaken people to the reality that there is no intellectual philosophy that will change society. The philosopher's stone is a recognition that all people are spiritual beings who have a Christ potential.

Gautama, show my mental state
that does give rise to love and hate,
your exposé I do endure,
so my perception will be pure.

**Gautama, Flame of Cosmic Peace,
unruly thoughts do hereby cease,
we radiate from you and me
the peace to still Samsara's Sea.**

2. Saint Germain, awaken people to the reality that we cannot co-create the abundant life by using the resources already available or redistributing them according to some man-made scheme. We must reach beyond the physical realm and draw forth the light of God to increase the amount of resources.

> Gautama, in your Flame of Peace,
> the struggling self I now release,
> the Buddha Nature I now see,
> it is the core of you and me.
>
> **Gautama, Flame of Cosmic Peace,**
> **unruly thoughts do hereby cease,**
> **we radiate from you and me**
> **the peace to still Samsara's Sea.**

3. Saint Germain, awaken people to the need for us to speak the higher truth that we know, in whatever form is suited to the people we are dealing with. Help us say what can enlighten them to the spiritual reality beyond the intellectual man-made doctrines.

> Gautama, I am one with thee,
> Mara's demons do now flee,
> your Presence like a soothing balm,
> my mind and senses ever calm.
>
> **Gautama, Flame of Cosmic Peace,**
> **unruly thoughts do hereby cease,**
> **we radiate from you and me**
> **the peace to still Samsara's Sea.**

4. Saint Germain, I call forth the judgment of Christ upon people in the scientific community who refuse to see that there could be some spiritual reality to life, that there could be something beyond the material universe.

> Gautama, I now take the vow,
> to live in the eternal now,
> with you I do transcend all time,
> to live in present so sublime.

> **Gautama, Flame of Cosmic Peace,**
> **unruly thoughts do hereby cease,**
> **we radiate from you and me**
> **the peace to still Samsara's Sea.**

5. Saint Germain, I call forth the judgment of Christ upon people in the scientific community who will not acknowledge that their own science has already pointed to the spiritual reality—if only they would look at it through the objectivity that they claim is the cornerstone of science.

> Gautama, I have no desire,
> to nothing earthly I aspire,
> in non-attachment I now rest,
> passing Mara's subtle test.

> **Gautama, Flame of Cosmic Peace,**
> **unruly thoughts do hereby cease,**
> **we radiate from you and me**
> **the peace to still Samsara's Sea.**

6. Saint Germain, awaken the scientists who have seen the unreality and the limitations of the materialistic paradigm. Help them bring forth new observations and new theories.

> Gautama, I melt into you,
> my mind is one, no longer two,
> immersed in your resplendent glow,
> Nirvana is all that I know.

> **Gautama, Flame of Cosmic Peace,**
> **unruly thoughts do hereby cease,**
> **we radiate from you and me**
> **the peace to still Samsara's Sea.**

7. Saint Germain, I call forth the judgment of Christ upon people in the scientific community who deny the fact that a human being is not exclusively the product of the DNA, but that the cell itself has a form of consciousness.

> Gautama, in your timeless space,
> I am immersed in Cosmic Grace,
> I know the God beyond all form,
> to world I will no more conform.

> **Gautama, Flame of Cosmic Peace,**
> **unruly thoughts do hereby cease,**
> **we radiate from you and me**
> **the peace to still Samsara's Sea.**

8. Saint Germain, I call forth the judgment of Christ upon people in the scientific community who have been trapped into thinking that by promoting the materialistic paradigm, they are working for an ultimate cause, an ultimate truth.

> Gautama, I am now awake,
> I clearly see what is at stake,
> and thus I claim my sacred right
> to be on earth the Buddhic Light.
>
> **Gautama, Flame of Cosmic Peace,
> unruly thoughts do hereby cease,
> we radiate from you and me
> the peace to still Samsara's Sea.**

9. Saint Germain, I call forth the judgment of Christ upon people in the scientific community who refuse to see that they are being used in order to keep the people pacified because they believe they have no in-built ability to fundamentally change their situation in life.

> Gautama, with your thunderbolt,
> we give the earth a mighty jolt,
> I know that some will understand,
> and join the Buddha's timeless band.
>
> **Gautama, Flame of Cosmic Peace,
> unruly thoughts do hereby cease,
> we radiate from you and me
> the peace to still Samsara's Sea.**

Part 7

1. Saint Germain, I call forth the judgment of Christ upon people in the scientific community who see that the medieval churches kept people trapped in ignorance, but they fail to see that materialists have created another earthly institution, which now defines that there is no force beyond the material universe.

> O Saint Germain, you do inspire,
> my vision raised forever higher,
> with you I form a figure-eight,
> your Golden Age I co-create.

> **O Saint Germain, what love you bring,**
> **it truly makes all matter sing,**
> **your violet flame does all restore,**
> **with you we are becoming more.**

2. Saint Germain, I call forth the judgment of Christ upon people in the scientific community who will not see that if there is nothing beyond the material universe, then human beings have no possibility of ever becoming free of the limitations of the material realm.

> O Saint Germain, what Freedom Flame,
> released when we recite your name,
> acceleration is your gift,
> our planet it will surely lift.

> **O Saint Germain, what love you bring,**
> **it truly makes all matter sing,**
> **your violet flame does all restore,**
> **with you we are becoming more.**

3. Saint Germain, I call forth the judgment of Christ upon people in the scientific community who will not see that materialism can never free the people from those forces who form a power elite and who at any time are setting up their institutions to control the people, using whatever philosophy is prevalent in society.

> O Saint Germain, in love we claim,
> our right to bring your violet flame,
> from you Above, to us below,
> it is an all-transforming flow.

> **O Saint Germain, what love you bring,**
> **it truly makes all matter sing,**
> **your violet flame does all restore,**
> **with you we are becoming more.**

4. Saint Germain, I call forth the judgment of Christ upon the elite who have prevented the people from realizing and accepting their built-in divinity.

> O Saint Germain, I love you so,
> my aura filled with violet glow,
> my chakras filled with violet fire,
> I am your cosmic amplifier.

> **O Saint Germain, what love you bring,
> it truly makes all matter sing,
> your violet flame does all restore,
> with you we are becoming more.**

5. Saint Germain, awaken people to their Christ potential to escape any limitations, to go beyond any institutions on earth, by connecting to a reality that is beyond the material universe and therefore can never be subject to any institutions in this world.

> O Saint Germain, I am now free,
> your violet flame is therapy,
> transform all hang-ups in my mind,
> as inner peace I surely find.

> **O Saint Germain, what love you bring,
> it truly makes all matter sing,
> your violet flame does all restore,
> with you we are becoming more.**

6. Saint Germain, awaken the top 10 percent of the most spiritually aware people to see that only we can help the people who have lived in poverty their entire lives. Only we can bring forth a change that will spread to all levels of society.

> O Saint Germain, my body pure,
> your violet flame for all is cure,
> consume the cause of all disease,
> and therefore I am all at ease.

> O Saint Germain, what love you bring,
> it truly makes all matter sing,
> your violet flame does all restore,
> with you we are becoming more.

7. Saint Germain, awaken the people who have grown up under the most poor conditions from the lie that no matter how hard they work, they cannot get ahead, for they are boxed in by limitations over which they have no control.

> O Saint Germain, I'm karma-free,
> the past no longer burdens me,
> a brand new opportunity,
> I am in Christic unity.

> O Saint Germain, what love you bring,
> it truly makes all matter sing,
> your violet flame does all restore,
> with you we are becoming more.

8. Saint Germain, help the poorest people see that the universe is a mirror, and if we project into the cosmic mirror that we are boxed in by physical limitations over which we have no control, then the universe must reason that we want to experience physical conditions that box us in.

> O Saint Germain, we are now one,
> I am for you a violet sun,
> as we transform this planet earth,
> your Golden Age is given birth.

> O Saint Germain, what love you bring,
> it truly makes all matter sing,
> your violet flame does all restore,
> with you we are becoming more.

9. Saint Germain, help the poorest people overcome the sense of hopelessness, the sense that nothing matters, that they can never get ahead.

> O Saint Germain, the earth is free,
> from burden of duality,
> in oneness we bring what is best,
> your Golden Age is manifest.

> O Saint Germain, what love you bring,
> it truly makes all matter sing,
> your violet flame does all restore,
> with you we are becoming more.

Part 8

1. Saint Germain, I call forth a shift in society where there is a change in the people's mindset and there is a change in physical conditions and the laws of society, so that people can see that by working harder, by making an effort, they can actually get ahead.

> Gautama, show my mental state
> that does give rise to love and hate,
> your exposé I do endure,
> so my perception will be pure.

> Gautama, Flame of Cosmic Peace,
> unruly thoughts do hereby cease,
> we radiate from you and me
> the peace to still Samsara's Sea.

2. Saint Germain, I call forth a fundamental change, a very quick shift that brings society away from being weighted down by the consciousness of lack, instead moving into the consciousness of abundance.

> Gautama, in your Flame of Peace,
> the struggling self I now release,
> the Buddha Nature I now see,
> it is the core of you and me.

> **Gautama, Flame of Cosmic Peace,**
> **unruly thoughts do hereby cease,**
> **we radiate from you and me**
> **the peace to still Samsara's Sea.**

3. Saint Germain, shatter the vortex of poverty, the vortex of the consciousness of lack. Help people reverse the downward spiral so that it is no longer self-reinforcing, and so that people are not being pulled down.

> Gautama, I am one with thee,
> Mara's demons do now flee,
> your Presence like a soothing balm,
> my mind and senses ever calm.

> Gautama, Flame of Cosmic Peace,
> unruly thoughts do hereby cease,
> we radiate from you and me
> the peace to still Samsara's Sea.

4. Saint Germain, help people start building a positive momentum of the consciousness of abundance that allows them to shift their society into a state of growth that is sustainable and will accelerate gradually.

> Gautama, I now take the vow,
> to live in the eternal now,
> with you I do transcend all time,
> to live in present so sublime.

> Gautama, Flame of Cosmic Peace,
> unruly thoughts do hereby cease,
> we radiate from you and me
> the peace to still Samsara's Sea.

5. Saint Germain, awaken the people who see the fallacy of capitalism so they also see the restrictions of communism. Help them see the middle way between the two extremes and create a society that can give abundance to all people without selling their nation to the international financial elite.

> Gautama, I have no desire,
> to nothing earthly I aspire,
> in non-attachment I now rest,
> passing Mara's subtle test.

**Gautama, Flame of Cosmic Peace,
unruly thoughts do hereby cease,
we radiate from you and me
the peace to still Samsara's Sea.**

6. Saint Germain, awaken people from the illusion that a nation has to either sell its soul to capitalism and international banks or become a communist nation. There is always a middle way, but it can be found only through a recognition of the spiritual reality.

> Gautama, I melt into you,
> my mind is one, no longer two,
> immersed in your resplendent glow,
> Nirvana is all that I know.

**Gautama, Flame of Cosmic Peace,
unruly thoughts do hereby cease,
we radiate from you and me
the peace to still Samsara's Sea.**

7. Saint Germain, accelerate the nations that have already started this transformation. Awaken the people who are enlightened at inner levels, so they can make the switch in consciousness and know with their outer minds what they already know in their higher beings.

> Gautama, in your timeless space,
> I am immersed in Cosmic Grace,
> I know the God beyond all form,
> to world I will no more conform.

> Gautama, Flame of Cosmic Peace,
> unruly thoughts do hereby cease,
> we radiate from you and me
> the peace to still Samsara's Sea.

8. Saint Germain, awaken the mature beings who have volunteered to come into embodiment in some of the poorest nations, those who are your own, who are devoted to Saint Germain.

> Gautama, I am now awake,
> I clearly see what is at stake,
> and thus I claim my sacred right
> to be on earth the Buddhic Light.

> Gautama, Flame of Cosmic Peace,
> unruly thoughts do hereby cease,
> we radiate from you and me
> the peace to still Samsara's Sea.

9. Saint Germain, awaken them to their desire to help bring forth your vision as a physical reality. Help them see that they volunteered to embody in poor nations under very difficult conditions, so that they might demonstrate how to overcome those limitations and rise to manifest a more abundant life spiritually and materially.

> Gautama, with your thunderbolt,
> we give the earth a mighty jolt,
> I know that some will understand,
> and join the Buddha's timeless band.

**Gautama, Flame of Cosmic Peace,
unruly thoughts do hereby cease,
we radiate from you and me
the peace to still Samsara's Sea.**

Sealing

In the name of the I AM THAT I AM, I accept that Archangel Michael, Astrea and Shiva form an impenetrable shield around myself and all constructive people, sealing us from all fear-based energies in all four octaves. I accept that the Light of God is consuming and transforming all fear-based energies that make up the forces behind war!

5 | RECONNECT TO YOUR HIGHEST LOVE

Saint Germain I AM, and Saint Germain I is, for I AM One with the great flow of all that is the River of Life.

What does it mean to be poor? How can you be poor? Well my beloved, you can be poor only by being separated from the River of Life itself. The River of Life is designed to help all life become more. Of course, as long as you are becoming more, there can be no poverty. You know that even though you may not have the total abundance right now, surely you will have it, if you keep transcending your current state. One day you will indeed have greater abundance, but it will not stop there, for you know you are in the eternal flow of God.

Those who are trapped in the outer conditions of poverty, and in the consciousness of poverty, are trapped precisely because they are separated from that River of Life. They do not have the vision, the knowing, the experience that life is a constant process of becoming more. They see it as something static, and thus they think they are trapped at their current level of material abundance and their current level of spiritual abundance, their current level of ignorance. They do not even know enough to know that there is more to life, or they do not fully believe that there is more to life. They do not believe that they could have it, thinking – because they have been trapped in the lie – that it is reserved for the few, for the elite.

Human beings cannot generate love

Poverty is a consequence of being separated from the River of Life. How can you be separated from the River of Life when the River of Life is the great is that encompasses all that is, all that exists? You can be separated from the River of Life only when you do not have love—you have lost love. How can you lose love when love is all there is? Only through the illusion created by the mind of anti-Christ. This illusion has two levels.

The first level, which is again the perversion of the Alpha or the Father, is that it is possible to be separated from the River of Life. The illusion that it is possible for any part of the Allness – that is all that is – to be separated from all that is. When I present it to you this way, even your intellects can see that there is something here that does not add up. It is not logical that anything can be separated from all that is, as it is not logical that one drop can be separated from the ocean, or that one planet in this material universe can be separated from the material universe.

The next level of illusion, which is a perversion of the Omega or Mother aspect, is that you are a separate being. Because you are separate, you are not worthy of love, you are not worthy to be in the flow of love. When you look at the people on this planet who are firmly trapped in the consciousness, the illusion, of poverty – in the energy vortex of poverty

– you will see that they are among the people who have the least love. They dare not believe that they are worthy of love so how can they receive love?

My beloved, what is love? What most people consider to be love is not love at all. You hear so often people talk and say: "I love this" or "I love that person," or "I love chocolate" or "I love big fancy houses or fast cars." But you see, because people have become blinded by the illusions of duality, they do not realize that when they talk about love, they are not talking about love at all. Human love is not simply a perversion of Divine Love – human love is not simply separated from Divine Love – human love is not love at all.

I must tell you that it is not possible for a human being to generate love. Allow your minds to absorb this statement, my beloved. You may think that you can feel love for another human being. When you are in love, you may think that this is something you are generating, but it is not. You cannot create love, you cannot destroy love. Love is the very driving force of the universe itself. It is love that gave God the will to create, the will to be more. This is the Alpha aspect of love. The Omega aspect of love is that which draws all of the diversified creation back to union with its source. This is the Omega aspect that seeks to return everything in the material world to oneness with its source, oneness with the Father, instead of being separated from that Father.

Love is the very creative flow that you see as the figure-eight flow. Love starts with the Creator in the spiritual realm, as the outgoing, downward flow that flows from the upper figure of the figure-eight, down to the nexus and then into the material world. Here it manifests itself as many individual beings and as everything you see in the physical universe. Once you reach that bottom point, then the return current of the Omega love is meant to take over. It will then draw everything from the material universe back up the figure-eight flow. It then goes through the nexus of becoming the Christ, the living Christ, and then it can flow back up to greater and greater degrees of oneness with its source and oneness with all life.

This is the force of love, flowing through the Alpha and Omega. This force is the very driving force in creation. In fact, there really is no other force, there is nothing else that exists, for everything is simply different manifestations of love. Or as the case may be, when you have separated yourself from the River of Life, it is still love that has taken on a lesser manifestation and an appearance of something separated from the great flow of life. That is why I am saying that you, as a human being, cannot create or generate love.

What you *can* do is to open up your being, your mind and heart, to allow the force of life, the River of Life, to flow through you and find expression through you in love for other people, love for a cause, love for making something more beautiful. Your choice is not a choice of whether to create love or not create love, but to open yourself up to love and allow God to flow through you. In so doing, you must also be willing to let that flow of the River of Life take you wherever it wants to take you so that you can fulfill your Divine plan. This is the plan you created before you came into embodiment in this specific lifetime, and before you first descended into the material universe.

Why love does not seek to own

You cannot stand still when you are in the flow of the River of Life. When you are in the flow, you simply cannot be poor, for what is poverty? It is precisely a state of stillstand where people believe they are trapped and have neither the will nor the knowledge to change their situation.

Why do they believe they are trapped? How can they believe they are trapped? Because they are not open to love! They do not believe they are worthy to have more. They do not believe they are worthy to be in that flow of the River of Life. They somehow believe – perhaps because of a mistake they have made, perhaps because of a sense of being sinners, perhaps because of a sense of being merely highly evolved animals – that they either cannot be in that flow or that they are not worthy to be in that flow. They must accept that they have to stay at their current level for the rest of this lifetime, which they often believe is the rest of their opportunity on earth. They believe it is the only lifetime they have, as they have been taught by both materialistic science and dogmatic, mainstream religion.

For poverty to be overcome, there must be a willingness to reach for a higher understanding of oneself and of life. As one begins to gain that understanding, there must be a recognition, that the only way out of poverty is to once again open oneself up to the flow of the River of Life. Not that it is flowing outside of oneself, passing one by, but that it is flowing inside oneself because one has realized, that the Kingdom of God is within. The open door through which the River of Life can flow is inside of you, not somewhere outside of you.

You can look again at the people who are stuck in poverty, and you can say: "How can they possibly come to accept that God loves them when they have grown up believing that they are poor precisely because they are not worthy of God's love, and that is why he has punished them by making them poor?" Or perhaps they have grown up to believe that there is no God, there is no flow of God's love. How can they then overcome that sense of being stuck, of being separated from the flow of love?

Jesus' mission of love and your mission of love

Once again, it can be done only by them seeing examples of people who are willing to put themselves in the flow of the River of Life and to allow that River of Life to take them wherever they need to go in order to fulfill their Divine plans. One of the main reasons Jesus came to earth was to demonstrate to the people that God has love for them. Did he not say: "God so loved the world that he sent his only begotten son into the world so that the world through him might be saved."

We could say that the essence of Jesus' mission was to help all people understand and accept that God loves them, for they are worthy of God's love. God has sent his son into the world to show an example of one who loves unconditionally. Of course, this was meant to be much more than what it has been turned into by official Christianity. It perverted the inner teachings of Christ by turning Jesus into an exception. Christianity says that Jesus, the outer person of Jesus, was the only son of God, instead of the reality of Jesus' teaching, namely that it is the universal Christ consciousness that is the only begotten son of the Father.

Only this state of consciousness can recognize the reality of the Father while at the same time recognizing the unreality of those who have fallen into the duality consciousness and have separated themselves from the River of Life. The Christ consciousness is the only one who can bridge the gap between the Creator and those who have separated themselves from the River of Life, thereby serving as the open door through which they can get back into oneness with all life.

Jesus came to set forth the example of someone who loves unconditionally. With loving unconditionally we mean, of course, someone who will not accept current conditions as final or unchangeable. A Christed being always goes into a particular situation seeking to raise up that situation and the people in that situation to become more. The Christ realizes that it is not realistic that people can come from a state of extreme poverty to manifesting full Christhood in the blink of an eye. He or she meets them where they are, giving them a cup of cold water in Christ's name, giving them whatever they need at their current level of consciousness in order to raise themselves up to that next level and then continue from there.

Precisely because of the consciousness of separation, precisely because of the downward spiral of poverty, both spiritual and material poverty, people were not ready 2,000 years ago to understand the inner teachings of Christ. That is part of the reason Jesus' teachings were perverted so that he was set up as the exception. In reality, the hope was that many people would dare to follow in the footsteps of Christ and also express that unconditional love by saying: "We cannot accept current conditions, we need to change, we need to come up higher."

When you look at the past 2,000 years, my beloved, you will see that there have indeed been outstanding individuals who had that love of Christ to come into this world, into a particular society, and say: "Things must change! Things cannot remain the same! Things *must* become more because they *can* become more, and this is right!"

This is the greater right that is beyond any human discussion, or any human definition of the duality of human right or human wrong. It is right because it is right in God. You have seen a few individuals who have taken that stand, and you have also seen that, once in a while, a greater group of people were willing to take a stand for a greater cause, for something that was right. Every time you saw that happen, you saw a shift in the collective consciousness, and you saw that being outpictured in the physical reality so that society changed at least a little bit.

Speaking out for what is the greater right

Had the true teachings of Christ not been perverted, many more people would have come to that point where they had dared to speak out and take a stand for what is right. Thus, society would have changed even more. But again, we are not the ones who regret what did not happen in the past, for we are always in the flow of the great is. We are constantly looking at the situation on earth, looking at the problems from a realistic assessment, but also looking at the potential that those problems could be overcome – in many cases as in the blinking of an eye – through an expansion of awareness on a collective level.

That is why, as I have said in my previous discourses, we recognize that even though appearances might be grim in some areas of this planet, we see that underneath the surface, the past 2,000 years have not in any way been wasted. Even though there has not been an outer manifestation of millions of people taking a stand for Christ, there has been an inner growth. Millions of people have been prepared at inner levels to, in this age, finally take that stand and speak out against what is not right by simply stating what is not right.

We know, because we see the inner potential, that it is possible that, in a very short time span, millions of people can be awakened to the realization that certain problems in society simply are not right and that they are no longer acceptable. One of those problems is precisely poverty. When – and mind you, I do not say "if," I say "when" – that breakthrough occurs, you will see that everything will change. The collective consciousness will shift almost instantly, and thereby, within a very short time span, even the physical "reality" will shift.

The absolute need for a non-violent approach

This morning I inspired this messenger to read a speech given by Mahatma Gandhi many years ago when India was still very much suppressed by the British colonial empire. This was a situation where Gandhi was invited to give a speech in front of a group of all of the important people in India, all those who were part of the power elite. These were people who were not used to having anyone speak out against them, they were not used to having anyone speak the truth. Gandhi stood up in front of this group of people and very calmly and very humbly – and in a very straightforward, honest manner – expressed what he saw as the wrongs in Indian society, and how they needed to change and why they were not right.

My beloved, this was not in itself a great, magnificent speech, but it was a ground-breaking speech in the sense that, for the first time, someone dared to say publicly what many many Indians knew in their hearts to be true. They had dared to say this privately but had not dared to speak out in the public for fear of various kinds of reprisals, even fear of ridicule. Or they had the sense that this was not proper because a person from a lowly station in society surely should not speak out in front of those of a higher station—such was the consciousness of the time.

By the fact that one person dared to stand up in a public forum and simply speak the truth, there was a shift in the collective consciousness in India that started a chain reaction. By

Gandhi and others continuing to speak out, that shift gained momentum until it became an unstoppable force. What was significant about Gandhi and the reason why I bring him up as an example, was that at a very early stage in his career, he realized that he personally had a choice to make.

He knew that he had the ability to become an orator and a leader who could lead an uprising against British colonial rule. He knew that he had the potential to become a leader for those people who were willing to engage in a violent uprising against the British, even if it had little chance of success. He saw – very clearly – the handwriting on the wall, so to speak, of whether he would go the way of becoming a revolutionary leader in a violent revolution, or whether he would seek a different approach, a middle way of non-violence.

That is why he decided, at a very early stage, that the very foundation for his mission and service had to be non-violence. This is precisely why he was successful in setting India free from British rule. Had he gone the way of violence, then India would not have been free until much later. There would have been such bloodshed that it would be almost unimaginable, even to the British people. If such bloodshed had come about, the British would have ended up being so disgusted with themselves that it would have been a great detriment to that nation. It would also have been a great detriment to the Indian nation, for they too would have been disgusted with themselves and their capacity for violence.

Take stock of your life

What we are asking you to do today, as the spiritual people, is to look for that middle way, look beyond duality, but also realize that sitting in your cave and meditating on God is not in itself enough to change the world. As with everything else, there must be an Alpha and an Omega action. There must be the great flow of is where the energy of God, the love of God, flows down the figure-eight flow to the bottom. Those who catch that figure-eight flow in this world do not simply use it for their own growth, their own gratification. No, they use it, as Christ demonstrated, to go out into the world to "set my people free."

Jesus said: "Greater love has no man than to lay down his life for a friend." He was willing to go to the ultimate extent of laying down his physical life, but, as I have said before, in this Aquarian age, this is not what is needed. What is needed is that you lay down your human sense of life, your human sense of identity, so that you are willing to reconnect yourself to your Divine plan, the Divine plan that you made before you came into embodiment. You are willing to take stock of your life and say: "Is my present form of life, my present path of life, is it in alignment with my own Divine plan? Is it is alignment with the choices I made when I was not blinded by my current situation in the physical octave?"

If you find that there is a discrepancy, then I am asking you to reconnect to the higher love of your own being, to open yourself up to the flow of the River of Life so that you will feel that flow through your being. Through that flow you will effortlessly – *effortlessly*, my beloved – change your life to bring every aspect of your life into alignment with your Divine plan.

In the past – because of the lower state of consciousness of the people – many spiritual people have gone through extreme disciplines in order to force themselves to be more spiritual. Many have withdrawn from the world, engaging in a great battle within themselves to separate themselves from the lusts and the desires of the world. This was necessary at the time, but I am telling you that there is an alternative. It is to reconnect to the love, and to allow that love to flow through you, whereby you will effortlessly shift your life to bring yourself into alignment with your Divine plan. You will know that this is a much greater love of your being than the love that you might have for any activity on earth that gives you pleasure or comfort.

Saint Germain's love for all people

You see my beloved, I love you with an unconditional love. There are millions of people on this planet, and I speak to them all now: I, Saint Germain, love each one of you. You are my own. Before you came into this lifetime, you volunteered to be part of bringing the Golden Age of Saint Germain into physical manifestation. I know that this is the greatest love of your being and the very reason why you descended to this planet at this particular time.

I see many of you in your current state of consciousness and your current state of life. I see that some of you are burdened by problems. I see that others of you have obtained a certain state of contentment and comfortability where you think that, after all, you are spiritual, after all you are doing this, you are doing that. You are doing rosaries, you are doing prayers, you are doing yoga, you are doing decrees, you are visualizing, you are holding the balance for the planet, you are coming together and praying or singing with other people. You are working with this or that religion, or perhaps you are engaged in society doing this or that humanitarian work or political work, or in other ways trying to change society.

I am not in any way saying that you are not doing something positive, but because I love you unconditionally, I want to tell you that you are still not fulfilling your highest potential. This is what you yourself in cooperation with me defined before you came into embodiment. You have the potential to be more, and to express that more in the physical world, thereby bringing about the more of the Golden Age.

I speak especially to those of you who are content with your lives and your spiritual progress. I, Saint Germain, do not desire to see you come to me after the close of this embodiment and say: "Oh Saint Germain, I had a great time on earth, I enjoyed doing this, I enjoyed doing that!" Then, after you have expressed your enthusiasm, you will face what all of us face after embodiment, in the life review where we calmly and clearly compare what we actually did to what was defined in our Divine plan and our highest potential. I do not desire to see your contentment and your enthusiasm be replaced by the somber realization that you fulfilled but a small percentage of your true potential.

Because I love you unconditionally, I want you to fulfill *all* of your potential. Do not fall into the trap of thinking that your Divine plan defines some far-flung goal that is above and beyond you. No, when you create your Divine plan, you are not blinded by the illusions of duality. You see very realistically what is your potential, or rather the potential for what God can do through you. Do not think that when you create your Divine plan, you define some Utopian ideal that you cannot live up to. No, you look very realistically at who you are, where you are at in your spiritual maturity, and then you define what is truly your realistic potential—if you decide to be all that you can be.

What I am here to remind you of is that many of you have not yet made that decision to be all you can be. You have allowed yourself to become content being what you are right now. Again, I am not saying you are bad people, I am not saying you are wrong. I am simply saying that in my love for you – that is not blinded by any conditions – I know you can be more, and I know this is what you want. In my love for you, I would rather be tough on you right now while you are still in embodiment and have the potential to live up to your highest potential, rather than having to see you go through the disappointment when it is too late and cycles have turned and you are no longer in embodiment.

Decide to be all you can be

Greater love has no man or woman than to lay down his life for a greater cause. Greater love have none of you than to lay down your comfortable lifestyles for the greater cause of bringing the Golden Age into embodiment.

The reality is that poverty can be defined in different ways. I have talked about those who are trapped in extreme poverty, and all of you can truly see that there are millions of people on earth who live in such poor physical conditions that they are trapped in both material and spiritual poverty. Everything starts in the mind, and I would remind you that there are many more people who are trapped in a form of spiritual poverty where they have at least some material abundance, but they think that is all there is to life.

I would go even further and say: "Well, who are the most poor people on this planet?" Those are the people that I partly talked about earlier today where I said that there are many people who are partially awakened to the need for change. They have been trapped in some intellectual pursuit of change through man-made ideologies or belief systems, not realizing that true change can only be brought through the oneness of Spirit and matter, the oneness of Father and Mother, so that we close the figure-eight flow between Above and below.

Those that are the most poor are those who have the inner potential to be more, and to bring about a Golden Age, but who are trapped in some illusion of the outer mind that prevents them from expressing that potential. You who are the spiritual people might look in the mirror and say: "Am I also poor because I am not living up to my highest potential, being all that I can be?"

My beloved, listen to what I say, for I speak with a greater love than you will ever encounter on earth. I am not coming to you to make you feel bad about yourself and your service and your life up until this point. I love you. I am coming to you precisely because I love you. I want you to stop, to step back and to say: "Is my life truly in alignment with my Divine plan? Am I fulfilling my highest potential, or is there more?"

I can tell you that for each one of you there is more, it is only a matter of whether you are willing to separate yourself enough from the ego to acknowledge that there is more. If you realize that there is more, be willing to lay down your comfortable sense of life and change your life, shift your consciousness, shift your outer life to bring it into alignment with the highest vision you can see right now.

You must understand that there is hardly any person who has ever come to this earth with a full awareness of their Divine plan. Not even Jesus had this full awareness, even though the idolatry of many Christians and even the idolatry of many spiritual people would make it seem as if he knew even from early childhood who he was and what his full mission was, having this or that ability to do supernatural things even as a child. Hardly anyone has had a clear recognition of the fullness of their Divine plan. Part of your Divine plan is to demonstrate the path of becoming more, and the path of becoming more is precisely that you start where you are, and you do something with what you have. You take what you have and you make it more. Then, as you have made it more, you will gain a higher vision of how to take what you now have and make that more. *That* is how life progresses, my beloved.

Why poverty is so paralyzing

This is precisely the effect of poverty. It paralyses people so that they are not willing to work with what they have and make the best of it, thereby making even miserable poverty into more, into something better. Why are they not able or willing to do this? They are not attuned with the very basic force of the universe, which is love, the love which drives all life to become more and grow towards the fullness of the Creator's Being, as I already expressed.

Do you now see that if you are content with your life as it is, it is because you are lacking in love? You have shut off the flow of love through you, instead of allowing it to flow in full measure. Why have you done this? Because you are not willing to let go of what you have right now, because you are afraid that you might lose something. You are like the servant who buried his talents in the ground, instead of being willing to multiply them so that he would have more to show when the master came back. The stark reality is that it is possible to be a person who believes that he or she is a spiritual person – be it a good Christian, Hindu, Muslim or ascended master student – yet despite all of one's understanding of the path, despite all of one's outer practices, one is still lacking in love. One is not willing to let go of some aspect of life (that makes one feel comfortable) in order to become more.

We have said, over and over again, that if this planet is to change, that change must begin with the top 10 percent. That is why I am addressing the one condition that more than anything blocks the top 10 percent from taking their rightful role in society, being the true leaders and not allowing the people to be pulled down by the lowest ten percent. Through their force of will, through their force of wisdom, through their force of love they are compelling, *pulling* the people up higher. They have the love and the wisdom and the will to say: "We will not allow the current conditions to continue, for we know this planet could be more. Thus, we will lay down our lives and work selflessly for positive change on this planet, whatever that means for us individually according to our Divine plan."

Take note, my beloved, that I am not asking you to throw yourself head-long behind some kind of cause. I am not asking you to be unwise or unbalanced, to go out there and get yourself killed or spend the rest of your life promoting some sort of cause that is not an ultimate cause. I am asking you to tune in to your heart, to your higher being, to your own Divine plan and ask yourself: "What is it that God wants to do through me? What is it in my own being that is currently limiting what God can do through me."

Your mission is essential for the Golden Age

Why does this messenger stand here giving this message? Because many years ago he asked himself precisely those questions. He kept contemplating them until he had come to a state of resolution that allowed him to come into that total unconditional surrender that he has described. This was precisely the point where he laid down his human life and his human expectations of what his service to God should be. He allowed them to die, whereby he could be reborn into the great flow of is and start his mission. What one has done, all can do. You all have missions that are equally as important as any other mission. You all have something that you can do that is essential for bringing forth the Golden Age.

I am not necessarily talking about some grandiose scheme. You must understand – again – that everything has an Alpha and an Omega aspect. What you see in the messenger bringing forth teachings directly from the ascended masters is the Alpha expression. There are many of you who are meant to bring forth some Omega expression that may not be seemingly as grandiose, but I can assure you is just as important in bringing forth the Golden Age.

Contemplate my teachings on love, the difference between human love, which seeks to possess and hold on to things, and Divine love, which is willing to let go of anything and everything on earth—because it knows that there is so much more in Spirit. Letting go of what is limited can never be a loss, but can only be a gain. You gain, if nothing else, freedom from being entrapped in thinking that you could not live without that particular condition or possession on earth.

Do you see, my beloved? You cannot be free as long as you are holding on to anything on earth. You cannot be free as long as you are holding on to your life. It is only in laying down your life that you become truly free and become one with the River of Life. This is what Christ called eternal life. This form of life never seeks to hold on to any limitation, any condition. It is constantly transcending itself and becoming more, and only in becoming more can it continue to have life.

Once again, I thank you for your attention, for your willingness to be here. As the conclusion of this discourse, I simply send the call again into the planetary consciousness, and the individual consciousness of all those who are part of Saint Germain's bands. I say: "Wake up and know that you are more! Then, reconnect to the greater love whereby you *will* be more, you will be here below the greater love that you already are Above. Then the earth can be here below what it already is above so that the Golden Age that is already manifest in the etheric, mental and even to some degree the emotional realm, can break through and be manifest in the physical."

My beloved, I seal you in the love of Saint Germain, the love that is infused with the Freedom Flame. It is the love that will not allow anyone to be trapped in limitations but wants all people to experience ultimate freedom, the freedom that I AM.

6 | INVOKING THE LOVE TO OVERCOME POVERTY

In the name of the I AM THAT I AM, Jesus Christ, I call upon Saint Germain and Sanat Kumara for the transformation of the consciousness of poverty on earth. Awaken people to the reality that we are spiritual beings and that we can co-create a new future by working with the ascended masters. I especially call for …

[Make your own calls here.]

Part 1

1. Saint Germain, awaken people to the reality that one can be poor only by being separated from the River of Life.

O Saint Germain, you do inspire,
my vision raised forever higher,
with you I form a figure-eight,
your Golden Age I co-create.

**O Saint Germain, what love you bring,
it truly makes all matter sing,
your violet flame does all restore,
with you we are becoming more.**

2. Saint Germain, awaken people to the reality that as long as we are becoming more, there can be no poverty.

O Saint Germain, what Freedom Flame,
released when we recite your name,
acceleration is your gift,
our planet it will surely lift.

**O Saint Germain, what love you bring,
it truly makes all matter sing,
your violet flame does all restore,
with you we are becoming more.**

3. Saint Germain, awaken people to the reality that if we keep transcending our current state, one day we will have greater abundance, for we are in the eternal flow of God.

O Saint Germain, in love we claim,
our right to bring your violet flame,
from you Above, to us below,
it is an all-transforming flow.

**O Saint Germain, what love you bring,
it truly makes all matter sing,
your violet flame does all restore,
with you we are becoming more.**

4. Saint Germain, awaken people to the reality that those who are trapped in the outer conditions of poverty, and in the consciousness of poverty, are trapped precisely because they are separated from the River of Life.

O Saint Germain, I love you so,
my aura filled with violet glow,
my chakras filled with violet fire,
I am your cosmic amplifier.

**O Saint Germain, what love you bring,
it truly makes all matter sing,
your violet flame does all restore,
with you we are becoming more.**

5. Saint Germain, awaken people who do not have the vision, the knowing, the experience that life is a constant process of becoming more.

O Saint Germain, I am now free,
your violet flame is therapy,
transform all hang-ups in my mind,
as inner peace I surely find.

**O Saint Germain, what love you bring,
it truly makes all matter sing,
your violet flame does all restore,
with you we are becoming more.**

6. Saint Germain, awaken people who see life as something static, and thus they think they are trapped at their current level of material abundance and their current level of spiritual abundance, their current level of ignorance.

> O Saint Germain, my body pure,
> your violet flame for all is cure,
> consume the cause of all disease,
> and therefore I am all at ease.
>
> **O Saint Germain, what love you bring,**
> **it truly makes all matter sing,**
> **your violet flame does all restore,**
> **with you we are becoming more.**

7. Saint Germain, awaken people who do not know that there is more to life, or they do not fully believe that there is more to life.

> O Saint Germain, I'm karma-free,
> the past no longer burdens me,
> a brand new opportunity,
> I am in Christic unity.
>
> **O Saint Germain, what love you bring,**
> **it truly makes all matter sing,**
> **your violet flame does all restore,**
> **with you we are becoming more.**

8. Saint Germain, awaken people to the reality that we can be separated from the River of Life only when we do not have love—we have lost love.

O Saint Germain, we are now one,
I am for you a violet sun,
as we transform this planet earth,
your Golden Age is given birth.

**O Saint Germain, what love you bring,
it truly makes all matter sing,
your violet flame does all restore,
with you we are becoming more.**

9. Saint Germain, awaken people to the reality that we can lose love only through the illusion created by the mind of anti-Christ.

O Saint Germain, the earth is free,
from burden of duality,
in oneness we bring what is best,
your Golden Age is manifest.

**O Saint Germain, what love you bring,
it truly makes all matter sing,
your violet flame does all restore,
with you we are becoming more.**

Part 2

1. Saint Germain, awaken people from the Alpha illusion that it is possible to be separated from the River of Life, that it is possible for any part of the Allness to be separated from all that is.

Sanat Kumara, Ruby Fire,
I seek my place in love's own choir,
with open hearts we sing your praise,
together we the earth do raise.

**Sanat Kumara, Ruby Ray,
bring to earth a higher way,
light this planet with your fire,
clothe her in a new attire.**

2. Saint Germain, awaken people from the Omega illusion that we are separate beings, and because we are separate, we are not worthy of love, we are not worthy to be in the flow of love.

Sanat Kumara, Ruby Fire,
initiations I desire,
I am for you an electrode,
Shamballa is my true abode.

**Sanat Kumara, Ruby Ray,
bring to earth a higher way,
light this planet with your fire,
clothe her in a new attire.**

3. Saint Germain, awaken the people who are firmly trapped in the consciousness, the illusion, the energy vortex of poverty. Help them see that they are among the people who have the least love.

Sanat Kumara, Ruby Fire,
I follow path that you require,
initiate me with your love,
the open door for Holy Dove.

> **Sanat Kumara, Ruby Ray,
> bring to earth a higher way,
> light this planet with your fire,
> clothe her in a new attire.**

4. Saint Germain, awaken the people who dare not believe that they are worthy of love so they cannot receive love.

> Sanat Kumara, Ruby Fire,
> your great example all inspire,
> with non-attachment and great mirth,
> we give the earth a true rebirth.

> **Sanat Kumara, Ruby Ray,
> bring to earth a higher way,
> light this planet with your fire,
> clothe her in a new attire.**

5. Saint Germain, awaken people to the reality that human love is not simply a perversion of Divine Love, human love is not love at all.

> Sanat Kumara, Ruby Fire,
> you are this planet's purifier,
> consume on earth all spirits dark,
> reveal the inner Spirit Spark.

> **Sanat Kumara, Ruby Ray,
> bring to earth a higher way,
> light this planet with your fire,
> clothe her in a new attire.**

6. Saint Germain, awaken people to the reality that it is not possible for a human being to generate love.

> Sanat Kumara, Ruby Fire,
> you are a cosmic amplifier,
> the lower forces can't withstand,
> vibrations from Venusian band.

> **Sanat Kumara, Ruby Ray,**
> **bring to earth a higher way,**
> **light this planet with your fire,**
> **clothe her in a new attire.**

7. Saint Germain, awaken people to the reality that we cannot create love, we cannot destroy love. Love is the driving force of the universe.

> Sanat Kumara, Ruby Fire,
> I am on earth your magnifier,
> the flow of love I do restore,
> my chakras are your open door.

> **Sanat Kumara, Ruby Ray,**
> **bring to earth a higher way,**
> **light this planet with your fire,**
> **clothe her in a new attire.**

8. Saint Germain, awaken people to the reality that the Alpha aspect of love is what gave God the will to create. The Omega aspect of love is that which draws all of the diversified creation back to union with its source.

Sanat Kumara, Ruby Fire,
Venusian song the multiplier,
as we your love reverberate,
the densest minds we penetrate.

Sanat Kumara, Ruby Ray,
bring to earth a higher way,
light this planet with your fire,
clothe her in a new attire.

9. Saint Germain, awaken people to the reality that love starts with the Creator in the spiritual realm, as the outgoing Alpha flow. The return current of the Omega love is what draws everything from the material universe back up the figure-eight flow.

Sanat Kumara, Ruby Fire,
you are for all the sanctifier,
the earth is now a holy place,
purified by cosmic grace.

Sanat Kumara, Ruby Ray,
bring to earth a higher way,
light this planet with your fire,
clothe her in a new attire.

Part 3

1. Saint Germain, awaken people to the reality that the force of love, flowing through the Alpha and Omega is the very driving force in creation. There is no other force, there is nothing else that exists, for everything is simply different manifestations of love.

> O Saint Germain, you do inspire,
> my vision raised forever higher,
> with you I form a figure-eight,
> your Golden Age I co-create.

> **O Saint Germain, what love you bring,**
> **it truly makes all matter sing,**
> **your violet flame does all restore,**
> **with you we are becoming more.**

2. Saint Germain, awaken people to the reality that when we have separated ourselves from the River of Life, it is still love that has taken on a lesser manifestation and an appearance of something separated from the flow of life.

> O Saint Germain, what Freedom Flame,
> released when we recite your name,
> acceleration is your gift,
> our planet it will surely lift.

> **O Saint Germain, what love you bring,**
> **it truly makes all matter sing,**
> **your violet flame does all restore,**
> **with you we are becoming more.**

3. Saint Germain, awaken people to the reality that we cannot create or generate love. We can open our beings to allow the force of life, the River of Life, to flow through us and find expression through love for other people, love for a cause, love for making something more beautiful.

> O Saint Germain, in love we claim,
> our right to bring your violet flame,
> from you Above, to us below,
> it is an all-transforming flow.

> **O Saint Germain, what love you bring,**
> **it truly makes all matter sing,**
> **your violet flame does all restore,**
> **with you we are becoming more.**

4. Saint Germain, awaken people to the reality that our choice is not a choice of whether to create love or not to create love, but to open ourselves up to love and allow God to flow through us.

> O Saint Germain, I love you so,
> my aura filled with violet glow,
> my chakras filled with violet fire,
> I am your cosmic amplifier.

> **O Saint Germain, what love you bring,**
> **it truly makes all matter sing,**
> **your violet flame does all restore,**
> **with you we are becoming more.**

5. Saint Germain, awaken people to the reality that we must be willing to let the flow of the River of Life take us wherever it wants so we can fulfill our Divine plans.

> O Saint Germain, I am now free,
> your violet flame is therapy,
> transform all hang-ups in my mind,
> as inner peace I surely find.
>
> **O Saint Germain, what love you bring,**
> **it truly makes all matter sing,**
> **your violet flame does all restore,**
> **with you we are becoming more.**

6. Saint Germain, awaken people to the reality that when we are in the flow, we cannot be poor, for poverty is a state of still-stand where people believe they are trapped and have neither the will nor the knowledge to change their situation.

> O Saint Germain, my body pure,
> your violet flame for all is cure,
> consume the cause of all disease,
> and therefore I am all at ease.
>
> **O Saint Germain, what love you bring,**
> **it truly makes all matter sing,**
> **your violet flame does all restore,**
> **with you we are becoming more.**

7. Saint Germain, awaken people to the reality that we can believe we are trapped only because we are not open to love, we do not believe we are worthy to have more.

O Saint Germain, I'm karma-free,
the past no longer burdens me,
a brand new opportunity,
I am in Christic unity.

**O Saint Germain, what love you bring,
it truly makes all matter sing,
your violet flame does all restore,
with you we are becoming more.**

8. Saint Germain, awaken the people who believe that because of a mistake they have made, a sense of being sinners, a sense of being merely evolved animals, they either cannot be in the flow or they are not worthy to be in the flow.

O Saint Germain, we are now one,
I am for you a violet sun,
as we transform this planet earth,
your Golden Age is given birth.

**O Saint Germain, what love you bring,
it truly makes all matter sing,
your violet flame does all restore,
with you we are becoming more.**

9. Saint Germain, awaken the people who accept that they have to stay at their current level for the rest of this lifetime, which they believe is the only lifetime they have according to both materialistic science and dogmatic religion.

> O Saint Germain, the earth is free,
> from burden of duality,
> in oneness we bring what is best,
> your Golden Age is manifest.
>
> **O Saint Germain, what love you bring,**
> **it truly makes all matter sing,**
> **your violet flame does all restore,**
> **with you we are becoming more.**

Part 4

1. Saint Germain, awaken people to the reality that for poverty to be overcome, there must be a willingness to reach for a higher understanding of oneself and of life.

> Sanat Kumara, Ruby Fire,
> I seek my place in love's own choir,
> with open hearts we sing your praise,
> together we the earth do raise.
>
> **Sanat Kumara, Ruby Ray,**
> **bring to earth a higher way,**
> **light this planet with your fire,**
> **clothe her in a new attire.**

2. Saint Germain, awaken people to the reality that the only way out of poverty is to open ourselves to the flow of the River of Life because we have realized that the Kingdom of God is within us.

Sanat Kumara, Ruby Fire,
initiations I desire,
I am for you an electrode,
Shamballa is my true abode.

**Sanat Kumara, Ruby Ray,
bring to earth a higher way,
light this planet with your fire,
clothe her in a new attire.**

3. Saint Germain, awaken the people who have grown up believing that they are poor because they are not worthy of God's love and that God has punished them by making them poor.

Sanat Kumara, Ruby Fire,
I follow path that you require,
initiate me with your love,
the open door for Holy Dove.

**Sanat Kumara, Ruby Ray,
bring to earth a higher way,
light this planet with your fire,
clothe her in a new attire.**

4. Saint Germain, awaken the people who have grown up to believe that there is no God, there is no flow of God's love.

Sanat Kumara, Ruby Fire,
your great example all inspire,
with non-attachment and great mirth,
we give the earth a true rebirth.

> Sanat Kumara, Ruby Ray,
> bring to earth a higher way,
> light this planet with your fire,
> clothe her in a new attire.

5. Saint Germain, awaken people to the reality that one of the main reasons Jesus came to earth was to demonstrate to the people that God has love for them.

> Sanat Kumara, Ruby Fire,
> you are this planet's purifier,
> consume on earth all spirits dark,
> reveal the inner Spirit Spark.

> Sanat Kumara, Ruby Ray,
> bring to earth a higher way,
> light this planet with your fire,
> clothe her in a new attire.

6. Saint Germain, awaken people to the reality that the essence of Jesus' mission was to help all people understand and accept that God loves them, for they are worthy of God's love.

> Sanat Kumara, Ruby Fire,
> you are a cosmic amplifier,
> the lower forces can't withstand,
> vibrations from Venusian band.

> Sanat Kumara, Ruby Ray,
> bring to earth a higher way,
> light this planet with your fire,
> clothe her in a new attire.

7. Saint Germain, awaken people to the reality that official Christianity perverted the inner teachings of Christ by turning Jesus into an exception and saying he was the only son of God.

> Sanat Kumara, Ruby Fire,
> I am on earth your magnifier,
> the flow of love I do restore,
> my chakras are your open door.
>
> **Sanat Kumara, Ruby Ray,**
> **bring to earth a higher way,**
> **light this planet with your fire,**
> **clothe her in a new attire.**

8. Saint Germain, awaken people to the reality that the Christ consciousness is the only one who can bridge the gap between the Creator and those who have separated themselves from the River of Life.

> Sanat Kumara, Ruby Fire,
> Venusian song the multiplier,
> as we your love reverberate,
> the densest minds we penetrate.
>
> **Sanat Kumara, Ruby Ray,**
> **bring to earth a higher way,**
> **light this planet with your fire,**
> **clothe her in a new attire.**

9. Saint Germain, awaken people to the reality that Jesus came to set forth the example of someone who loves unconditionally, someone who will not accept current conditions as final or unchangeable.

Sanat Kumara, Ruby Fire,
you are for all the sanctifier,
the earth is now a holy place,
purified by cosmic grace.

**Sanat Kumara, Ruby Ray,
bring to earth a higher way,
light this planet with your fire,
clothe her in a new attire.**

Part 5

1. Saint Germain, awaken people to the reality that those who have the love of Christ say: "Things must change! Things cannot remain the same! Things must become more because they *can* become more, and this is right!"

O Saint Germain, you do inspire,
my vision raised forever higher,
with you I form a figure-eight,
your Golden Age I co-create.

**O Saint Germain, what love you bring,
it truly makes all matter sing,
your violet flame does all restore,
with you we are becoming more.**

2. Saint Germain, awaken people to the reality that every time an individual or a group of people are willing to take a stand for a greater cause, there is a shift in the collective consciousness. It will be outpictured in the physical reality so that society changes.

> O Saint Germain, what Freedom Flame,
> released when we recite your name,
> acceleration is your gift,
> our planet it will surely lift.
>
> **O Saint Germain, what love you bring,**
> **it truly makes all matter sing,**
> **your violet flame does all restore,**
> **with you we are becoming more.**

3. Saint Germain, awaken people to the reality that millions of people have been prepared at inner levels to take that stand and speak out against poverty by simply stating what is not right.

> O Saint Germain, in love we claim,
> our right to bring your violet flame,
> from you Above, to us below,
> it is an all-transforming flow.
>
> **O Saint Germain, what love you bring,**
> **it truly makes all matter sing,**
> **your violet flame does all restore,**
> **with you we are becoming more.**

4. Saint Germain, awaken people to the possibility that millions of people can be awakened to the realization that poverty is not right and that it is no longer acceptable.

> O Saint Germain, I love you so,
> my aura filled with violet glow,
> my chakras filled with violet fire,
> I am your cosmic amplifier.

> **O Saint Germain, what love you bring,**
> **it truly makes all matter sing,**
> **your violet flame does all restore,**
> **with you we are becoming more.**

5. Saint Germain, awaken people to the reality that there is great value in someone daring to say publicly what many people know in their hearts to be true.

> O Saint Germain, I am now free,
> your violet flame is therapy,
> transform all hang-ups in my mind,
> as inner peace I surely find.

> **O Saint Germain, what love you bring,**
> **it truly makes all matter sing,**
> **your violet flame does all restore,**
> **with you we are becoming more.**

6. Saint Germain, awaken people to the reality that when one person dares to stand up in a public forum and speak the truth, there will be a shift in the collective consciousness that starts a chain reaction.

O Saint Germain, my body pure,
your violet flame for all is cure,
consume the cause of all disease,
and therefore I am all at ease.

**O Saint Germain, what love you bring,
it truly makes all matter sing,
your violet flame does all restore,
with you we are becoming more.**

7. Saint Germain, awaken people to the reality that by others continuing to speak out, the shift gains momentum until it becomes an unstoppable force.

O Saint Germain, I'm karma-free,
the past no longer burdens me,
a brand new opportunity,
I am in Christic unity.

**O Saint Germain, what love you bring,
it truly makes all matter sing,
your violet flame does all restore,
with you we are becoming more.**

8. Saint Germain, awaken people to the reality that there is an absolute necessity for those who want to bring about change in this age to walk the middle way of non-violence.

O Saint Germain, we are now one,
I am for you a violet sun,
as we transform this planet earth,
your Golden Age is given birth.

> O Saint Germain, what love you bring,
> it truly makes all matter sing,
> your violet flame does all restore,
> with you we are becoming more.

9. Saint Germain, awaken the spiritual people to look for the middle way, to look beyond duality and to realize that sitting in a cave and meditating on God is not in itself enough to change the world.

> O Saint Germain, the earth is free,
> from burden of duality,
> in oneness we bring what is best,
> your Golden Age is manifest.

> O Saint Germain, what love you bring,
> it truly makes all matter sing,
> your violet flame does all restore,
> with you we are becoming more.

Part 6

1. Saint Germain, awaken people to the reality that in the Aquarian age, we do not need to lay down our physical lives. We need to lay down our human sense of life, our human sense of identity, so that we are willing to reconnect to our Divine plans.

Sanat Kumara, Ruby Fire,
I seek my place in love's own choir,
with open hearts we sing your praise,
together we the earth do raise.

**Sanat Kumara, Ruby Ray,
bring to earth a higher way,
light this planet with your fire,
clothe her in a new attire.**

2. Saint Germain, awaken the spiritual people to the need to take stock of our lives and say: "Is my present form of life in alignment with my Divine plan? Is it in alignment with the choices I made when I was not blinded by my current situation in the physical octave?"

Sanat Kumara, Ruby Fire,
initiations I desire,
I am for you an electrode,
Shamballa is my true abode.

**Sanat Kumara, Ruby Ray,
bring to earth a higher way,
light this planet with your fire,
clothe her in a new attire.**

3. Saint Germain, help the spiritual people reconnect to the higher love of our own beings, so we will effortlessly change our lives to bring every aspect into alignment with our Divine plans.

Sanat Kumara, Ruby Fire,
I follow path that you require,
initiate me with your love,
the open door for Holy Dove.

**Sanat Kumara, Ruby Ray,
bring to earth a higher way,
light this planet with your fire,
clothe her in a new attire.**

4. Saint Germain, awaken the people who, before they came into this lifetime, volunteered to be part of bringing your Golden Age into physical manifestation. Help us see that this is the greatest love of our beings and the very reason we descended to this planet at this particular time.

Sanat Kumara, Ruby Fire,
your great example all inspire,
with non-attachment and great mirth,
we give the earth a true rebirth.

**Sanat Kumara, Ruby Ray,
bring to earth a higher way,
light this planet with your fire,
clothe her in a new attire.**

5. Saint Germain, awaken the people who are doing something spiritual but who are not fulfilling their highest potential because they can be more and express that more in the physical world.

> Sanat Kumara, Ruby Fire,
> you are this planet's purifier,
> consume on earth all spirits dark,
> reveal the inner Spirit Spark.
>
> **Sanat Kumara, Ruby Ray,**
> **bring to earth a higher way,**
> **light this planet with your fire,**
> **clothe her in a new attire.**

6. Saint Germain, awaken the people who are content with their lives and their spiritual progress and help them see the true potential in their Divine plans.

> Sanat Kumara, Ruby Fire,
> you are a cosmic amplifier,
> the lower forces can't withstand,
> vibrations from Venusian band.
>
> **Sanat Kumara, Ruby Ray,**
> **bring to earth a higher way,**
> **light this planet with your fire,**
> **clothe her in a new attire.**

7. Saint Germain, awaken people to the reality that our Divine plans do not define some far-flung goal that is above and beyond us. They are based on a realistic view of our potential, or rather the potential for what God can do through us.

> Sanat Kumara, Ruby Fire,
> I am on earth your magnifier,
> the flow of love I do restore,
> my chakras are your open door.

**Sanat Kumara, Ruby Ray,
bring to earth a higher way,
light this planet with your fire,
clothe her in a new attire.**

8. Saint Germain, awaken the people who have not yet made the decision to be all they can be. They have allowed themselves to become content being what they are right now.

Sanat Kumara, Ruby Fire,
Venusian song the multiplier,
as we your love reverberate,
the densest minds we penetrate.

**Sanat Kumara, Ruby Ray,
bring to earth a higher way,
light this planet with your fire,
clothe her in a new attire.**

9. Saint Germain, awaken people to the reality that greater love has none of us than to lay down our comfortable lifestyles for the greater cause of bringing the Golden Age into manifestation.

Sanat Kumara, Ruby Fire,
you are for all the sanctifier,
the earth is now a holy place,
purified by cosmic grace.

**Sanat Kumara, Ruby Ray,
bring to earth a higher way,
light this planet with your fire,
clothe her in a new attire.**

Part 7

1. Saint Germain, awaken the people who are trapped in extreme poverty, those who live in such poor physical conditions that they are stuck in both material and spiritual poverty.

> O Saint Germain, you do inspire,
> my vision raised forever higher,
> with you I form a figure-eight,
> your Golden Age I co-create.
>
> **O Saint Germain, what love you bring,**
> **it truly makes all matter sing,**
> **your violet flame does all restore,**
> **with you we are becoming more.**

2. Saint Germain, awaken the people who are trapped in a form of spiritual poverty where they have at least some material abundance, but they think that is all there is to life.

> O Saint Germain, what Freedom Flame,
> released when we recite your name,
> acceleration is your gift,
> our planet it will surely lift.
>
> **O Saint Germain, what love you bring,**
> **it truly makes all matter sing,**
> **your violet flame does all restore,**
> **with you we are becoming more.**

3. Saint Germain, awaken people to the reality that the most poor people on this planet are those who are partially awakened to the need for change, but they have been trapped in some intellectual pursuit of change through man-made ideologies, not realizing that true change can only be brought through the oneness of Spirit and matter.

> O Saint Germain, in love we claim,
> our right to bring your violet flame,
> from you Above, to us below,
> it is an all-transforming flow.

> **O Saint Germain, what love you bring,**
> **it truly makes all matter sing,**
> **your violet flame does all restore,**
> **with you we are becoming more.**

4. Saint Germain, awaken the people who have the inner potential to be more and to bring about a Golden Age, but they are trapped in some illusion of the outer mind that prevents them from expressing that potential.

> O Saint Germain, I love you so,
> my aura filled with violet glow,
> my chakras filled with violet fire,
> I am your cosmic amplifier.

> **O Saint Germain, what love you bring,**
> **it truly makes all matter sing,**
> **your violet flame does all restore,**
> **with you we are becoming more.**

5. Saint Germain, awaken people to the reality that for each one of us there is more, it is only a matter of whether we are willing to separate ourselves from the ego and then bring our consciousness and life into alignment with our highest vision.

> O Saint Germain, I am now free,
> your violet flame is therapy,
> transform all hang-ups in my mind,
> as inner peace I surely find.

> **O Saint Germain, what love you bring,**
> **it truly makes all matter sing,**
> **your violet flame does all restore,**
> **with you we are becoming more.**

6. Saint Germain, awaken people to the reality that part of our Divine plan is to demonstrate the path of becoming more, the path of starting where we are and doing something with what we have.

> O Saint Germain, my body pure,
> your violet flame for all is cure,
> consume the cause of all disease,
> and therefore I am all at ease.

> **O Saint Germain, what love you bring,**
> **it truly makes all matter sing,**
> **your violet flame does all restore,**
> **with you we are becoming more.**

7. Saint Germain, awaken people to the reality that poverty paralyzes people so that they are not willing to work with what they have and make the best of it, thereby making even miserable poverty into more, into something better.

> O Saint Germain, I'm karma-free,
> the past no longer burdens me,
> a brand new opportunity,
> I am in Christic unity.

> **O Saint Germain, what love you bring,**
> **it truly makes all matter sing,**
> **your violet flame does all restore,**
> **with you we are becoming more.**

8. Saint Germain, awaken the people who are not attuned with the basic force of the universe, which is love, the love that drives all life to become more and grow towards the fullness of the Creator's Being.

> O Saint Germain, we are now one,
> I am for you a violet sun,
> as we transform this planet earth,
> your Golden Age is given birth.

> **O Saint Germain, what love you bring,**
> **it truly makes all matter sing,**
> **your violet flame does all restore,**
> **with you we are becoming more.**

9. Saint Germain, awaken people to the reality that if we are content with our lives as they are, it is because we are lacking in love. We have shut off the flow of love through us, instead of allowing it to flow in full measure.

> O Saint Germain, the earth is free,
> from burden of duality,
> in oneness we bring what is best,
> your Golden Age is manifest.
>
> **O Saint Germain, what love you bring,**
> **it truly makes all matter sing,**
> **your violet flame does all restore,**
> **with you we are becoming more.**

Part 8

1. Saint Germain, awaken people to the reality that we have shut off the flow of love because we are not willing to let go of what we have right now, we are afraid that we might lose something.

> Sanat Kumara, Ruby Fire,
> I seek my place in love's own choir,
> with open hearts we sing your praise,
> together we the earth do raise.
>
> **Sanat Kumara, Ruby Ray,**
> **bring to earth a higher way,**
> **light this planet with your fire,**
> **clothe her in a new attire.**

2. Saint Germain, awaken people who believe they are spiritual, yet despite all of their understanding and practice, they are still lacking in love.

> Sanat Kumara, Ruby Fire,
> initiations I desire,
> I am for you an electrode,
> Shamballa is my true abode.

**Sanat Kumara, Ruby Ray,
bring to earth a higher way,
light this planet with your fire,
clothe her in a new attire.**

3. Saint Germain, awaken people to the reality that if this planet is to change, that change must begin with the top 10 percent.

> Sanat Kumara, Ruby Fire,
> I follow path that you require,
> initiate me with your love,
> the open door for Holy Dove.

**Sanat Kumara, Ruby Ray,
bring to earth a higher way,
light this planet with your fire,
clothe her in a new attire.**

4. Saint Germain, awaken the top 10 percent to their Divine plans of taking their rightful role in society, being the true leaders and not allowing the people to be pulled down by the lowest ten percent.

Sanat Kumara, Ruby Fire,
your great example all inspire,
with non-attachment and great mirth,
we give the earth a true rebirth.

**Sanat Kumara, Ruby Ray,
bring to earth a higher way,
light this planet with your fire,
clothe her in a new attire.**

5. Saint Germain, awaken the people who have the love, wisdom and will to say: "We will not allow the current conditions to continue, for we know this planet could be more. Thus, we will lay down our lives and work selflessly for positive change on this planet, whatever that means for us individually according to our Divine plans."

Sanat Kumara, Ruby Fire,
you are this planet's purifier,
consume on earth all spirits dark,
reveal the inner Spirit Spark.

**Sanat Kumara, Ruby Ray,
bring to earth a higher way,
light this planet with your fire,
clothe her in a new attire.**

6. Saint Germain, awaken the top 10 percent to the need to tune in to our hearts, higher beings and Divine plans and ask: "What is it that God wants to do through me? What is it in my own being that is currently limiting what God can do through me."

Sanat Kumara, Ruby Fire,
you are a cosmic amplifier,
the lower forces can't withstand,
vibrations from Venusian band.

**Sanat Kumara, Ruby Ray,
bring to earth a higher way,
light this planet with your fire,
clothe her in a new attire.**

7. Saint Germain, awaken people to the reality that we all have missions that are equally as important as any other mission. We all have something that we can do that is essential in bringing forth the Golden Age.

Sanat Kumara, Ruby Fire,
I am on earth your magnifier,
the flow of love I do restore,
my chakras are your open door.

**Sanat Kumara, Ruby Ray,
bring to earth a higher way,
light this planet with your fire,
clothe her in a new attire.**

8. Saint Germain, awaken people to the reality that human love seeks to possess and hold on to things. Divine love is willing to let go of anything and everything on earth—because it knows there is so much more in Spirit.

Sanat Kumara, Ruby Fire,
Venusian song the multiplier,
as we your love reverberate,
the densest minds we penetrate.

**Sanat Kumara, Ruby Ray,
bring to earth a higher way,
light this planet with your fire,
clothe her in a new attire.**

9. Saint Germain, awaken people to the reality that we cannot be free as long as we are holding on to our lives. It is only in laying down our lives that we become truly free and one with the River of Life. The river is constantly transcending itself and becoming more, and only in becoming more can it continue to have life.

Sanat Kumara, Ruby Fire,
you are for all the sanctifier,
the earth is now a holy place,
purified by cosmic grace.

**Sanat Kumara, Ruby Ray,
bring to earth a higher way,
light this planet with your fire,
clothe her in a new attire.**

Sealing

In the name of the I AM THAT I AM, I accept that Archangel Michael, Astrea and Shiva form an impenetrable shield around myself and all constructive people, sealing us from all fear-based energies in all four octaves. I accept that the Light of God is consuming and transforming all fear-based energies that make up the forces behind war!

7 | POVERTY IS HATRED OF THE MOTHER

Saint Germain I AM, and I come in the great Flame of Freedom. This is the flame of the great is, the is of all life, the River of Life that flows from Spirit to matter and back to Spirit, thus raising up all creation as it flows. The Seventh Ray is the integration of the first six rays, but before you can integrate the six rays and graduate to the initiations of the Seventh Ray, you must integrate the first three and win your freedom on the Fourth Ray of God Purity.

In my first three discourses on this topic, I have spoken about winning your freedom on the First Ray of God Power, the Second Ray of God Wisdom and the Third Ray of God Love. I have talked about the need to overcome poverty on those rays, and poverty, of course, is that which keeps you trapped at a certain level and thus prevents you from winning the freedom that allows you – that *empowers* you – to rise beyond that level.

Understanding the Fourth Ray

We now come to the Fourth Ray of Purity, and it is represented by the white light. You know what happens when you send a ray of white light into a glass prism: you split it into all the colors of the rainbow. The Fourth Ray is in the middle, with three rays before it and three rays after it. What happens to a new lifestream that descends into the matter sphere, is that it must first be tested on the First Ray and learn to express God power. When it has some proficiency in God power, it will begin to be tested on the Second Ray and express wisdom. Then it moves on to love. The first three rays are, so to speak, the beginning of the path of initiation. We know well that as a lifestream begins those first three rays, it has not yet attained Christhood, or even a certain degree of mastery. Therefore, there is – in an ideal situation – a great deal of guidance that is offered to such a lifestream.

If the lifestream takes advantage of this guidance, then it will integrate the lessons of the first three rays and be well prepared for the initiations of the Fourth Ray where it must begin to stand on its own. On the Fourth Ray of Purity a lifestream cannot be tutored in every little detail, for it must of necessity show that it has integrated what it has learned as a result of its tutorship on the first three rays. On the first three rays – when the lifestream experiments with expressing Power, Wisdom and Love – there is a great deal of forgiveness. When a lifestream makes a mistake, it is instantly forgiven and helped by the teacher to see its mistake so that it can rise above it. That is, of course, a lifestream can be helped by the teacher – the true spiritual teacher – only according to its free-will choices and its willingness to learn from the mentorship of the teacher.

7 | Poverty Is Hatred of the Mother

Understanding the fall on the Fourth Ray

As a lifestream experiments and learns on the first three rays, we allow the lifestream to make mistakes and we are quite tolerant of these mistakes. We are not the kind of teachers, that you might know on earth, who come down hard on you and punish you for every little mistake, my beloved. It is not our goal to turn you into robots who can stand attention or march in sync with others, as if you had no individuality. It is our goal to raise you up so that – when you pass the initiations on the Seventh Ray – you are free to express your divine individuality in this world. This is not a mechanical process that can be forced, which is why free will reigns supreme.

It is possible that a lifestream – as it experiments with the first three rays – can build up a certain momentum and habit on misusing those first three rays—in other words, expressing power, wisdom and love in an unbalanced way. A lifestream may begin to feel a certain kind of fear that causes it to express power in order to control other people or its outer situation. This misuse of power – this fear-based expression of power – is the beginning of poverty. When you seek to take by force in the material world, then the more force you express, the more that force will limit yourself and your own spiritual freedom.

As you begin to express power in an unbalanced manner, you will cut yourself off from the power of God. You will not be able to have the power of God flow through you and thereby manifest in the material universe all you desire. Of course, when you experience that you cannot manifest what you desire, you begin to feel poverty. You begin to seek to use even more force in order to control your outer situation. Many lifestreams can come to the point where they go to the next level and start misusing wisdom, which then allows them to use the mind of anti-christ to come up with a sophisticated reasoning for why they do not need or do not want God Power; they simply want power in the material universe. They can gain that power, at least to some degree, by misusing the power of the First Ray through the unbalanced wisdom of the mind of anti-christ, the perversion of God Wisdom.

This perversion of wisdom can lead to the next step where the lifestream begins to feel that it does not love God and that God does not love it. It begins to believe that if God really loved me, God should give me everything I want and should not force me to face the consequences of my own choices—and my own misuse of power and wisdom. You now see the triangle of the misuse – the abuse, the unbalanced use – of power, wisdom and love, which causes the lifestream to sink into a state of spiritual poverty, of feeling cut off from the power, wisdom and love of God. This is a state that sets the stage for the lifestream failing the initiations on the Fourth Ray, which is the ray of purity.

Impure motives

The abuse of power, wisdom and love causes the lifestream to build a momentum of impurity. It begins to express its co-creative abilities in an impure manner that is focused on raising up the self – the separate sense of self, the ego – rather than raising up the All. This, my beloved, is essential to understand. When you reach the initiations of the Fourth Ray, you will face precisely the test of whether you will purify yourself from all imbalanced use of power, wisdom and love, and thereby begin to express your creative abilities in a more pure manner. What do I mean when I say more pure? I mean whether you express your creative abilities in order to gain an advantage for your separate self, or whether you rise to the higher level of using your creative abilities to raise up the All, seeking to have everything in the material universe become more.

Do you see the essential difference here? When you use your creative abilities in an impure manner, you are seeking to gather more and more to the separate self – around the separate self – so that you build an impenetrable wall that isolates the separate self from the return of its own karma, from the return of the consequences of its own choices. You seek to use the energies of the material realm to isolate and insulate yourself from the spiritual path and its initiations.

Why do you do this? Because the separate self, of course, cannot see the true purpose of the spiritual path. It therefore believes that the initiations – the return of your karma, the cosmic mirror sending back to you whatever you send out – is a punishment by an angry God in the sky. The reality is that the return of the consequences of your own choices is precisely how you learn, and therefore it is an opportunity, my beloved.

When you receive a return current from the cosmic mirror that is not pure according to your highest vision, then that is an opportunity for you to realize that what you sent into the cosmic mirror was not a pure impulse.

That is why the mirror reflects back an impure material manifestation. You now have the opportunity to rise up and purify your co-creative efforts. That is, of course, if you are willing to allow what comes back from the cosmic mirror to awaken you to the need to look in the personal mirror and do what Jesus said, namely look for the beam in your own eye. You see where you have allowed impurities to gather in your eye – in your vision, in your mind – thus causing those impurities to form a colored film that inevitably colors your mind. Thereby, it colors everything you send into that cosmic mirror, making it inevitable that the mirror can only reflect back to you an impure manifestation.

Taking full responsibility on the Fourth Ray

The Fourth Ray is the ray of God Purity and the ray of the white light of the Mother. What happens when a lifestream has built this momentum of misusing power, wisdom and love and when the lifestream – when faced with the Fourth Ray initiations – refuses to look in the personal mirror, when the lifestream refuses to purify itself? If the lifestream will not purify itself, there can be only one reason. It is that the lifestream is not willing to take full responsibility for itself and its use of its creative power.

If you are not willing to take full responsibility and recognize the fact of life – that what comes back to you in the material universe, in the world of matter, in the world of Mother, is a reflection of what you have sent out – then what must you do? Very simple, for if what comes back to you from the cosmic mirror is not your fault – because you are not willing to recognize that you could have sent out an impure impulse – then it must be someone else's fault, must it not?

This is one of the core issues of the ego. When something is not to living up to the ego's expectations of how the material world should be, then there must be something wrong and therefore it must be someone's fault. If you are not willing to consider that it might be your fault – in the sense that you have used your co-creative abilities in an unbalanced manner – then you must place blame outside yourself—on someone else.

My beloved, who is that someone else? Well, it is quite simple. It is precisely the white light of the Mother that forces you, so to speak, to face the initiations on the Fourth Ray. The initiation of whether you will raise your co-creative abilities to a higher level and use them to raise up the All, raise up all life, or whether you will use them to gather more to the separate self. Will you seek to gather more of the things of this world to the separate self? Or will you rise to the higher level of seeking to make everything in this world more – meaning more of God's light, more of God's abundance – and thereby raising up all life, even raising up the material sphere to the perfection of the Kingdom of God, as Maitreya explains in his book.

It is precisely the white light that forces you to face the necessity to look at how you have used your co-creative abilities in expressing power, wisdom and love. It is the white light that gives you a sense of co-measurement, for is it not so that in most cultures on this planet white is associated with purity? When you do your laundry, do you not want it to be white, rather than gray or dirtied by other colors?

How hatred of the Mother begins

When you rise to the initiations of the Fourth Ray, what will happen is that your spiritual teachers and your I AM Presence will release a greater amount of the white light of purity into your energy field. This is much like shining a bright light into a dark room. When the room – when your energy field – was still in the shadows – when it was not brightly lit – it was more difficult to see what was pure and what was impure in your energy field. It was more difficult to see where you had expressed power, wisdom and love in an impure manner and where you had expressed it in purity. This allowed your ego to hide in the shadows, so to speak, and find excuses for saying that an imbalanced expression was not really that bad, and therefore you did not have to face it and change it right now.

When that white light of purity descends, you can no longer hide in the shadows. You are forced to take stock of yourself and see what is pure and what is impure. You now have the white light as a sense of co-measurement for what true purity means, even what true power, what true wisdom and what true love means. As the white light shines into your energy field, it will naturally brighten the colors that are there. You know well that as the sun rises in the morning, at first everything looks gray, but as the light intensifies, you now begin to see all of the colors of the flowers and the sky. Naturally, the white light will make it easier for you to see where you have an impure manifestation of the blue color of God Power, an impure manifestation of the golden color of God Wisdom and an impure manifestation of the pink ray of God Love. Thus, your ego cannot so easily deny the need for change.

Of course, if you are not willing to look in the mirror, then the ego always can present you with an easy way out. That easy way out is to place blame on the white light itself, the white light of the Mother. The reasoning from the mind of antichrist, which the ego believes and seeks to make you believe, is that it is not *you* who imposed an impure image on the Ma-ter light. It is the light itself that has manifested an imperfect manifestation that now burdens you, or does not give you what you want. It is the Mother who is against you and who is refusing to give you what you want.

The reasoning is that the Mother is wrong, that there is something wrong with the Mother and that you should seek to use your creative abilities to control, even punish, the Mother. You should do this instead of immersing yourself in the pure white light of the Mother so that you can purify your energy field and have the clear colors of the first three rays shining through the brightness of the Fourth Ray, thereby expressing your co-creative abilities with a higher degree of selflessness.

When you are not willing to look in the mirror and pass the initiations on the Fourth Ray, then the inevitable outcome is what we call hatred of the Mother. When you believe in the lie that the Mother is not merely reflecting back to you what you send out – but that the Mother is deliberately forcing you to encounter an imperfect manifestation – you will almost inevitably turn your fear into hatred of the Mother.

How Lucifer fell

In hating the Mother, you can avoid looking in the mirror—seeing your own impurity. Instead of recognizing that the impurity is inside your own mind and energy field, you do what the ego does best. You project the impurity outside yourself, projecting it onto the Mother Light, saying: "Oh this planet earth is such a low place. There is such a lack of resources. There is such an imbalance in nature. Our bodies are so limited and manifest disease so easily. There is not enough money for everyone. There is not enough resources. There is not enough oil. Everything is so limited and restricted. This is the Mother's fault, this is the fault of Mother Earth because she will not give us the abundant life."

You have an entire class of lifestreams that fell on the initiations of the Fourth Ray. Most of them fell in higher spheres, but it was the same basic initiation. You may know that Lucifer himself fell on the Fourth Ray, and he fell because of the pride of not being willing to look at his own impurities and therefore projecting those impurities on the Mother Light, building up hatred of the Mother.

This is where you need to understand how ingenious God's universe is designed and how ingeniously the Law of Free Will actually works. When a lifestream refuses to voluntarily look at the beam in its own eye, then that lifestream has put itself beyond the reach of the true spiritual teachers of humankind.

We cannot reach that lifestream, for we work exclusively within the framework of the Law of Free Will. There is no point in that lifestream remaining in the mystery school, and that is why the lifestream then falls or descends into a lower sphere, or outside of the mystery school. What happens to that lifestream is that it descends precisely into a sphere that corresponds to its level of consciousness.

When a lifestream has hatred of the Mother, it will descend into the most dense level of the world of form, which is currently the material universe, where it encounters the lowest vibration of the Mother Light. It therefore has an opportunity to learn by encountering precisely that which it has come to believe is responsible for all of its problems. By being forced, so to speak, to face that which it was not willing to face in the mystery school, the lifestream has the only remaining opportunity left open to it to pass its initiations—and overcome the false beliefs that caused it to fall in the first place.

The question, of course, is whether the lifestream will actually do so or whether it will continue to build upon the momentum of denial, thereby building up more and more hatred of the Mother. It can do this until its time runs out and there is no opportunity left for that lifestream to become more, making it necessary for the lifestream – the separate lifestream – to be dissolved in the final act of dissolution in the Court of Sacred Fire. Here, the intensity of the white light of purity burns away all impurities that have been built up over what would be corresponding to millions of lifetimes on earth.

7 | Poverty Is Hatred of the Mother

How poverty relates to God Purity

Can you now see how poverty relates to the initiations of the Fourth Ray of God Purity? Poverty is precisely caused by the fact that you are projecting an impure image onto the Ma-ter light. When you do this, you pull the white light of the Mother down to a lower vibration that is not according to – or in alignment with, in attunement with – the abundant life.

When the white light – a beam of white light – hits a glass prism and is split into the colors of the rainbow, what you see as the colors of the rainbow are not the pure colors that you find in the higher realms. They are a symbol for the impurities in humankind's consciousness, and these impurities project imperfect images onto the Ma-ter light. As more and more of such images are projected onto the Ma-ter light, more and more limitations are created on the physical earth. This is why people come to feel that the earth is a limited place.

The earth is only limited as long as imperfect images are projected onto it. The earth has no desire whatsoever to limit or restrict you. The earth would gladly outpicture the abundant life of God in the twinkling of an eye. The earth has vowed to take on the role of being a substitute teacher for those lifestreams who have cut themselves off from their spiritual teachers—and therefore cannot learn through the School of Divine Direction. They must learn in the School of Hard Knocks by experiencing the mirroring back of what they are sending out. This is what they have allowed to build up in their own consciousness, namely the impurities and the imbalances. When you look at the people on this earth who have the greatest degree of material poverty, you will see that many of them are often being pulled into some very impure activities, as a way to sort of compensate for the fact that they feel boxed in by their daily lives. They seek an escape, for example through alcohol, drugs, gambling, imperfect music, perverted sexual practices or anything else that can be done without a great amount of money. The more poor people become in the material sense, the more insensitive they often become to their own lives, including to their environment. You will see this in a lack of personal hygiene, an unwillingness to dress cleanly, even when this is actually possible according to their material means. You will see it in an inattentiveness to their environment, to the cleanliness of their houses, the beauty of their houses and their surroundings.

Breaking the spiral of poverty

I full well understand that there are many people on this earth who have grown up in poverty and who will say: "But Saint Germain, I do not have the money to build a house, to live in a beautiful house." But I say to you: "There is not one person on this earth who is so poor that they could not do something with what they have to make their lives more, to make their lives better!"

When you look at Jesus' parable about the talents, you will see that the lord gave ten talents to one servant, five to another and two to another. *All* have something that they can multiply. What you see is often that those who feel that they have too little are the ones who say: "We have so little, we can do nothing." They do not even try to do the best with what they have, thus burying their talents in the ground. Thereby, that which they have is taken from them—not because an angry God does so, but because they themselves take from them what they have. They refuse to use what they have to multiply what they have so that they connect themselves to the River of Life.

The River of Life is the process of becoming more. Even if you have very little, if you do the best with what you have, you reconnect yourself to the River of Life. Being connected to the River of Life is not a matter of having a certain amount of money and material possessions. It is only a matter of one thing: your willingness to use what you have and make it more. No matter how few talents you have, even if you have next to nothing, you can always do something more with what you have – some kind of kindness, some kind of unwillingness to participate in impure activities – and thereby reconnect yourself to the River of Life. Then, what you have will inevitably be multiplied by the law of God, which is unfailing.

Those who feel they are poor are like the person sitting in front of a mirror, refusing to smile at the mirror, saying: "Until the image of myself in the mirror smiles at me, I will not smile at the mirror." Do you see that this will never happen, for the mirror will unfailingly reflect back to you what *you* project into the mirror? You must smile at the mirror, you must smile at the world before the world can smile back at you and give you more. When you *do* smile, the world *will* smile back—although, as Mother Mary explains in her book, it may take some time. The impulse has to cycle through the three higher levels before it reaches the material universe. Depending on how many impurities you have built up in those higher levels, that will determine when and how pure of an impulse the mirror can reflect back to you.

There is always something you can do to make things better. This is precisely why you see that in many countries in the world, the people in general are less poor today than they were a hundred, five hundred, or a thousand years ago. That is because a critical mass of the people, in what you call the rich nations, have been willing to do more with what they had, no matter how little they had.

This my beloved, is love. This is the culmination of the Third Ray where you integrate that love so that you say: "We are willing to learn how to express our creative abilities in a more pure way and therefore bring forth more than what we have right now, thereby raising up all of life, even the environment in which we live, by beautifying it and purifying it."

The power elite are the most poor people

No matter how little you have, you can always do more. The reverse of that is, of course, that no matter how much you have, you can still refuse to do more with what you have. You will see that some of the richest people in the world – in terms of money and material possessions – are in reality as poor spiritually, mentally, emotionally as those who are poor physically. I can assure you that when you look at the wealthiest people, the members of the power elite, you will see that if they are not sharing their wealth and seeking to raise up all life, but are using that wealth to control life, then I can assure you that they have taken that wealth by force. Although a lifestream can build up a momentum that allows it to gather material wealth through force, I can assure you that by doing so a lifestream will diminish its spiritual wealth.

Precisely because of the time delay built into the material universe, it is possible that a lifestream can misuse its co-creative abilities to take material abundance from other people by exploiting those people. The lifestream can get away with doing this for several lifetimes. That is why many people have come to believe that there must be some injustice in the universe that allows certain people to be very rich or inherit great riches, even if they have done nothing to help other parts of life. The law of God is unfailing, and it works two ways. If you have little but do more with what you have, it is unfailing that the law will in the future give you more. The reverse, of course, is that if you have much and refuse to do something for others with what you have, then in time – as cycles move on, – it is inevitable that what you have will be taken away from you.

When you look at the history of the world, you will often see that there have been societies that had a power elite who seemed to be ontouchable. They were simply so above the ordinary population that it seemed like their power and privileges could never be taken away from them. Yet, suddenly things shifted in that society. Through some natural occurrence, a revolution or other occurrence in society, suddenly some of the richest people lost all they had and now stood with nothing. They were worse off than the people, for they had never had to work for what they had. They were not able to handle that situation psychologically—often going to pieces, as they say, instead of picking up the pieces and starting the path of initiation, the path of doing more with whatever you have, no matter how little or how much you have.

Breaking the downward spiral

This is what I spoke about in my previous discourses, namely how poverty becomes a self-reinforcing downward spiral. When people begin to feel that they have too little – and that they have too little because of some injustice, because the Mother Light will not give them more abundance – they manifest hatred of the Mother. They refuse to take care of the Mother, which is their physical environment, their physical bodies, other people, their own children. They begin to become neglectful of the Mother and the expressions of the Mother. What do they do? They project that hatred, that impurity, onto the Ma-ter light and they must inevitably receive a return.

Beyond this is also the very physical neglect of their environment whereby their environment becomes more and more impure, more and more dirty, more and more disorganized, more and more non-functional. By living in an environment that is dirty and disorganized, their consciousness is affected to the point where their vision is impaired. They cannot envision a way out, they cannot envision something better, they cannot envision the reality that the white light simply reflects back what is projected upon it. They cannot see that if they are willing to change their minds, they will change their lives, their outer situations. This, of course, sets the stage whereby they reinforce the downward spiral through their failed initiations on the Fourth Ray, setting the stage for the next level where they fail the initiations on the Fifth Ray of God Vision. This, of course, will be the topic of my next discourse.

For now, I want you to ponder the importance of overcoming hatred of the Mother by looking at everything in the material universe as an expression of Mother. You can then realize that whatever you do to any part of life, you are doing to God the Mother, to the Divine Mother.

A technique for overcoming hatred of the Mother

If you wish to overcome any momentum of hatred of the Mother, here is a simple technique. If you have any love for any representative of the Divine Mother, then use that love. For example, I know many of you have a great love for Mother Mary, who is the highest representative of the Divine Mother for the evolutions on this planet. See Mother Mary behind every outer manifestation.

Allow yourself to realize that whatever you do to any part of life, whatever you do to your physical environment, whatever you do even to a stone, or even by throwing a piece of garbage onto the ground, you are doing to Mother Mary. Then ask yourself: "Do I love Mother Mary more than this activity?" If you do, my beloved, then of course you will know that it is time to stop that activity.

If you cannot yet come to that realization, then ask Mother Mary – with all the fervor of your heart, with all the purity of your heart – to help you see and overcome the momentums of hatred of the Mother that you have in your own being. Use her invocations for this purpose, my beloved. You have so many invocations (see *www.transcendencetoolbox.com*), and you must realize that each invocation is designed to help you overcome a specific aspect of hatred of the Mother.

You are beginning to see, I trust, that any imperfection you encounter in the material universe is an expression – is a variant – of hatred of the Mother. Use those invocations, pray to Mother Mary who is here with me and wants to extend her love and gratitude to you, those of you who have already used her invocations.

She implores you to use them more consciously in the future, to use them specifically to give her a matrix that she can use to enlighten you and to purify you of the illusions and momentums of hatred of the Mother. This is the hatred of the Mother that you will almost inevitably pick up by being in embodiment on this planet. It is currently so weighted down and polluted by hatred of the Mother in all areas of human society, of individual lives, and even in nature herself, as I spoke about some time ago in California when I talked about the imbalances of nature.

There are no material means for overcoming poverty

I trust you can see that the only way to overcome poverty is to be willing to take responsibility by recognizing that your material circumstances are a reflection of your state of consciousness. The only true way to overcome poverty is to look in the mirror, to look at the beam in your own eye and raise your consciousness. That is why there is no material means for overcoming poverty. You cannot create a government program that will automatically eradicate poverty in a particular nation. No government program can force the people to change their consciousness. However, it is possible to institute a government program that suddenly somewhat shakes the people out of the sense of hopelessness and lack of vision. Thereby, it changes their consciousness and changes their vision. What I want to help you see is that it is not actually the outer program that eradicates poverty, but the fact that the outer program has an impact on changing people's vision.

Imagine that you combined the kind of programs you have seen so far on this planet with an educational program that taught the people how to take command over their own psychology and mind so that you have both the Alpha and the Omega effect. The Alpha being teaching people of the power of the mind, and the Omega being instituting actual physical programs to give them better jobs and a better source of physical income or a better physical environment.

What has been done so far on this planet has been only the Omega aspect of eradicating poverty. That is why in many nations it has had such a limited effect. Many well-meaning people (who have a great understanding that things need to change) have been seduced into supporting such government programs. Although they can have a limited effect, they cannot ultimately fulfill the goal of eradicating poverty—for poverty can only be eradicated through both the Alpha and the Omega. Therefore, you must step up. The people who really want to help eradicate poverty must step up and realize that it is necessary to bring in the Alpha by educating the people. This does not mean that all people need to come into a particular religious or spiritual belief, or recognize a particular religion or even recognize the ascended masters. All people need to understand the simple fact that the human psyche has an impact on everything they do personally and on everything that goes on in society, even on what goes on in nature.

You cannot truly change the physical conditions on this earth unless you deal with the human psyche and educate people. They need to learn how to use the power of their minds to create a pure state, both materially and spiritually, instead of continuing to create impurity both spiritually and materially. Only when you combine the Alpha and the Omega, only when you enlighten people to the power of their minds, will you be successful in any government program or even any planetary effort to eradicate poverty and bring forth the abundant life that many of the most aware people in the top 10 percent know should be manifest on this planet.

No freedom without purity

I have spoken my peace on the topic of freedom, for now you see that there can be no freedom without purity, the purity that comes by overcoming hatred of the Mother and building that unconditional love of the Mother. You realize that the Mother has unconditional love for you and will reflect back to you whatever conditions you project upon the Ma-ter light. The conditions and limitations you experience in the matter sphere are simply the reflections of the conditions in your own mind. They are not conditions of the Mother—who loves you unconditionally and will gladly and lovingly give you the abundant life materially when you are willing to reach for the abundant life spiritually.

It is not the responsibility of the Mother to give you the abundant life spiritually. It is only the responsibility of the Mother to give you the abundant life materially. She can do so only by reflecting back to you what you send out. It is your responsibility to purify your mind so that you can project pure images upon the Ma-ter light—that the Mother will then reflect back to you as material circumstances.

When you overcome hatred of the Mother, you see that the Mother has unconditional love for you and will give you anything you desire in the material world. She will do so according to the laws of nature that define what can be created on this planet and according not only to the state of your own consciousness but also to the collective state of consciousness of humankind, as it is currently manifest.

It is indeed possible for people to rise high above the collective consciousness and manifest far greater material abundance than what you see in the general population. Unfortunately, what you have seen so far is that those who have manifested greater material wealth have done so by taking it through force. This is precisely why many spiritual people do not want material wealth. They think it can be taken only through force. If you study Mother Mary's books [*A Course in Abundance*], you will see that her entire purpose is to show you that you can indeed have the abundant life materially. You can have it, not through force but through love—the unconditional love of the Father-Mother God. This is the perfect love that will set you free through the purity of the Fourth Ray.

I seal you, my beloved, in that purity. I thank you for your attention, for your willingness to be the open doors so that I might anchor an extraordinary portion of the Freedom Flame, expressed through the Fourth Ray of Purity. It will radiate out from this physical place but will in an instant, in the twinkling of an eye, cover the entire planet. Thereby, it will accelerate the process of setting people free, of empowering them to overcome the hatred of the Mother and the sense that the Mother will never give them the abundant life. It will help them come to the point of realization that the Mother Light can manifest abundance—the abundance that it is the Father's good pleasure to give you when you are willing to be One with your own higher being.

Be sealed in the Fourth Ray of God Purity, reinforced by the Seventh Ray of Freedom. Go forth and sin no more! Overcome your hatred of the Mother! Be willing to see it and let it pass into that Fourth Ray of the intensity of the white light that burns away all hatred of the Mother, for it burns away all unlike itself. Be sealed! BE FREE!

8 | INVOKING PURITY TO CONSUME HATRED OF THE MOTHER

In the name of the I AM THAT I AM, Jesus Christ, I call upon Saint Germain and Elohim Astrea for the transformation of the consciousness of poverty on earth. Awaken people to the reality that we are spiritual beings and that we can co-create a new future by working with the ascended masters. I especially call for …

[Make your own calls here.]

Part 1

1. Saint Germain, I call forth the judgment of Christ upon those people who have a momentum of misusing the first three rays, those who are expressing power, wisdom and love in an unbalanced way.

O Saint Germain, you do inspire,
my vision raised forever higher,
with you I form a figure-eight,
your Golden Age I co-create.

**O Saint Germain, what love you bring,
it truly makes all matter sing,
your violet flame does all restore,
with you we are becoming more.**

2. Saint Germain, I call forth the judgment of Christ upon those people who feel fear that causes them to express power in order to control other people or their outer situation.

O Saint Germain, what Freedom Flame,
released when we recite your name,
acceleration is your gift,
our planet it will surely lift.

**O Saint Germain, what love you bring,
it truly makes all matter sing,
your violet flame does all restore,
with you we are becoming more.**

3. Saint Germain, awaken people to the reality that this fear-based expression of power is the beginning of poverty.

O Saint Germain, in love we claim,
our right to bring your violet flame,
from you Above, to us below,
it is an all-transforming flow.

> **O Saint Germain, what love you bring,**
> **it truly makes all matter sing,**
> **your violet flame does all restore,**
> **with you we are becoming more.**

4. Saint Germain, awaken people to the reality that when we seek to take by force in the material world, then the more force we express, the more that force will limit ourselves and our own spiritual freedom.

> O Saint Germain, I love you so,
> my aura filled with violet glow,
> my chakras filled with violet fire,
> I am your cosmic amplifier.

> **O Saint Germain, what love you bring,**
> **it truly makes all matter sing,**
> **your violet flame does all restore,**
> **with you we are becoming more.**

5. Saint Germain, awaken people to the reality that as we begin to express power in an unbalanced manner, we will cut ourselves off from the power of God. When we do not have the power of God flowing through us, we cannot manifest what we desire.

> O Saint Germain, I am now free,
> your violet flame is therapy,
> transform all hang-ups in my mind,
> as inner peace I surely find.

**O Saint Germain, what love you bring,
it truly makes all matter sing,
your violet flame does all restore,
with you we are becoming more.**

6. Saint Germain, awaken people to the reality that when we experience that we cannot manifest what we desire, we begin to feel poverty. We begin to use even more force in order to control our outer situation.

O Saint Germain, my body pure,
your violet flame for all is cure,
consume the cause of all disease,
and therefore I am all at ease.

**O Saint Germain, what love you bring,
it truly makes all matter sing,
your violet flame does all restore,
with you we are becoming more.**

7. Saint Germain, I call forth the judgment of Christ upon those people who have gone to the next level and started misusing wisdom, which allows them to use the mind of anti-christ to justify why they want power in the material universe.

O Saint Germain, I'm karma-free,
the past no longer burdens me,
a brand new opportunity,
I am in Christic unity.

**O Saint Germain, what love you bring,
it truly makes all matter sing,
your violet flame does all restore,
with you we are becoming more.**

8. Saint Germain, I call forth the judgment of Christ upon those people who have gained power by misusing the power of the First Ray through the unbalanced wisdom of the mind of anti-christ, the perversion of God Wisdom.

O Saint Germain, we are now one,
I am for you a violet sun,
as we transform this planet earth,
your Golden Age is given birth.

**O Saint Germain, what love you bring,
it truly makes all matter sing,
your violet flame does all restore,
with you we are becoming more.**

9. Saint Germain, I call forth the judgment of Christ upon those people who feel they do not love God and that God does not love them.

O Saint Germain, the earth is free,
from burden of duality,
in oneness we bring what is best,
your Golden Age is manifest.

**O Saint Germain, what love you bring,
it truly makes all matter sing,
your violet flame does all restore,
with you we are becoming more.**

Part 2

1. Saint Germain, I call forth the judgment of Christ upon those people who believe that if God really loved them, God should give them everything they want and should not force them to face the consequences of their own choices—and their own misuse of power and wisdom.

> Astrea, loving Being white,
> your Presence is my pure delight,
> your sword and circle white and blue,
> the astral plane is cutting through.

> **Astrea, come accelerate,**
> **with purity I do vibrate,**
> **release the fire so blue and white,**
> **my aura filled with vibrant light.**

2. Saint Germain, I call forth the judgment of Christ upon those people who have gone to the next level and have created a triangle of the misuse of power, wisdom and love.

> Astrea, calm the raging storm,
> so purity will be the norm,
> my aura filled with blue and white,
> with shining armor, like a knight.

> **Astrea, come accelerate,**
> **with purity I do vibrate,**
> **release the fire so blue and white,**
> **my aura filled with vibrant light.**

3. Saint Germain, I call forth the judgment of Christ upon those people who have sunk into a state of spiritual poverty, of feeling cut off from the power, wisdom and love of God. This is a state that sets the stage for people failing the initiations of the Fourth Ray.

> Astrea, come and cut me free,
> from every binding entity,
> let astral forces all be bound,
> true freedom I have surely found.
>
> **Astrea, come accelerate,**
> **with purity I do vibrate,**
> **release the fire so blue and white,**
> **my aura filled with vibrant light.**

4. Saint Germain, I call forth the judgment of Christ upon those people who have abused power, wisdom and love and who have built a momentum of impurity.

> Astrea, I sincerely urge,
> from demons all, do me purge,
> consume them all and take me higher,
> I will endure your cleansing fire.
>
> **Astrea, come accelerate,**
> **with purity I do vibrate,**
> **release the fire so blue and white,**
> **my aura filled with vibrant light.**

5. Saint Germain, I call forth the judgment of Christ upon those people who express their co-creative abilities in an impure manner that is focused on raising up the ego rather than raising up the All.

> Astrea, do all spirits bind,
> so that I am no longer blind,
> I see the spirit and its twin,
> the victory of Christ I win.
>
> **Astrea, come accelerate,**
> **with purity I do vibrate,**
> **release the fire so blue and white,**
> **my aura filled with vibrant light.**

6. Saint Germain, awaken people to the need to purify our intentions so we do not express our creative abilities in order to gain an advantage for the separate self. Help us rise to the higher level of using our creative abilities to raise up the All, seeking to have everything in the material universe become more.

> Astrea, clear my every cell,
> from energies of death and hell,
> my body is now free to grow,
> each cell emits an inner glow.
>
> **Astrea, come accelerate,**
> **with purity I do vibrate,**
> **release the fire so blue and white,**
> **my aura filled with vibrant light.**

8 | Invoking Purity to Consume Hatred of the Mother

7. Saint Germain, I call forth the judgment of Christ upon those people who are seeking to gather more and more to the separate self so that they build an impenetrable wall that isolates the separate self from the return of its own karma, the consequences of its own choices.

> Astrea, clear my feeling mind,
> in purity my peace I find,
> with higher feeling you release,
> I co-create in perfect peace.
>
> **Astrea, come accelerate,**
> **with purity I do vibrate,**
> **release the fire so blue and white,**
> **my aura filled with vibrant light.**

8. Saint Germain, I call forth the judgment of Christ upon those people who seek to use the energies of the material realm to isolate and insulate themselves from the spiritual path and its initiations.

> Astrea, clear my mental realm,
> my Christ self always at the helm,
> I see now how to manifest,
> the matrix that for all is best.
>
> **Astrea, come accelerate,**
> **with purity I do vibrate,**
> **release the fire so blue and white,**
> **my aura filled with vibrant light.**

9. Saint Germain, I call forth the judgment of Christ upon those people who believe the return of their karma, the cosmic mirror sending back to them whatever they have sent out, is a punishment by an angry God in the sky.

> Astrea, with great clarity,
> I claim a new identity,
> etheric blueprint I now see,
> I co-create more consciously.
>
> **Astrea, come accelerate,**
> **with purity I do vibrate,**
> **release the fire so blue and white,**
> **my aura filled with vibrant light.**

Part 3

1. Saint Germain, awaken people to the reality that the return of the consequences of our own choices is how we learn, and therefore it is an opportunity.

> O Saint Germain, you do inspire,
> my vision raised forever higher,
> with you I form a figure-eight,
> your Golden Age I co-create.
>
> **O Saint Germain, what love you bring,**
> **it truly makes all matter sing,**
> **your violet flame does all restore,**
> **with you we are becoming more.**

2. Saint Germain, awaken people to the reality that when we receive a return current from the cosmic mirror that is not pure, then it is an opportunity for us to realize that what we sent into the mirror was not a pure impulse. We can now rise up and purify our co-creative efforts.

> O Saint Germain, what Freedom Flame,
> released when we recite your name,
> acceleration is your gift,
> our planet it will surely lift.
>
> **O Saint Germain, what love you bring,**
> **it truly makes all matter sing,**
> **your violet flame does all restore,**
> **with you we are becoming more.**

3. Saint Germain, I call forth the judgment of Christ upon those people who are not willing to allow what comes back from the cosmic mirror to awaken them to the need to look in the personal mirror and do what Jesus said, namely look for the beam in our own eye.

> O Saint Germain, in love we claim,
> our right to bring your violet flame,
> from you Above, to us below,
> it is an all-transforming flow.
>
> **O Saint Germain, what love you bring,**
> **it truly makes all matter sing,**
> **your violet flame does all restore,**
> **with you we are becoming more.**

4. Saint Germain, I call forth the judgment of Christ upon those people who refuse to look in the personal mirror because they are not willing to take full responsibility for themselves and the use of their creative power.

> O Saint Germain, I love you so,
> my aura filled with violet glow,
> my chakras filled with violet fire,
> I am your cosmic amplifier.

> **O Saint Germain, what love you bring,**
> **it truly makes all matter sing,**
> **your violet flame does all restore,**
> **with you we are becoming more.**

5. Saint Germain, I call forth the judgment of Christ upon those people who will not accept that what comes back is a reflection of what they have sent out. They project that it is someone else's fault.

> O Saint Germain, I am now free,
> your violet flame is therapy,
> transform all hang-ups in my mind,
> as inner peace I surely find.

> **O Saint Germain, what love you bring,**
> **it truly makes all matter sing,**
> **your violet flame does all restore,**
> **with you we are becoming more.**

6. Saint Germain, I call forth the judgment of Christ upon those people who refuse to let the white light of the Mother expose their impurities. They blame the Mother Light itself.

8 | Invoking Purity to Consume Hatred of the Mother

O Saint Germain, my body pure,
your violet flame for all is cure,
consume the cause of all disease,
and therefore I am all at ease.

**O Saint Germain, what love you bring,
it truly makes all matter sing,
your violet flame does all restore,
with you we are becoming more.**

7. Saint Germain, I call forth the judgment of Christ upon those people who project that it is not them who have imposed an impure image on the Ma-ter light. It is the light itself that has manifested an imperfect manifestation that now burdens them, or does not give them what they want.

O Saint Germain, I'm karma-free,
the past no longer burdens me,
a brand new opportunity,
I am in Christic unity.

**O Saint Germain, what love you bring,
it truly makes all matter sing,
your violet flame does all restore,
with you we are becoming more.**

8. Saint Germain, I call forth the judgment of Christ upon those people who project that the Mother is wrong, that there is something wrong with the Mother and that they should seek to use their creative abilities to control, even punish, the Mother.

O Saint Germain, we are now one,
I am for you a violet sun,
as we transform this planet earth,
your Golden Age is given birth.

**O Saint Germain, what love you bring,
it truly makes all matter sing,
your violet flame does all restore,
with you we are becoming more.**

9. Saint Germain, I call forth the judgment of Christ upon those people who are not willing to look in the mirror and who have turned their fear into hatred of the Mother.

O Saint Germain, the earth is free,
from burden of duality,
in oneness we bring what is best,
your Golden Age is manifest.

**O Saint Germain, what love you bring,
it truly makes all matter sing,
your violet flame does all restore,
with you we are becoming more.**

Part 4

1. Saint Germain, I call forth the judgment of Christ upon those people who project the impurity outside themselves, thinking planet earth is a low place with imbalance in nature, imperfect bodies and a lack of money and resources.

8 | Invoking Purity to Consume Hatred of the Mother

> Astrea, loving Being white,
> your Presence is my pure delight,
> your sword and circle white and blue,
> the astral plane is cutting through.
>
> **Astrea, come accelerate,**
> **with purity I do vibrate,**
> **release the fire so blue and white,**
> **my aura filled with vibrant light.**

2. Saint Germain, I call forth the judgment of Christ upon those people who project that it is the fault of Mother Earth that she will not give them the abundant life.

> Astrea, calm the raging storm,
> so purity will be the norm,
> my aura filled with blue and white,
> with shining armor, like a knight.
>
> **Astrea, come accelerate,**
> **with purity I do vibrate,**
> **release the fire so blue and white,**
> **my aura filled with vibrant light.**

3. Saint Germain, I call forth the judgment of Christ upon the entire class of lifestreams that fell on the initiations of the Fourth Ray, including those who fell in higher spheres.

> Astrea, come and cut me free,
> from every binding entity,
> let astral forces all be bound,
> true freedom I have surely found.

**Astrea, come accelerate,
with purity I do vibrate,
release the fire so blue and white,
my aura filled with vibrant light.**

4. Saint Germain, I call forth the judgment of Christ upon those who are still holding on to the Luciferian consciousness, the pride of not being willing to look at their own impurities. They are projecting those impurities upon the Mother Light, building up hatred of the Mother.

Astrea, I sincerely urge,
from demons all, do me purge,
consume them all and take me higher,
I will endure your cleansing fire.

**Astrea, come accelerate,
with purity I do vibrate,
release the fire so blue and white,
my aura filled with vibrant light.**

5. Saint Germain, I call forth the judgment of Christ upon those who have continued to build upon the momentum of denial, thereby building up more and more hatred of the Mother.

Astrea, do all spirits bind,
so that I am no longer blind,
I see the spirit and its twin,
the victory of Christ I win.

**Astrea, come accelerate,
with purity I do vibrate,
release the fire so blue and white,
my aura filled with vibrant light.**

6. Saint Germain, awaken people to the reality that poverty is caused by the fact that we are projecting an impure image onto the Ma-ter light. When we do this, we pull the white light of the Mother down to a lower vibration that is not in alignment with the abundant life.

Astrea, clear my every cell,
from energies of death and hell,
my body is now free to grow,
each cell emits an inner glow.

**Astrea, come accelerate,
with purity I do vibrate,
release the fire so blue and white,
my aura filled with vibrant light.**

7. Saint Germain, awaken people to the reality that as more and more impure images are projected onto the Ma-ter light, more and more limitations are created on the physical earth. This is why people come to feel that the earth is a limited place.

Astrea, clear my feeling mind,
in purity my peace I find,
with higher feeling you release,
I co-create in perfect peace.

**Astrea, come accelerate,
with purity I do vibrate,
release the fire so blue and white,
my aura filled with vibrant light.**

8. Saint Germain, awaken people to the reality that the earth is only limited as long as imperfect images are projected onto it. The earth has no desire to limit or restrict us. The earth would gladly outpicture the abundant life in the twinkling of an eye.

Astrea, clear my mental realm,
my Christ self always at the helm,
I see now how to manifest,
the matrix that for all is best.

**Astrea, come accelerate,
with purity I do vibrate,
release the fire so blue and white,
my aura filled with vibrant light.**

9. Saint Germain, awaken people to the reality that the earth has vowed to take on the role of being a substitute teacher for those who have cut themselves off from their spiritual teachers and must learn in the School of Hard Knocks.

Astrea, with great clarity,
I claim a new identity,
etheric blueprint I now see,
I co-create more consciously.

**Astrea, come accelerate,
with purity I do vibrate,
release the fire so blue and white,
my aura filled with vibrant light.**

Part 5

1. Saint Germain, I call forth the judgment of Christ upon those people who have the greatest degree of material poverty, and who are engaging in some very impure activities as a way to compensate for feeling boxed in.

> O Saint Germain, you do inspire,
> my vision raised forever higher,
> with you I form a figure-eight,
> your Golden Age I co-create.
>
> **O Saint Germain, what love you bring,
> it truly makes all matter sing,
> your violet flame does all restore,
> with you we are becoming more.**

2. Saint Germain, I call forth the judgment of Christ upon those people who seek to escape poverty through alcohol, drugs, gambling, imperfect music, perverted sexual practices or anything else that can be done without a great amount of money.

O Saint Germain, what Freedom Flame,
released when we recite your name,
acceleration is your gift,
our planet it will surely lift.

**O Saint Germain, what love you bring,
it truly makes all matter sing,
your violet flame does all restore,
with you we are becoming more.**

3. Saint Germain, I call forth the judgment of Christ upon those people who have used their poverty as an excuse for becoming insensitive to their own lives, their environment, personal hygiene or dress.

O Saint Germain, in love we claim,
our right to bring your violet flame,
from you Above, to us below,
it is an all-transforming flow.

**O Saint Germain, what love you bring,
it truly makes all matter sing,
your violet flame does all restore,
with you we are becoming more.**

4. Saint Germain, I call forth the judgment of Christ upon those people who refuse to do something with what they have to make their lives more, to make their lives better.

O Saint Germain, I love you so,
my aura filled with violet glow,
my chakras filled with violet fire,
I am your cosmic amplifier.

8 | Invoking Purity to Consume Hatred of the Mother

**O Saint Germain, what love you bring,
it truly makes all matter sing,
your violet flame does all restore,
with you we are becoming more.**

5. Saint Germain, I call forth the judgment of Christ upon those people who feel they have so little that they can do nothing and who do not even try to do the best with what they have, thus burying their talents in the ground.

O Saint Germain, I am now free,
your violet flame is therapy,
transform all hang-ups in my mind,
as inner peace I surely find.

**O Saint Germain, what love you bring,
it truly makes all matter sing,
your violet flame does all restore,
with you we are becoming more.**

6. Saint Germain, I call forth the judgment of Christ upon those people who believe an angry God is taking from them what they have and who will not see that they themselves take from them what they have.

O Saint Germain, my body pure,
your violet flame for all is cure,
consume the cause of all disease,
and therefore I am all at ease.

> O Saint Germain, what love you bring,
> it truly makes all matter sing,
> your violet flame does all restore,
> with you we are becoming more.

7. Saint Germain, I call forth the judgment of Christ upon those people who refuse to multiply what they have and connect themselves to the River of Life.

> O Saint Germain, I'm karma-free,
> the past no longer burdens me,
> a brand new opportunity,
> I am in Christic unity.

> **O Saint Germain, what love you bring,**
> **it truly makes all matter sing,**
> **your violet flame does all restore,**
> **with you we are becoming more.**

8. Saint Germain, awaken people to the reality that being connected to the River of Life is not a matter of having a certain amount of money and material possessions. It is only a matter of the willingness to use what we have and make it more.

> O Saint Germain, we are now one,
> I am for you a violet sun,
> as we transform this planet earth,
> your Golden Age is given birth.

> **O Saint Germain, what love you bring,**
> **it truly makes all matter sing,**
> **your violet flame does all restore,**
> **with you we are becoming more.**

9. Saint Germain, I call forth the judgment of Christ upon those people who are like the person sitting in front of a mirror, refusing to smile at the mirror, saying: "Until the image of myself in the mirror smiles at me, I will not smile at the mirror."

> O Saint Germain, the earth is free,
> from burden of duality,
> in oneness we bring what is best,
> your Golden Age is manifest.
>
> **O Saint Germain, what love you bring,
> it truly makes all matter sing,
> your violet flame does all restore,
> with you we are becoming more.**

Part 6

1. Saint Germain, awaken people to the reality that when we do smile at the world, the world will smile back—although it may take some time for the impulse to cycle through the three higher levels before it reaches the material universe.

> Astrea, loving Being white,
> your Presence is my pure delight,
> your sword and circle white and blue,
> the astral plane is cutting through.

**Astrea, come accelerate,
with purity I do vibrate,
release the fire so blue and white,
my aura filled with vibrant light.**

2. Saint Germain, awaken people to the reality that it is the amount of impurities we have built up in the higher levels that will determine when and how pure of an impulse the mirror can reflect back to us.

Astrea, calm the raging storm,
so purity will be the norm,
my aura filled with blue and white,
with shining armor, like a knight.

**Astrea, come accelerate,
with purity I do vibrate,
release the fire so blue and white,
my aura filled with vibrant light.**

3. Saint Germain, awaken people to the reality that people in richer countries are less poor today than they were in the past because they have been willing to do more with what they had, no matter how little they had.

Astrea, come and cut me free,
from every binding entity,
let astral forces all be bound,
true freedom I have surely found.

> **Astrea, come accelerate,**
> **with purity I do vibrate,**
> **release the fire so blue and white,**
> **my aura filled with vibrant light.**

4. Saint Germain, I call forth the judgment of Christ upon those who are the richest people in the world in terms of money and material possessions, but who are as poor spiritually, mentally and emotionally as those who are poor physically.

> Astrea, I sincerely urge,
> from demons all, do me purge,
> consume them all and take me higher,
> I will endure your cleansing fire.

> **Astrea, come accelerate,**
> **with purity I do vibrate,**
> **release the fire so blue and white,**
> **my aura filled with vibrant light.**

5. Saint Germain, I call forth the judgment of Christ upon those people who are not sharing their wealth and seeking to raise up all life, but are using that wealth to control life.

> Astrea, do all spirits bind,
> so that I am no longer blind,
> I see the spirit and its twin,
> the victory of Christ I win.

> **Astrea, come accelerate,**
> **with purity I do vibrate,**
> **release the fire so blue and white,**
> **my aura filled with vibrant light.**

6. Saint Germain, I call forth the judgment of Christ upon those people who have built up a momentum that allows them to gather material wealth through force.

> Astrea, clear my every cell,
> from energies of death and hell,
> my body is now free to grow,
> each cell emits an inner glow.
>
> **Astrea, come accelerate,**
> **with purity I do vibrate,**
> **release the fire so blue and white,**
> **my aura filled with vibrant light.**

7. Saint Germain, I call forth the judgment of Christ upon those people who are misusing their co-creative abilities to take material abundance from other people by exploiting those people.

> Astrea, clear my feeling mind,
> in purity my peace I find,
> with higher feeling you release,
> I co-create in perfect peace.
>
> **Astrea, come accelerate,**
> **with purity I do vibrate,**
> **release the fire so blue and white,**
> **my aura filled with vibrant light.**

8. Saint Germain, I call forth the judgment of Christ upon those societies that have a power elite whose members seem to be ontouchable. They are so above the ordinary population that it seems like their power and privileges can never be taken away from them.

> Astrea, clear my mental realm,
> my Christ self always at the helm,
> I see now how to manifest,
> the matrix that for all is best.

> **Astrea, come accelerate,**
> **with purity I do vibrate,**
> **release the fire so blue and white,**
> **my aura filled with vibrant light.**

9. Saint Germain, I call forth the judgment of Christ upon those people who refuse to do more with whatever they have, and who therefore turn poverty into a self-reinforcing downward spiral.

> Astrea, with great clarity,
> I claim a new identity,
> etheric blueprint I now see,
> I co-create more consciously.

> **Astrea, come accelerate,**
> **with purity I do vibrate,**
> **release the fire so blue and white,**
> **my aura filled with vibrant light.**

Part 7

1. Saint Germain, I call forth the judgment of Christ upon those people who feel they have too little, and that it is an injustice that the Mother Light will not give them more abundance.

> O Saint Germain, you do inspire,
> my vision raised forever higher,
> with you I form a figure-eight,
> your Golden Age I co-create.
>
> **O Saint Germain, what love you bring,**
> **it truly makes all matter sing,**
> **your violet flame does all restore,**
> **with you we are becoming more.**

2. Saint Germain, I call forth the judgment of Christ upon those people who manifest hatred of the Mother and refuse to take care of the Mother, which is their physical environment, bodies, other people and children.

> O Saint Germain, what Freedom Flame,
> released when we recite your name,
> acceleration is your gift,
> our planet it will surely lift.
>
> **O Saint Germain, what love you bring,**
> **it truly makes all matter sing,**
> **your violet flame does all restore,**
> **with you we are becoming more.**

3. Saint Germain, I call forth the judgment of Christ upon those people who are neglectful of the Mother and the expressions of the Mother. They project that hatred onto the Ma-ter light, meaning they must inevitably receive a return.

> O Saint Germain, in love we claim,
> our right to bring your violet flame,
> from you Above, to us below,
> it is an all-transforming flow.
>
> **O Saint Germain, what love you bring,**
> **it truly makes all matter sing,**
> **your violet flame does all restore,**
> **with you we are becoming more.**

4. Saint Germain, I call forth the judgment of Christ upon those people who feel no gratitude or appreciation for the opportunity to be in embodiment in the Mother realm.

> O Saint Germain, I love you so,
> my aura filled with violet glow,
> my chakras filled with violet fire,
> I am your cosmic amplifier.
>
> **O Saint Germain, what love you bring,**
> **it truly makes all matter sing,**
> **your violet flame does all restore,**
> **with you we are becoming more.**

5. Saint Germain, I call forth the judgment of Christ upon those people who show such physical neglect of their environment that it becomes more and more impure, dirty, disorganized and non-functional.

> O Saint Germain, I am now free,
> your violet flame is therapy,
> transform all hang-ups in my mind,
> as inner peace I surely find.
>
> **O Saint Germain, what love you bring,
> it truly makes all matter sing,
> your violet flame does all restore,
> with you we are becoming more.**

6. Saint Germain, I call forth the judgment of Christ upon those people who have allowed their vision to become so impaired that they cannot see a way out, they cannot imagine something better, they cannot acknowledge the reality that the Mother Light simply reflects back what is projected upon it.

> O Saint Germain, my body pure,
> your violet flame for all is cure,
> consume the cause of all disease,
> and therefore I am all at ease.
>
> **O Saint Germain, what love you bring,
> it truly makes all matter sing,
> your violet flame does all restore,
> with you we are becoming more.**

7. Saint Germain, I call forth the judgment of Christ upon those people who will not overcome hatred of the Mother by looking at everything in the material universe as an expression of Mother. They will not see that whatever they do to any part of life, they are doing to the Divine Mother.

8 | Invoking Purity to Consume Hatred of the Mother

O Saint Germain, I'm karma-free,
the past no longer burdens me,
a brand new opportunity,
I am in Christic unity.

**O Saint Germain, what love you bring,
it truly makes all matter sing,
your violet flame does all restore,
with you we are becoming more.**

8. Saint Germain, awaken people to the reality that the way to overcome hatred of the Mother is to see Mother Mary, or any representative of the Divine Mother, behind every outer manifestation.

O Saint Germain, we are now one,
I am for you a violet sun,
as we transform this planet earth,
your Golden Age is given birth.

**O Saint Germain, what love you bring,
it truly makes all matter sing,
your violet flame does all restore,
with you we are becoming more.**

9. Saint Germain, awaken people to the reality that the only way to overcome poverty is to be willing to take responsibility by recognizing that our material circumstances are a reflection of our state of consciousness.

O Saint Germain, the earth is free,
from burden of duality,
in oneness we bring what is best,
your Golden Age is manifest.

**O Saint Germain, what love you bring,
it truly makes all matter sing,
your violet flame does all restore,
with you we are becoming more.**

Part 8

1. Saint Germain, awaken people to the reality that there is no material means for overcoming poverty. We cannot create a government program that will automatically eradicate poverty in a particular nation. No government program can force the people to change their consciousness.

Astrea, loving Being white,
your Presence is my pure delight,
your sword and circle white and blue,
the astral plane is cutting through.

**Astrea, come accelerate,
with purity I do vibrate,
release the fire so blue and white,
my aura filled with vibrant light.**

2. Saint Germain, awaken people to the reality that it is not possible to institute a government program that shakes the people out of the sense of hopelessness and lack of vision, thereby changing their consciousness.

> Astrea, calm the raging storm,
> so purity will be the norm,
> my aura filled with blue and white,
> with shining armor, like a knight.

> **Astrea, come accelerate,**
> **with purity I do vibrate,**
> **release the fire so blue and white,**
> **my aura filled with vibrant light.**

3. Saint Germain, awaken people to the need to combine different kinds of programs with an educational program that teaches the people how to take command over their own psychology and mind so that we have both the Alpha and the Omega effect.

> Astrea, come and cut me free,
> from every binding entity,
> let astral forces all be bound,
> true freedom I have surely found.

> **Astrea, come accelerate,**
> **with purity I do vibrate,**
> **release the fire so blue and white,**
> **my aura filled with vibrant light.**

4. Saint Germain, awaken people to the reality that the Alpha is teaching people about the power of the mind, and the Omega is physical programs to give them better jobs, a better source of physical income or a better physical environment.

> Astrea, I sincerely urge,
> from demons all, do me purge,
> consume them all and take me higher,
> I will endure your cleansing fire.
>
> **Astrea, come accelerate,**
> **with purity I do vibrate,**
> **release the fire so blue and white,**
> **my aura filled with vibrant light.**

5. Saint Germain, awaken people to the reality that what has been done so far on this planet has been only the Omega aspect of eradicating poverty. That is why this has had such a limited effect in many nations.

> Astrea, do all spirits bind,
> so that I am no longer blind,
> I see the spirit and its twin,
> the victory of Christ I win.
>
> **Astrea, come accelerate,**
> **with purity I do vibrate,**
> **release the fire so blue and white,**
> **my aura filled with vibrant light.**

6. Saint Germain, awaken the many well-meaning people who have been seduced into supporting such government programs. Help them step up and realize that it is necessary to bring in the Alpha by educating the people.

> Astrea, clear my every cell,
> from energies of death and hell,
> my body is now free to grow,
> each cell emits an inner glow.

> **Astrea, come accelerate,**
> **with purity I do vibrate,**
> **release the fire so blue and white,**
> **my aura filled with vibrant light.**

7. Saint Germain, awaken people to the reality that only when we enlighten people to the power of their minds, will we be successful in any government program or even any planetary effort to eradicate poverty. Only then can we bring forth the abundant life that many people know should be manifest on this planet.

> Astrea, clear my feeling mind,
> in purity my peace I find,
> with higher feeling you release,
> I co-create in perfect peace.

> **Astrea, come accelerate,**
> **with purity I do vibrate,**
> **release the fire so blue and white,**
> **my aura filled with vibrant light.**

8. Saint Germain, awaken the spiritual people who do not want material wealth because they think it can be taken only through force. Help them see that we can have abundance through love—the unconditional love of the Father-Mother God.

> Astrea, clear my mental realm,
> my Christ self always at the helm,
> I see now how to manifest,
> the matrix that for all is best.

> **Astrea, come accelerate,**
> **with purity I do vibrate,**
> **release the fire so blue and white,**
> **my aura filled with vibrant light.**

9. Saint Germain, I invoke and multiply your Freedom Flame, expressed through the Fourth Ray of Purity, to accelerate the process of setting people free, of empowering us to overcome the hatred of the Mother and come to the point of accepting the abundance that it is the Father's good pleasure to give us when we are willing to be one with our own higher beings.

> Astrea, with great clarity,
> I claim a new identity,
> etheric blueprint I now see,
> I co-create more consciously.

> **Astrea, come accelerate,**
> **with purity I do vibrate,**
> **release the fire so blue and white,**
> **my aura filled with vibrant light.**

Sealing

In the name of the I AM THAT I AM, I accept that Archangel Michael, Astrea and Shiva form an impenetrable shield around myself and all constructive people, sealing us from all fear-based energies in all four octaves. I accept that the Light of God is consuming and transforming all fear-based energies that make up the forces behind war!

9 | WITH PURE VISION YOU MANIFEST A GOLDEN AGE

As I have discoursed with you previously, when a lifestream goes through the first three rays – the initiations on those rays – it has sort of a Divine grace period. It has great freedom to experiment with its creative powers in order to hopefully find some sense of balance between power, wisdom and love on its own. It can have as much guidance from the spiritual teacher as it desires. On the Fourth Ray the lifestream must face the initiation of purifying its creative efforts, but more than that: purifying its intentions, its entire sense of purpose. "Why do I co-create? Is it to gain some advantage for the separate self, or to raise up the All and fulfill the greater purpose for which I descended into these dense matter spheres?"

In the natural, ideal scenario a lifestream will pass the initiation on the Fourth Ray. It will purify its motives, and therefore it can move on to the Fifth Ray of God Vision with a pure motive, a pure intention—to co-create that which is best for the All, for the overall purposes of God. This will empower the lifestream to develop a pure vision, so that – as it begins to express that vision in the material realm – it will be based on a pure understanding of how creation works.

Why pure intentions are so important

The Fifth Ray is the first ray in the upper half, so to speak, of the seven rays, the one that comes after the nexus point of the Fourth Ray. Although – in a linear fashion – the rays naturally ascend in a series, in order to fully understand the mystery of creation we need to turn the scale upside down. We need to realize that what truly happens is that a lifestream starts its co-creative efforts in a higher sphere of God's Will. Then, when it has passed those initiations, it descends to the next lower sphere, and so on until it reaches the fourth. This is precisely the place – as you have been told – where Lucifer and many other angels fell. They fell out of their pride of thinking they knew better than God, thus condemning God for his creation and his intention for that creation.

After the fall happened in the fourth sphere – which is a representation, a symbol if you will, of the Fourth Ray – then lifestreams descended into the fifth sphere. When you consider a figure-eight, the Fourth Ray, the fourth sphere is the nexus. The first three rays, love, wisdom and power are in the upper half of the figure-eight, which is the realm that we might call the realm of Spirit. The Fifth, Sixth and Seventh rays are in the lower half of the figure-eight, which we – for the purposes of this discussion – will call the realm of Ma-ter, the realm of Mother.

In the ideal scenario, a lifestream would face the opportunity to truly start using the Ma-ter light in its co-creative efforts. When used with pure intention, the lifestream would formulate a pure vision of what it wanted to co-create, and then impose that vision upon the Ma-ter light. When a lifestream separates itself from the flow of the River of Life, from the flow of the great is, and begins to think it is a separate being, then of course it cannot formulate a pure vision. Instead of having the vision and the intention to co-create that which raises up the All, the lifestream is now blinded by the spiritual pride it developed as a result of failing the initiations on the Fourth Ray. The lifestream cannot see beyond the separate self, it cannot see that it is truly one with the All, and one with God.

It sees itself as separate from all other beings in the sphere where it abides, and it inevitably sees a sort of competition or conflict between itself and others. Precisely because of the pride, it now attempts to use its co-creative efforts – to use the momentum it developed on the first four rays – in order to impose images and visions upon the Ma-ter light. This creates the impression that it is more important than other beings and thus elevated above them in some sense.

Impure vision leads to divisions in the psyche

Such a lifestream, inevitably, is not seeking to raise up the All. Its vision – its eye – is not single; it is divided, it is dualistic. When thine eye be single, thy whole body shall be full of light and only light. When thine eye be divided into the dualities of the mind of anti-christ, thy whole body will not be full of light. There will be a duality in your body, which of course is not the physical body but your being. There will be room for both light and darkness.

Even when a being falls, it is not instantly stripped of the momentums and attainment it has gathered before the fall. It is allowed to keep that momentum of light, but along with it comes the darkness. Listen carefully: When a being is of one mind, it has the intention to raise up the All because it has the clear vision to see that it is one with the All. The only way to truly raise up yourself is to work on raising up the All. The more you raise up others, the more you will be raised, for this is what we have spoken about many times—the principle of multiplying the talents so that God can give you more.

When you have clear vision, pure vision, you see this principle as the most fundamental principle of life in the Ma-ter realm. You see that the purpose is to raise up a particular sphere in the Ma-ter realm to express the full perfection of the Kingdom of God so that the sphere is so filled with light that it ascends and becomes part of the spiritual realm. You are willing to be that open door for the light of your higher being, the light of God, to stream through you. You become – as Jesus said – the open door, the Way, the Truth and the Life. You know then that the more you actually give to raise up other parts of life, the more you receive from the true source of life, which is God itself, through your higher being.

When your vision is divided, you obviously cannot see this truth. You are not unified in your creative efforts. When your vision is unified, your co-creative efforts are unified. You have no conflict in your being, you have no evaluation of: "Should I really give to this other person because will that raise up the other person to be more important than myself or to have more than myself?" You know that the more you give, the more you receive from God. There is no point in even evaluating who has more and who has less, for you are simply focused on being all you can be and expressing that in the Ma-ter realm.

When your vision has become divided, then you see a duality and suddenly begin to think in an entirely different way. You begin to pass value judgments and say that something is better than something else—some people, some beings, are better or more important than someone else. The more you are trapped in pride, the more you want to belong to those who are more important or who have more or who can do more. You now seek to express your light, the momentum you gathered on the first four rays, in a way that not only seeks to raise up life but has a duality because you are seeking to raise up yourself while putting others down, by limiting them so they will not grow.

A divided mind cannot have God power

It is not possible to truly express God Power, when you have separated yourself from oneness with God. How, my beloved, could this possibly be done? Those who have fallen into duality, can express their co-creative efforts by using the momentums they gathered before they fell. They cannot receive more from the source, for they are not multiplying the talents.

It is inevitable that – when they express their creative efforts in order to put down other forms of life – they will bury their talents in the ground. That which they have will be taken from them, in the sense that they lose that portion of their light and momentum—which they have now used to put down and limit other forms of life. This is very simple, this is simple mathematics. If you do not multiply, you cannot have more. If you divide, you have less. You learned this in some of the first grades of your school system, my beloved.

You now see why those who have fallen into duality must seek to put down others in order to elevate themselves. If they were focused on raising up the All, the more they give, the more they would receive and that would raise themselves up. When they cannot do that, when they cannot multiply the talents, then they cannot be raised up, can they? The only way they can seem more important, or seem to have more than others, is to limit others. Those who have separated themselves from the River of Life, and have fallen into the consciousness of poverty, must now seek to trap all other beings in that same state of consciousness. They must get others to believe in the illusion of separation, the illusion of lack, thinking that this material realm is separated from the abundance of God, the River of Life. Thus, there are limits to what can be done.

The origin of inequality in society

In many past ages it has happened that those who were the dualistic leaders managed to create a society in which they had set themselves up in leadership positions. These positions were ontouchable because the people could not challenge them. They either did not have the physical power or they believed that they could or should not challenge the leaders.

The Jews of Jesus' time had created precisely such a society. It was a society in which they were very comfortable. Even though they had the concept that a Messiah would come, they were not actually looking forward to the coming of the Messiah. Of course, they would not have admitted this consciously, but subconsciously they were not willing to lose their comfortability, to lose their mortal lives, in order to follow the Messiah. Subconsciously, they were happy to believe that the Messiah would come sometime in the distant future.

When Jesus suddenly appeared and said: "I AM the Messiah and I am here NOW," they came up with all kinds of excuses for ignoring him. They allowed the fallen leaders to kill his physical body in an attempt to prevent that he would overthrow status quo by overturning those tables of the spiritual money-changers. These leaders had taken away not the money of the people but the consciousness of abundance of the people. They had separated them from the flow of the River of Life so that no one among the people could gather enough light, enough Christhood, to stand up and challenge those fallen beings in leadership positions.

A subtle secret about fallen beings

I will now give you a subtle truth that very few people on this earth have understood. I do not say this to cause any kind of pride in your being, although I do say it with the intention of giving you a test of whether you will respond with pride or not. What exactly is it that happens when a culture, society or lifewave separates itself from the flow of the River of Life? They obviously are cut off from the creative forces of God, namely the expanding force of the Father and the contracting force of the Mother. They cannot be the open door for this creative force, and thus they cannot bring more abundance into their sphere, into the sphere of their planet. More than that, you need to understand exactly what is going on in the minds of such beings.

To illustrate this, let me ask you to imagine something. Imagine that you had a gun as you know them on earth. Imagine you were walking in the forest – and you were starving and your family and community were starving – and you saw a deer that could provide nutrition to your community. You took aim with the gun and fired the gun, and then the gun would fire and the deer would be killed. But if you flew into anger and raised that gun to shoot one of your fellow men, then the gun would refuse to fire. This is how it is with the creative power of God, the flow of the River of Life. If you co-create with a pure intention and pure vision, then the power of God and the love of God – in perfect balance – will gladly and lovingly flow through you. They will flow with the eagerness of the God who wants to express itself through all of its sons and daughters. You will have the power of God for which nothing is impossible.

When you try to express your co-creative abilities with impure vision, an impure intent, then the power of God will not flow through you. We might say that the cosmic gun will not fire, and thus you will not have the power of God. You will only have the power you have garnered in your own being through your initiations on the first rays before you fell. Those who were the original fallen beings – who realized this mechanism after they had descended into the matter spheres – realized that they would soon run out of power if they did not do something. Here is the plan they came up with in order to prolong their own existence in the matter realm for as long as possible.

We might say that the River of Life – the creative force of God – is creative, and by creative I mean something that is not predictable, that is not mechanical. This creative force will work only when you have pure intention. It will not work for those who are trapped in duality and seek to limit other forms of life and raise up themselves. What they decided to create was a sphere in the material realm – not limited to planet earth, but including planet earth – where they had created a mechanical force in imitation of the creative force of God. A force that allowed them to express power with impure intentions.

The mechanization consciousness

This is precisely the beginning of what we of the ascended masters have called the mechanization concept. To return to my previous analogy of a gun, you know that a gun is a mechanical device. If it is properly loaded and functioning, it will fire anytime you pull the trigger, whether you are shooting to get food, shooting to kill another human being or shooting for the mere sport of killing an animal even though you do not need the nourishment.

This is precisely what the beings trapped in duality love—something that allows them to express their power without any of what they would call restrictions. When you are separated from the flow of the River of Life, you think that the laws of God are restrictions of your creativity. In reality, they are not restrictions of your creativity. What you are expressing is not creativity; it is a mechanical display of power, a dualistic display of power. This concept, this consciousness of mechanization, has permeated virtually every aspect of life on this planet. It is a clear perversion of the Fifth Ray. The Fifth Ray of God Vision is precisely what is meant to empower beings to use their powers in a creative manner, by tuning in to their higher beings, thus expressing their creative powers in accordance with the laws of God so that they multiply all life.

As a perversion of that, you have the creation of a mechanical device, which does not even have to be a physical device, where you do not have to be in alignment with the laws of God. You do not have to have pure intentions in order to express power, forcing the Ma-ter light into an impure matrix, into an impure form. This is a consciousness that is very subtle. It has been given many subtle disguises, and in today's world – especially in the more technological part of the world – it has deceived the majority of the population into believing that it is necessary, that it is good and that there is no alternative to it.

This is why you have an entire group of leaders on this planet – not only political leaders, but leaders in science, in the media, even in religion – who believe in, are blinded by – and thus are continually promoting – an approach to life that springs from the mechanization consciousness. They are attempting to maintain their positions of leadership, privilege and power by keeping the people in a state of consciousness where they are not being co-creators with God, for they dare not or cannot express their true creative powers.

They are literally living as mechanized beings, as a kind of biological robots, who are doing the same thing over and over, never breaking out of certain boundaries. They have, like computers, like robots, been programmed to stay within their program and do what they were programmed to do and nothing more, nothing beyond it, nothing creative. They are mechanically repeating the same actions, the same beliefs, the same patterns over and over and over again.

Discernment about technology

This is most clearly expressed in technology where you have grown up, from you were "this big," with technological devices that are entirely mechanical in nature. When you push the switch on the wall, the light will come on. If it does not, then you know there is something wrong that has to be fixed somewhere. This is where you need to use the discernment of the Christ mind. I am not saying that all technology is wrong. At this particular stage in the unfoldment of the growth of humankind and of this planet, technology does give many people freedom from the drudgery of physical, mechanical labor.

If you go back to older times, you will see that many people lived in an agricultural society where they were literally having to work night and day to scratch out a living from the meager conditions provided by the unbalanced state of nature. Most of their time was caught up in simple survival so they had little left over for spirituality of any kind. In my embodiments as

Roger Bacon and Francis Bacon, I did indeed set the stage for the emergence of modern science, which has brought forth much technology. What I realized those centuries ago was that humankind was so trapped in the mechanization consciousness that it would not be possible to bring them out of it through spirituality alone. I determined to – for a time – literally fight fire with fire by bringing forth the scientific method and thereby creating technological, mechanical devices that could set people free from the mechanical labor of scratching out a living from the earth.

My beloved, it – of course – was not my plan or my intention that people should be trapped in this technological wonder age. I did not want them to be so used to, so addicted to, technology that they would refuse to develop the creative powers of their minds to the point where they no longer needed technology. I wanted them to use technology wisely to bring forth only that which could not – at the time – be brought forth through the powers of the mind alone.

Turning a teaching into a mechanical doctrine

It is necessary for you who are the spiritual people to realize that there are many of the things you see on this earth that are by no means ideal whatsoever. Even we of the ascended masters have to adapt our efforts for freeing humankind to what is possible to bring forth at a particular time, in a particular culture. One aspect of this is, of course, that when we bring forth a spiritual teaching, it is adapted to the consciousness of the people of the time. It is not meant to be turned into an infallible doctrine that can stand for all time.

When human beings turn a spiritual teaching into such a fixed dogma, then they turn a spiritual teaching into a mechanical "device." Now – instead of using a mechanical device to produce food or take them from one place to another on the earth – they seek to use a mechanical device to take them from earth to heaven. They believe that the outer path – what Jesus called the broad way that leads to destruction, the outer religion – can lead them to salvation. They fail to see that it will never lead them to salvation because it is a mechanical path, my beloved.

You must understand that this concept of a mechanical, outer religion that will guarantee your salvation was developed by a very small minority of the people in embodiment and the disembodied beings who are controlling them, as Maitreya explains in his book. It was not developed because these beings actually believe that they can force their way into heaven through a mechanical path. They – in their pride – have no intention of going to heaven. They do not want to have anything to do with God. They want to stay separated from God for as long as possible. How can they do this? They can do this only when they turn the majority of the population into mechanical people, and especially when they do this to the top 10 percent—those who have the greater connection to their higher beings, to the spiritual realm.

The top 10 percent are those who still have some connection to their higher beings, who have a pure intention of doing what is right for the All. They have been tricked into expressing that pure intention through an impure vision that is affected by the mechanization consciousness. They believe that if they do what is prescribed by an outer religion, then they will not only be doing what is right to raise up other people, but they will also be securing their own salvation. The fallen beings do not believe that a mechanical religion will work. They have only created a mechanical religion in order to trap especially the top 10 percent, but also the majority of the population into approaching salvation in a mechanical manner, thereby expressing whatever light they have through the mechanization consciousness.

Thereby, people are misqualifying their light with a dualistic, human vibration that allows the fallen beings – who are cut off from the flow of light – to steal the misqualified light, use it to sustain their own beings, their own existence, use it to sustain their own leadership positions. They can use it to secure their position as the money-changers in the temple who control the people because they have managed to make the people believe that the people cannot enter the Kingdom of God without going through the outer religion and its leaders.

Growing up in a mechanistic society

My beloved, you have been brought up in a society, in a religion, that is almost completely inundated with this mechanization consciousness. It is time for you to come to a higher level of understanding of the spiritual path. It is time for you to make a sincere effort, an all-out effort, to shake off this yoke of the mechanization consciousness. It is time to take a stand and say: "I am not a robot. I am not a mechanical being. I am a son or daughter of God. I am a spiritual being. I am a creative being. I see who I AM, and I am willing to purify my vision, so that I will no longer express the power of God from my heart through the impurities of this mechanization consciousness. I see that it causes me to use my co-creative powers in a way that seeks to maintain a society, a culture – and even nature – in a state that is less than the actual potential for this earth."

This is keeping the earth cut off from the flow of the River of Life, serving to maintain status quo that allows a small power elite to control the population and to keep this planet in a state of physical, material, spiritual, emotional and mental poverty.

This causes the majority of the population to live at a much lower level materially and spiritually than is necessary. This is done in order to make it possible to create the illusion that the elite is raised above the people. Even though the reality is that the elite are more poor than all those below them. They are more trapped in the consciousness of poverty, the consciousness of mechanization, than any of the people that are being led by these blind leaders. These leaders are truly heading for the ditch of duality, either the ditch on the one side of the road or the ditch on the other side.

Raising your vision above mechanization

We have given you the teachings that you need to accomplish this task, especially in Mother Mary's book [*A Course in Abundance*], which speaks on the psychological level, and in Maitreya's book, which speaks on the overall level of understanding what is going on here on earth. You have the tools, you have the teachings. What is left is to grasp the vision of the need to reach beyond that mechanization consciousness and to become creative beings—instead of continuing these patterns of mechanization that have been programmed into you for many lifetimes.

Make that effort, make the determination, right now to reach for the vision. If you are willing to make this decision, then I want to hear it from you, spoken physically. Call to me, Saint Germain, now, and ask me to assist you in showing you the vision of what is beyond duality, what is beyond the mechanization concept so that I may have the authority to give you that assistance, to give you the vision that will set you free from the mechanization concept. [Audience makes calls]

9 | With Pure Vision You Manifest a Golden Age

My beloved, now that I have the authority to assist you – and have achieved the double goal of waking you up – I will continue my discourse. You see, the task I am asking you to engage in is not easy. For eons, very few people on this planet have freed themselves entirely from this mechanization consciousness. You need to think about the teachings we have given you—of how all of you have volunteered to come into embodiment to take on specific aspects of the collective consciousness. I now give you the understanding that what you have taken on is some aspect of the mechanization consciousness. Really, there is no other state of consciousness on earth but the mechanization consciousness and the Christ consciousness, the creative consciousness.

When you have this overall understanding, it will be easier for you to gain a greater understanding of the particular aspect of the mechanization consciousness that you have taken on. When you begin to understand, so to speak, the mechanics of the mechanization concept, you will be able to apply it to any aspect of your personal situation, any aspect of society.

There is no greater service, there is no greater need, on planet earth right now than to have some people who will not only free themselves from the mechanization consciousness, but who will begin to speak out against that mechanization consciousness. They must point out how it has influenced every aspect of society and how it has caused human beings to limit themselves in a multitude of ways. First of all, it has caused them to deny the very reality that they are spiritual beings who have the creative powers of God, and therefore do not in many cases need a mechanical device to produce what they want on earth.

This has influenced every aspect of society where, for example, you still believe that in order to have energy to run your cars, heat your houses or produce electricity, you need oil. I tell you that if people could free themselves from the mechanization concept, they would be able to tap into a far greater source of energy that would make oil obsolete. You would see a state where there was free and unlimited amounts of energy ready for creative efforts.

Understanding true healing

Likewise, my beloved, you see it in the field of health where people have been seduced by modern medicine and materialistic science into believing that their bodies are a kind of biological robot, a kind of mechanical device. If some kind of disease manifests, it is because something has gone wrong with the body machine. We need to have the mechanics in the garage – called a hospital – go in with their mechanical devices or their chemicals and fix what has gone wrong with the machine so it can again run properly.

This, of course, is a total denial of the true art of healing, which is also the expression of the Fifth Ray. True healing is not a mechanical process; it is a creative process. It starts with the realization that you are more than the physical body because you are a spiritual being.

It also starts with the realization that the body is not a mechanical device through which your spiritual being is expressing itself. No, the human body is not a device. It is an expression, a projection, of the state of consciousness of the spiritual being that inhabits the body.

Your physical body is like the movie on a screen in a theater. It is a projection of what is on the film strip in the projection room. The projection room, of course, is the four levels of your mind, as we have explained many times, the lowest of the minds being the physical mind. Your physical body is a projection of what is occurring on the four levels of your consciousness – what we have also called your four lower bodies – that simply converge to create the physical body as a projection upon the Ma-ter light.

As science has now proven over and over again, there is a limit to what can be achieved through mechanical approaches to healing. When you introduce a chemical into the body, that chemical might remove a specific symptom, but it will have side effects that might be as severe or more severe than the disease that is being attempted to be cured. Likewise, it is, of course, a very primitive procedure to cut open the body with a knife and seek to remove some part from the body that you think has gone wrong. It needs to be realized – as many people in the spiritual field have already started to realize – that healing needs to be approached in a new way. So far this has often been called a holistic way where you realize that the only way to truly heal the body is to also work on the mind, including all levels of the mind.

If the people who are in the healing field would heed the teachings I have given in this discourse – about the mechanization consciousness – and would seek to truly understand what I am saying here, and would then seek to apply it according to their expertise in whatever field of healing they have experience, then you could see a tremendous acceleration of the alternative or holistic healing field. Suddenly, when the healers themselves are willing to remove the beam from their own eyes – are willing to remove the mechanization consciousness from their own minds – they will be inspired by their higher beings to bring forth new healing methods that work at an entirely higher level.

The problem with alternative healing

Let me tell you what is the single most important problem with the field of alternative or holistic healing today. The problem is that most of the people who are healers in that field – and most of the people who come to the healers – are still trapped in the mechanization consciousness. They are looking for the easy way out – the guaranteed path to salvation, the mechanical path to salvation, the magical formula – that will allow people to either take some natural remedy or do some kind of exercise, be it physical or mental, and suddenly, puff, the disease is gone.

In order to have true healing, you need to rise above the mechanization consciousness. This can only be done when you are willing to follow the true spiritual path, the inner path to Christhood. Only then can you rise above that mechanization consciousness. You can avoid being seduced by the oh-so-subtle illusions created to reinforce that mechanization consciousness and make people believe that this material world functions according to mechanical laws.

The laws of nature are not mechanical

My beloved, science has created the concept of the laws of nature. Certainly, there are laws that guide the evolution of nature. The problem with materialistic science is that it has given people the impression – the fundamental belief, the paradigm – that even the laws of nature are mechanical. They always function in a certain way and therefore nothing can override the laws of nature.

This is what has caused several past societies – that had achieved a high level of sophistication – to actually lose the abundance they had attained. Some of these societies were so abundant and so sophisticated that, compared to your current civilization, you would have said that they were a golden age society. To some degree they were, but what happened was that those societies were eventually taken over by the people who had an imbalance of power. These are the people who are unbalanced in power, and they will seek to control those who are unbalanced in love—and who therefore become passive followers of the blind leaders.

When the blind leaders had taken over, they created a society in which the people were very comfortable. They were comfortable because they had used the mechanization consciousness to create mechanical, technological devices that gave them what they needed to sustain their lifestyle. They had been seduced by the mechanization consciousness to believe that there was nothing beyond their current lifestyle, that there was no greater abundance to be had. According to the laws of nature – and the limitations built into nature on this planet – they could not have more than what they had.

This is the scenario expressed in the saying that ignorance is bliss. The people were ignorant of the potential to have more, and therefore they had reached a certain state of contentment, a certain state of comfortability with what they had. This was to a large degree the case with the Jews at the time that Jesus appeared. That is why he had to perform certain miracles that shook people out of the consciousness that there were certain limitations, that there were certain things that were impossible for a human being.

Today, those who are trapped in the aspect of the mechanization consciousness called materialistic science look back at Jesus' time and deny his miracles. They say: "This would go against the laws of nature, and therefore, clearly, it could not be possible that someone could raise the dead, heal the sick by a simple command, or walk on water or turn water into wine. Thus, Jesus must have been a phony, he must have been a charlatan, he must have hypnotized the people to believe in his miracles. Or the gospel writers simply made it all up to make Jesus look special."

The reality is that the laws of nature are not mechanical. When you attain some measure of Christ consciousness, you can go beyond what science currently calls the laws of nature. You can use the infinite creative power of the expanding and contracting forces of the Father-Mother God – through the balance of the Christ mind – to bring forth a much higher manifestation than what is currently possible on earth.

What science currently sees as the laws of nature are not actually the laws of God. They are the laws that are created out of the duality of the mechanization consciousness where an action must have an opposite reaction. Any action will be limited by the reaction. There are certain limitations that human beings cannot go beyond—as long as they are trapped in the dualistic state of consciousness, the mechanization consciousness. Jesus came to demonstrate that with men it is impossible to go beyond the current limitations of nature, but with God all things are possible.

It is time to accept your creative power

This is the message that Jesus gave 2,000 years ago. We of the ascended masters knew that 2,000 years ago, there were very few people who were ready to understand the fullness of Jesus' message. We also know that today there are many people among the top 10 percent who are ready to understand this message. They are ready to embody that message and to go out and make good on Jesus' promise, namely that those who believe on him shall do the works that he did and even greater works than he did. Humankind has progressed in consciousness over the past 2,000 years, and therefore it is possible to bring forth even greater abundance, even greater so-called miracles, than Jesus could bring forth 2,000 years ago.

This is the reality that can be attained by you when you truly understand the Fifth Ray of creative vision and of holistic healing. You do this through a total change in consciousness that frees you, that raises you, above the duality of the mechanization consciousness of action and reaction. It sets you free to be the open door for the Father-Mother God to express itself through you, as that infinite power that is completely one with the love. It brings forth a balanced manifestation through the Son that raises up all sons and daughters of God. The consciousness of the Son is precisely what sees all life as one and empowers you to see yourself as one with the Father and as one with all life. You are seeing that it is only by raising up the All that you truly raise up yourself.

My beloved, I seal you in the Fifth Ray of Vision and healing, infused with the Seventh Ray of Freedom and the entire momentum of freedom that I, Saint Germain, embody for this planet. I AM in the great is of freedom. Therefore, I *is* freedom for the earth. I am willing to give that flow of is to those who will reach for total freedom from the mechanization consciousness that is anti-freedom. Be sealed in that Freedom Flame that cannot be stopped by anything—except the free will of the individual and the free will of a society. I seal you in the love of my heart.

10 | INVOKING VISION TO OVERCOME POVERTY

In the name of the I AM THAT I AM, Jesus Christ, I call upon Saint Germain and the Divine Director for the transformation of the consciousness of poverty on earth. Awaken people to the reality that we are spiritual beings and that we can co-create a new future by working with the ascended masters. I especially call for …

[Make your own calls here.]

Part 1

1. Saint Germain, help people develop a pure vision so that their co-creative efforts will be based on a pure understanding of how creation works.

O Saint Germain, you do inspire,
my vision raised forever higher,
with you I form a figure-eight,
your Golden Age I co-create.

**O Saint Germain, what love you bring,
it truly makes all matter sing,
your violet flame does all restore,
with you we are becoming more.**

2. Saint Germain, help people develop pure intention and formulate a pure vision of what they want to co-create before they impose that vision upon the Ma-ter light.

O Saint Germain, what Freedom Flame,
released when we recite your name,
acceleration is your gift,
our planet it will surely lift.

**O Saint Germain, what love you bring,
it truly makes all matter sing,
your violet flame does all restore,
with you we are becoming more.**

3. Saint Germain, I call forth the judgment of Christ upon those who are blinded by the spiritual pride they developed as a result of failing the initiations on the Fourth Ray, those who cannot see beyond the separate self.

O Saint Germain, in love we claim,
our right to bring your violet flame,
from you Above, to us below,
it is an all-transforming flow.

> **O Saint Germain, what love you bring,**
> **it truly makes all matter sing,**
> **your violet flame does all restore,**
> **with you we are becoming more.**

4. Saint Germain, I call forth the judgment of Christ upon those who see themselves as separate from all other human beings and who see a competition or conflict between themselves and others.

> O Saint Germain, I love you so,
> my aura filled with violet glow,
> my chakras filled with violet fire,
> I am your cosmic amplifier.

> **O Saint Germain, what love you bring,**
> **it truly makes all matter sing,**
> **your violet flame does all restore,**
> **with you we are becoming more.**

5. Saint Germain, I call forth the judgment of Christ upon those who, out of pride, attempt to create the impression that they are more important than other beings and therefore elevated above them.

> O Saint Germain, I am now free,
> your violet flame is therapy,
> transform all hang-ups in my mind,
> as inner peace I surely find.

> O Saint Germain, what love you bring,
> it truly makes all matter sing,
> your violet flame does all restore,
> with you we are becoming more.

6. Saint Germain, I call forth the judgment of Christ upon those who are not seeking to raise up the All because their vision is dualistic.

O Saint Germain, my body pure,
your violet flame for all is cure,
consume the cause of all disease,
and therefore I am all at ease.

> O Saint Germain, what love you bring,
> it truly makes all matter sing,
> your violet flame does all restore,
> with you we are becoming more.

7. Saint Germain, awaken people to the reality that the only way to truly raise up ourselves is to work on raising up the All. The more we raise up others, the more we will be raised.

O Saint Germain, I'm karma-free,
the past no longer burdens me,
a brand new opportunity,
I am in Christic unity.

> O Saint Germain, what love you bring,
> it truly makes all matter sing,
> your violet flame does all restore,
> with you we are becoming more.

8. Saint Germain, awaken people to the reality that the principle of multiplying our talents is the most fundamental principle of life in the Ma-ter realm.

> O Saint Germain, we are now one,
> I am for you a violet sun,
> as we transform this planet earth,
> your Golden Age is given birth.
>
> **O Saint Germain, what love you bring,**
> **it truly makes all matter sing,**
> **your violet flame does all restore,**
> **with you we are becoming more.**

9. Saint Germain, awaken people to the reality that the more we give to raise up other parts of life, the more we receive from the true source of life, our own higher beings.

> O Saint Germain, the earth is free,
> from burden of duality,
> in oneness we bring what is best,
> your Golden Age is manifest.
>
> **O Saint Germain, what love you bring,**
> **it truly makes all matter sing,**
> **your violet flame does all restore,**
> **with you we are becoming more.**

Part 2

1. Saint Germain, I call forth the judgment of Christ upon those whose vision has become divided and who pass value judgments, saying that some people are better or more important than others.

> Divine Director, I now see,
> the world is unreality,
> in my heart I now truly feel,
> the Spirit is all that is real.
>
> **Divine Director, send the light,**
> **from blindness clear my inner sight,**
> **my vision free, my vision clear,**
> **your guidance is forever here.**

2. Saint Germain, I call forth the judgment of Christ upon those who are so trapped in pride that they want to belong to those who are more important or who have more or who can do more than others.

> Divine Director, vision give,
> in clarity I want to live,
> I now behold my plan Divine,
> the plan that is uniquely mine.
>
> **Divine Director, send the light,**
> **from blindness clear my inner sight,**
> **my vision free, my vision clear,**
> **your guidance is forever here.**

3. Saint Germain, I call forth the judgment of Christ upon those who seek to express the momentum they gathered on the first four rays in a dualistic way. They are seeking to raise up themselves by putting others down.

> Divine Director, show in me,
> the ego games, and set me free,
> help me escape the ego's cage,
> to help bring in the golden age.

> **Divine Director, send the light,**
> **from blindness clear my inner sight,**
> **my vision free, my vision clear,**
> **your guidance is forever here.**

4. Saint Germain, I call forth the judgment of Christ upon those who have fallen into duality and who can express their co-creative efforts only by using the momentums they gathered before they fell. They cannot receive more from the source, for they are not multiplying the talents.

> Divine Director, I'm with you,
> my vision one, no longer two,
> as karma's veil you do disperse,
> I see a whole new universe.

> **Divine Director, send the light,**
> **from blindness clear my inner sight,**
> **my vision free, my vision clear,**
> **your guidance is forever here.**

5. Saint Germain, I call forth the judgment of Christ upon those who have fallen into duality and who can only make themselves seem more important than others by limiting them.

> Divine Director, I go up,
> electric light now fills my cup,
> consume in me all shadows old,
> bestow on me a vision bold.
>
> **Divine Director, send the light,**
> **from blindness clear my inner sight,**
> **my vision free, my vision clear,**
> **your guidance is forever here.**

6. Saint Germain, I call forth the judgment of Christ upon those who have separated themselves from the River of Life. They have fallen into the consciousness of poverty and are now seeking to trap all other beings in that same state of consciousness.

> Divine Director, heart of gold,
> my sacred labor I unfold,
> o blessed Guru, I now see,
> where my own plan is taking me.
>
> **Divine Director, send the light,**
> **from blindness clear my inner sight,**
> **my vision free, my vision clear,**
> **your guidance is forever here.**

7. Saint Germain, I call forth the judgment of Christ upon those who are seeking to get others to believe in the illusion of separation, the illusion of lack, the illusion that the material realm is separated from Spirit.

> Divine Director, by your grace,
> in grander scheme I find my place,
> my individual flame I see,
> uniqueness God has given me.
>
> **Divine Director, send the light,**
> **from blindness clear my inner sight,**
> **my vision free, my vision clear,**
> **your guidance is forever here.**

8. Saint Germain, I call forth the judgment of Christ upon the dualistic leaders in past ages who managed to create a society in which they had set themselves up in leadership positions.

> Divine Director, vision one,
> I see that I AM God's own Sun,
> with your direction so Divine,
> I am now letting my light shine.
>
> **Divine Director, send the light,**
> **from blindness clear my inner sight,**
> **my vision free, my vision clear,**
> **your guidance is forever here.**

9. Saint Germain, I call forth the judgment of Christ upon those who create leadership positions that seem ontouchable because the people cannot challenge them. The people either do not have the physical power or believe they cannot or should not challenge the leaders.

> Divine Director, what a gift,
> to be a part of Spirit's lift,
> to raise mankind out of the night,
> to bask in Spirit's loving sight.
>
> **Divine Director, send the light,**
> **from blindness clear my inner sight,**
> **my vision free, my vision clear,**
> **your guidance is forever here.**

Part 3

1. Saint Germain, I call forth the judgment of Christ upon those who are not willing to lose their comfortability, to lose their mortal lives, in order to follow Christ.

> O Saint Germain, you do inspire,
> my vision raised forever higher,
> with you I form a figure-eight,
> your Golden Age I co-create.
>
> **O Saint Germain, what love you bring,**
> **it truly makes all matter sing,**
> **your violet flame does all restore,**
> **with you we are becoming more.**

10 | *Invoking Vision to Overcome Poverty*

2. Saint Germain, I call forth the judgment of Christ upon those who believe that the Messiah will come sometime in the distant future, making up excuses for ignoring the savior that is always present.

> O Saint Germain, what Freedom Flame,
> released when we recite your name,
> acceleration is your gift,
> our planet it will surely lift.
>
> **O Saint Germain, what love you bring,**
> **it truly makes all matter sing,**
> **your violet flame does all restore,**
> **with you we are becoming more.**

3. Saint Germain, I call forth the judgment of Christ upon the fallen leaders who killed Jesus' physical body in an attempt to prevent him from overturning the tables of the spiritual money-changers.

> O Saint Germain, in love we claim,
> our right to bring your violet flame,
> from you Above, to us below,
> it is an all-transforming flow.
>
> **O Saint Germain, what love you bring,**
> **it truly makes all matter sing,**
> **your violet flame does all restore,**
> **with you we are becoming more.**

4. Saint Germain, I call forth the judgment of Christ upon the leaders who had taken away not only the money of the people but the abundant consciousness of the people.

O Saint Germain, I love you so,
my aura filled with violet glow,
my chakras filled with violet fire,
I am your cosmic amplifier.

**O Saint Germain, what love you bring,
it truly makes all matter sing,
your violet flame does all restore,
with you we are becoming more.**

5. Saint Germain, I call forth the judgment of Christ upon the leaders who had separated the people from the flow of the River of Life so that no one among them could gather enough light, enough Christhood, to stand up and challenge the fallen beings in leadership positions.

O Saint Germain, I am now free,
your violet flame is therapy,
transform all hang-ups in my mind,
as inner peace I surely find.

**O Saint Germain, what love you bring,
it truly makes all matter sing,
your violet flame does all restore,
with you we are becoming more.**

6. Saint Germain, I call forth the judgment of Christ upon the original fallen beings who realized that they cannot use the power of God for selfish purposes, meaning they would soon run out of power if they did not find a way to prolong their existence in the matter realm.

> O Saint Germain, my body pure,
> your violet flame for all is cure,
> consume the cause of all disease,
> and therefore I am all at ease.
>
> **O Saint Germain, what love you bring,
> it truly makes all matter sing,
> your violet flame does all restore,
> with you we are becoming more.**

7. Saint Germain, I call forth the judgment of Christ upon the fallen beings who created a sphere in the material realm where they had generated a mechanical force that allowed them to express power with impure intentions.

> O Saint Germain, I'm karma-free,
> the past no longer burdens me,
> a brand new opportunity,
> I am in Christic unity.
>
> **O Saint Germain, what love you bring,
> it truly makes all matter sing,
> your violet flame does all restore,
> with you we are becoming more.**

8. Saint Germain, I call forth the judgment of Christ upon the fallen beings who are the masterminds behind the mechanization consciousness and the mechanization concept.

> O Saint Germain, we are now one,
> I am for you a violet sun,
> as we transform this planet earth,
> your Golden Age is given birth.

> O Saint Germain, what love you bring,
> it truly makes all matter sing,
> your violet flame does all restore,
> with you we are becoming more.

9. Saint Germain, I call forth the judgment of Christ upon the fallen beings who wanted a sphere where they could express their power without any of what they would call restrictions.

> O Saint Germain, the earth is free,
> from burden of duality,
> in oneness we bring what is best,
> your Golden Age is manifest.

> O Saint Germain, what love you bring,
> it truly makes all matter sing,
> your violet flame does all restore,
> with you we are becoming more.

Part 4

1. Saint Germain, I call forth the judgment of Christ upon the fallen beings who think that the laws of God are restrictions of their creativity.

> Divine Director, I now see,
> the world is unreality,
> in my heart I now truly feel,
> the Spirit is all that is real.

> **Divine Director, send the light,**
> **from blindness clear my inner sight,**
> **my vision free, my vision clear,**
> **your guidance is forever here.**

2. Saint Germain, I call forth the judgment of Christ upon the fallen beings who are not expressing creativity, but a mechanical display of power, a dualistic display of power.

> Divine Director, vision give,
> in clarity I want to live,
> I now behold my plan Divine,
> the plan that is uniquely mine.

> **Divine Director, send the light,**
> **from blindness clear my inner sight,**
> **my vision free, my vision clear,**
> **your guidance is forever here.**

3. Saint Germain, I call forth the judgment of Christ upon the fallen beings who have managed to get the consciousness of mechanization to permeate virtually every aspect of life on this planet.

> Divine Director, show in me,
> the ego games, and set me free,
> help me escape the ego's cage,
> to help bring in the golden age.

> **Divine Director, send the light,**
> **from blindness clear my inner sight,**
> **my vision free, my vision clear,**
> **your guidance is forever here.**

4. Saint Germain, I call forth the judgment of Christ upon the fallen beings who are behind the creation of a mechanical device, which does not even have to be a physical device, where they do not have to be in alignment with the laws of God or have pure intentions.

> Divine Director, I'm with you,
> my vision one, no longer two,
> as karma's veil you do disperse,
> I see a whole new universe.
>
> **Divine Director, send the light,**
> **from blindness clear my inner sight,**
> **my vision free, my vision clear,**
> **your guidance is forever here.**

5. Saint Germain, I call forth the judgment of Christ upon the fallen beings who have given the mechanization consciousness many subtle disguises that have deceived the majority of the population into believing that it is necessary and good, and that there is no alternative to it.

> Divine Director, I go up,
> electric light now fills my cup,
> consume in me all shadows old,
> bestow on me a vision bold.
>
> **Divine Director, send the light,**
> **from blindness clear my inner sight,**
> **my vision free, my vision clear,**
> **your guidance is forever here.**

6. Saint Germain, I call forth the judgment of Christ upon the leaders in politics, economics, science, the media and religion who are blinded by and are promoting an approach to life that springs from the mechanization consciousness.

> Divine Director, heart of gold,
> my sacred labor I unfold,
> o blessed Guru, I now see,
> where my own plan is taking me.
>
> **Divine Director, send the light,**
> **from blindness clear my inner sight,**
> **my vision free, my vision clear,**
> **your guidance is forever here.**

7. Saint Germain, I call forth the judgment of Christ upon the leaders who are attempting to maintain their positions of leadership, privilege and power by keeping the people in a state of consciousness where they are not being co-creators with God, for they cannot express their true creative powers.

> Divine Director, by your grace,
> in grander scheme I find my place,
> my individual flame I see,
> uniqueness God has given me.
>
> **Divine Director, send the light,**
> **from blindness clear my inner sight,**
> **my vision free, my vision clear,**
> **your guidance is forever here.**

8. Saint Germain, I call forth the judgment of Christ upon the leaders who keep people living as mechanized beings, as a kind of biological robots, who are doing the same thing over and over, never breaking out of certain boundaries.

> Divine Director, vision one,
> I see that I AM God's own Sun,
> with your direction so Divine,
> I am now letting my light shine.
>
> **Divine Director, send the light,**
> **from blindness clear my inner sight,**
> **my vision free, my vision clear,**
> **your guidance is forever here.**

9. Saint Germain, I call forth the judgment of Christ upon the fallen beings who have programmed the people to be like computers and stay within their program, doing what they were programmed to do, mechanically repeating the same actions, the same beliefs, the same patterns over and over.

> Divine Director, what a gift,
> to be a part of Spirit's lift,
> to raise mankind out of the night,
> to bask in Spirit's loving sight.
>
> **Divine Director, send the light,**
> **from blindness clear my inner sight,**
> **my vision free, my vision clear,**
> **your guidance is forever here.**

Part 5

1. Saint Germain, I call forth the judgment of Christ upon the fallen beings who are seeking to use technology to trap people even more firmly instead of allowing it to give them free time to pursue spiritual growth.

> O Saint Germain, you do inspire,
> my vision raised forever higher,
> with you I form a figure-eight,
> your Golden Age I co-create.
>
> **O Saint Germain, what love you bring,**
> **it truly makes all matter sing,**
> **your violet flame does all restore,**
> **with you we are becoming more.**

2. Saint Germain, I call forth the judgment of Christ upon the fallen beings behind the addiction to technology that is causing people to refuse to develop the creative powers of their minds. Thus, they never come to the point where they no longer need technology.

> O Saint Germain, what Freedom Flame,
> released when we recite your name,
> acceleration is your gift,
> our planet it will surely lift.
>
> **O Saint Germain, what love you bring,**
> **it truly makes all matter sing,**
> **your violet flame does all restore,**
> **with you we are becoming more.**

3. Saint Germain, I call forth the judgment of Christ upon the fallen beings who take a spiritual teaching and turn it into an infallible doctrine and claim it can stand for all time.

> O Saint Germain, in love we claim,
> our right to bring your violet flame,
> from you Above, to us below,
> it is an all-transforming flow.
>
> **O Saint Germain, what love you bring,**
> **it truly makes all matter sing,**
> **your violet flame does all restore,**
> **with you we are becoming more.**

4. Saint Germain, I call forth the judgment of Christ upon the fallen beings who turn a spiritual teaching into a fixed dogma and thereby turn it into a mechanical "device."

> O Saint Germain, I love you so,
> my aura filled with violet glow,
> my chakras filled with violet fire,
> I am your cosmic amplifier.
>
> **O Saint Germain, what love you bring,**
> **it truly makes all matter sing,**
> **your violet flame does all restore,**
> **with you we are becoming more.**

5. Saint Germain, I call forth the judgment of Christ upon the fallen beings who seek to use a mechanical device to take them from earth to heaven, believing that the outer path, the outer religion can lead them to salvation.

O Saint Germain, I am now free,
your violet flame is therapy,
transform all hang-ups in my mind,
as inner peace I surely find.

**O Saint Germain, what love you bring,
it truly makes all matter sing,
your violet flame does all restore,
with you we are becoming more.**

6. Saint Germain, I call forth the judgment of Christ upon the fallen beings who developed the concept of a mechanical, outer religion that will guarantee our salvation.

O Saint Germain, my body pure,
your violet flame for all is cure,
consume the cause of all disease,
and therefore I am all at ease.

**O Saint Germain, what love you bring,
it truly makes all matter sing,
your violet flame does all restore,
with you we are becoming more.**

7. Saint Germain, I call forth the judgment of Christ upon the fallen beings who do not even believe that they can force their way into heaven through a mechanical path.

O Saint Germain, I'm karma-free,
the past no longer burdens me,
a brand new opportunity,
I am in Christic unity.

> O Saint Germain, what love you bring,
> it truly makes all matter sing,
> your violet flame does all restore,
> with you we are becoming more.

8. Saint Germain, I call forth the judgment of Christ upon the fallen beings who in their pride have no intention of going to heaven. They do not want to have anything to do with God. They want to stay separated from God as long as possible.

> O Saint Germain, we are now one,
> I am for you a violet sun,
> as we transform this planet earth,
> your Golden Age is given birth.

> **O Saint Germain, what love you bring,**
> **it truly makes all matter sing,**
> **your violet flame does all restore,**
> **with you we are becoming more.**

9. Saint Germain, I call forth the judgment of Christ upon the fallen beings who are seeking to turn the majority of the population and the top 10 percent into mechanical beings.

> O Saint Germain, the earth is free,
> from burden of duality,
> in oneness we bring what is best,
> your Golden Age is manifest.

> **O Saint Germain, what love you bring,**
> **it truly makes all matter sing,**
> **your violet flame does all restore,**
> **with you we are becoming more.**

Part 6

1. Saint Germain, I call forth the judgment of Christ upon all people who believe that if they do what is prescribed by an outer religion, then they will be raising up other people and securing their own salvation.

> Divine Director, I now see,
> the world is unreality,
> in my heart I now truly feel,
> the Spirit is all that is real.
>
> **Divine Director, send the light,**
> **from blindness clear my inner sight,**
> **my vision free, my vision clear,**
> **your guidance is forever here.**

2. Saint Germain, I call forth the judgment of Christ upon the fallen beings who do not believe that a mechanical religion will work. They have only created a mechanical religion in order to trap the top 10 percent and the majority into approaching salvation in a mechanical manner, thereby expressing their light through the mechanization consciousness.

> Divine Director, vision give,
> in clarity I want to live,
> I now behold my plan Divine,
> the plan that is uniquely mine.

> **Divine Director, send the light,**
> **from blindness clear my inner sight,**
> **my vision free, my vision clear,**
> **your guidance is forever here.**

3. Saint Germain, I call forth the judgment of Christ upon all people who are misqualifying their light with a dualistic, human vibration that allows the fallen beings to steal the misqualified light and use it to sustain their positions.

> Divine Director, show in me,
> the ego games, and set me free,
> help me escape the ego's cage,
> to help bring in the golden age.

> **Divine Director, send the light,**
> **from blindness clear my inner sight,**
> **my vision free, my vision clear,**
> **your guidance is forever here.**

4. Saint Germain, I call forth the judgment of Christ upon the fallen beings who use the light of the people to secure their position as the money-changers in the temple. They control the people because they have managed to make them believe that they cannot enter the Kingdom of God without going through the outer religion and its leaders.

> Divine Director, I'm with you,
> my vision one, no longer two,
> as karma's veil you do disperse,
> I see a whole new universe.

> Divine Director, send the light,
> from blindness clear my inner sight,
> my vision free, my vision clear,
> your guidance is forever here.

5. Saint Germain, awaken people to the reality that we have been brought up in a society and religion that is almost completely inundated with the mechanization consciousness.

> Divine Director, I go up,
> electric light now fills my cup,
> consume in me all shadows old,
> bestow on me a vision bold.

> **Divine Director, send the light,**
> **from blindness clear my inner sight,**
> **my vision free, my vision clear,**
> **your guidance is forever here.**

6. Saint Germain, awaken people to the need to shake off the yoke of the mechanization consciousness and say: "I am not a robot. I am not a mechanical being. I am a son or daughter of God. I am a spiritual being. I am a creative being."

> Divine Director, heart of gold,
> my sacred labor I unfold,
> o blessed Guru, I now see,
> where my own plan is taking me.

> **Divine Director, send the light,**
> **from blindness clear my inner sight,**
> **my vision free, my vision clear,**
> **your guidance is forever here.**

7. Saint Germain, awaken people to the need to say: "I see who I AM, and I am willing to purify my vision so that I will no longer express the power of God from my heart through the impurities of this mechanization consciousness that causes me to use my co-creative powers in a way that seeks to maintain everything in a state that is less than the actual potential for this earth."

> Divine Director, by your grace,
> in grander scheme I find my place,
> my individual flame I see,
> uniqueness God has given me.

> **Divine Director, send the light,**
> **from blindness clear my inner sight,**
> **my vision free, my vision clear,**
> **your guidance is forever here.**

8. Saint Germain, I call forth the judgment of Christ upon the fallen beings who are keeping the earth cut off from the flow of the River of Life. They are seeking to maintain status quo that allows a small power elite to control the population and keep this planet in a state of physical, material, spiritual, emotional and mental poverty.

> Divine Director, vision one,
> I see that I AM God's own Sun,
> with your direction so Divine,
> I am now letting my light shine.

**Divine Director, send the light,
from blindness clear my inner sight,
my vision free, my vision clear,
your guidance is forever here.**

9. Saint Germain, I call forth the judgment of Christ upon the fallen beings who are causing the majority of the population to live at a much lower material and spiritual level than necessary.

Divine Director, what a gift,
to be a part of Spirit's lift,
to raise mankind out of the night,
to bask in Spirit's loving sight.

**Divine Director, send the light,
from blindness clear my inner sight,
my vision free, my vision clear,
your guidance is forever here.**

Part 7

1. Saint Germain, I call forth the judgment of Christ upon the fallen beings who are seeking to create the illusion that the elite is raised above the people.

O Saint Germain, you do inspire,
my vision raised forever higher,
with you I form a figure-eight,
your Golden Age I co-create.

**O Saint Germain, what love you bring,
it truly makes all matter sing,
your violet flame does all restore,
with you we are becoming more.**

2. Saint Germain, I call forth the judgment of Christ upon the fallen beings who are trapped in the consciousness of poverty, the consciousness of mechanization, and are heading for the ditch of duality, either the ditch on the one side of the road or the ditch on the other side.

O Saint Germain, what Freedom Flame,
released when we recite your name,
acceleration is your gift,
our planet it will surely lift.

**O Saint Germain, what love you bring,
it truly makes all matter sing,
your violet flame does all restore,
with you we are becoming more.**

3. Saint Germain, I am determining right now to reach for the vision that is beyond duality. I call to you and I give you the authority to assist me and show me the vision of what is beyond duality, what is beyond mechanization. Give me the vision that will set me free from the mechanization concept.

O Saint Germain, in love we claim,
our right to bring your violet flame,
from you Above, to us below,
it is an all-transforming flow.

**O Saint Germain, what love you bring,
it truly makes all matter sing,
your violet flame does all restore,
with you we are becoming more.**

4. Saint Germain, help me understand the particular aspect of the mechanization consciousness that I have taken on. Help me free myself from the mechanization consciousness, and I will begin to speak out against the mechanization concept.

O Saint Germain, I love you so,
my aura filled with violet glow,
my chakras filled with violet fire,
I am your cosmic amplifier.

**O Saint Germain, what love you bring,
it truly makes all matter sing,
your violet flame does all restore,
with you we are becoming more.**

5. Saint Germain, help me point out how the mechanization consciousness has influenced every aspect of society, and how it has caused human beings to limit ourselves by denying that we are spiritual beings who have the creative powers of God, and therefore do not need a mechanical device to produce what we want on earth.

O Saint Germain, I am now free,
your violet flame is therapy,
transform all hang-ups in my mind,
as inner peace I surely find.

> O Saint Germain, what love you bring,
> it truly makes all matter sing,
> your violet flame does all restore,
> with you we are becoming more.

6. Saint Germain, I call forth the judgment of Christ upon the fallen beings who have influenced every aspect of society, causing people to believe that in order to have energy, we need oil.

O Saint Germain, my body pure,
your violet flame for all is cure,
consume the cause of all disease,
and therefore I am all at ease.

> O Saint Germain, what love you bring,
> it truly makes all matter sing,
> your violet flame does all restore,
> with you we are becoming more.

7. Saint Germain, I call forth the judgment of Christ upon the fallen beings who have used modern medicine and materialistic science to seduce people into believing that their bodies are a kind of biological robot, a kind of mechanical device.

O Saint Germain, I'm karma-free,
the past no longer burdens me,
a brand new opportunity,
I am in Christic unity.

> O Saint Germain, what love you bring,
> it truly makes all matter sing,
> your violet flame does all restore,
> with you we are becoming more.

8. Saint Germain, I call forth the judgment of Christ upon the fallen beings who are denying that healing is a creative process, thereby blocking an understanding of the mechanization consciousness and delaying an acceleration of the holistic healing field.

> O Saint Germain, we are now one,
> I am for you a violet sun,
> as we transform this planet earth,
> your Golden Age is given birth.
>
> **O Saint Germain, what love you bring,**
> **it truly makes all matter sing,**
> **your violet flame does all restore,**
> **with you we are becoming more.**

9. Saint Germain, I call forth the judgment of Christ upon the people in the field of holistic healing who will not see that they are still trapped in the mechanization consciousness and are looking for the easy way out.

> O Saint Germain, the earth is free,
> from burden of duality,
> in oneness we bring what is best,
> your Golden Age is manifest.
>
> **O Saint Germain, what love you bring,**
> **it truly makes all matter sing,**
> **your violet flame does all restore,**
> **with you we are becoming more.**

Part 8

1. Saint Germain, I call forth the judgment of Christ upon the fallen beings who have created very subtle illusions in order to reinforce the mechanization consciousness and make people believe that this material world functions according to mechanical laws.

> Divine Director, I now see,
> the world is unreality,
> in my heart I now truly feel,
> the Spirit is all that is real.
>
> **Divine Director, send the light,**
> **from blindness clear my inner sight,**
> **my vision free, my vision clear,**
> **your guidance is forever here.**

2. Saint Germain, I call forth the judgment of Christ upon the fallen beings who have created materialistic science and the paradigm that the laws of nature are mechanical, saying they always function in a certain way and therefore nothing can override the laws of nature.

> Divine Director, vision give,
> in clarity I want to live,
> I now behold my plan Divine,
> the plan that is uniquely mine.

**Divine Director, send the light,
from blindness clear my inner sight,
my vision free, my vision clear,
your guidance is forever here.**

3. Saint Germain, I call forth the judgment of Christ upon the fallen beings who are unbalanced in power and who seek to control those who are unbalanced in love—making people passive followers of the blind leaders.

Divine Director, show in me,
the ego games, and set me free,
help me escape the ego's cage,
to help bring in the golden age.

**Divine Director, send the light,
from blindness clear my inner sight,
my vision free, my vision clear,
your guidance is forever here.**

4. Saint Germain, I call forth the judgment of Christ upon the fallen beings who created a society in which the people were comfortable because they had used the mechanization consciousness to create technological devices that gave them what they needed to sustain their lifestyle.

Divine Director, I'm with you,
my vision one, no longer two,
as karma's veil you do disperse,
I see a whole new universe.

**Divine Director, send the light,
from blindness clear my inner sight,
my vision free, my vision clear,
your guidance is forever here.**

5. Saint Germain, I call forth the judgment of Christ upon the fallen beings who have seduced people into believing that according to the laws of nature they cannot have more than what they have.

Divine Director, I go up,
electric light now fills my cup,
consume in me all shadows old,
bestow on me a vision bold.

**Divine Director, send the light,
from blindness clear my inner sight,
my vision free, my vision clear,
your guidance is forever here.**

6. Saint Germain, I call forth the judgment of Christ upon the fallen beings who deny Jesus' miracles and say this would go against the laws of nature, and therefore it is not possible that someone could raise the dead, heal the sick, walk on water or turn water into wine.

Divine Director, heart of gold,
my sacred labor I unfold,
o blessed Guru, I now see,
where my own plan is taking me.

> Divine Director, send the light,
> from blindness clear my inner sight,
> my vision free, my vision clear,
> your guidance is forever here.

7. Saint Germain, awaken people to the reality that the laws of nature are not mechanical. When we attain some measure of Christ consciousness, we can go beyond the laws of nature. We can use the infinite creative power of the expanding and contracting forces of the Father-Mother God to bring forth a much higher manifestation than what is currently possible on earth.

> Divine Director, by your grace,
> in grander scheme I find my place,
> my individual flame I see,
> uniqueness God has given me.

> Divine Director, send the light,
> from blindness clear my inner sight,
> my vision free, my vision clear,
> your guidance is forever here.

8. Saint Germain, awaken the top 10 percent to the reality that the laws of nature are not the laws of God. They are created out of the duality of the mechanization consciousness where an action must have an opposite reaction.

> Divine Director, vision one,
> I see that I AM God's own Sun,
> with your direction so Divine,
> I am now letting my light shine.

> Divine Director, send the light,
> from blindness clear my inner sight,
> my vision free, my vision clear,
> your guidance is forever here.

9. Saint Germain, awaken the top 10 percent to the potential to go through a total change in consciousness that raises us above the duality of the mechanization consciousness and sets us free to bring forth a balanced manifestation through the Christ consciousness.

> Divine Director, what a gift,
> to be a part of Spirit's lift,
> to raise mankind out of the night,
> to bask in Spirit's loving sight.

> Divine Director, send the light,
> from blindness clear my inner sight,
> my vision free, my vision clear,
> your guidance is forever here.

Sealing

In the name of the I AM THAT I AM, I accept that Archangel Michael, Astrea and Shiva form an impenetrable shield around myself and all constructive people, sealing us from all fear-based energies in all four octaves. I accept that the Light of God is consuming and transforming all fear-based energies that make up the forces behind war!

11 | TRUE SERVICE MEANS ACCELERATION INTO UNITY

Saint Germain I AM, and I come to discourse with you on the poverty consciousness and how it relates to the Sixth Ray. I come with fire and determination, for my beloved, in my previous discourses I have attempted to give you understanding, but it is necessary to give you more than understanding. It is necessary to give you a quickening, an acceleration that goes beyond the intellectual understanding. If the intellect itself could raise the world into the Kingdom of God, then surely this would already have happened—considering the amount of intellectual people that have walked this earth and taken up positions in society.

You who are the spiritual people on earth have been told that the Sixth Ray is the ray of ministration—of ministering to life, of giving service to life. While this is true, I come to give you a higher understanding. I must tell you that there is not one amongst you who have understood the fullness and the reality of the Sixth Ray and what it means to give service to life. You have all adopted – through subtle means coming from the culture – a view of the Sixth Ray that is distinctly anti-service—that is even anti-Christ. It – precisely – springs from the mechanization consciousness that I spoke about yesterday.

Stepping up to a higher vision of service

My beloved, what does it mean to give service to life? You have all come to believe that when you are serving someone, you are being somewhat passive, you are helping them according to their need, the need that you see as a physical manifestation. The true need of people is not to have some human, bodily or worldly need fulfilled. The true need of people is to have an acceleration so that they are awakened to their lack of vision and so that they can see beyond the separate self—the separate self that has these worldly needs.

You need to step up to the realization that there is service and there is *service*. There is worldly service, mechanical service, and there is spiritual service, creative service. You will not serve life in an ultimate capacity by fulfilling people's outer needs through mechanical means. You will give ultimate service to life only – *only* – if you step up your vision of service to where you realize that you need to accelerate people beyond their current needs—instead of simply seeking to fulfill those needs.

When you seek to fulfill people's needs, even the needs of the poor, the infirm or the sick, you are enabling them to stay in the consciousness that has precipitated their outer physical condition. This is an essential realization, and I, Saint Germain, have come this day to literally draw a line in the sand and say: "Those who are not willing to accelerate their vision of service, should no longer count themselves students of the ascended masters!"

From this day forward, I want all of you – who call yourself students of the ascended masters – to step up to a higher vision of service, a higher love, a higher power. I want you to realize that in order to give true service, you must have that balance of love and power so you do not go out and serve with a passivity of love, human love. You go out with the power of God and say: "What is the situation here, what is the spiritual, psychological cause of it? What needs to be done to accelerate these people out of their current limitations, out of their current state of consciousness so that they can begin to co-create a better situation through the mind of Christ. How can they rise above being stuck in the current situation that they have co-created through the mind of anti-Christ, through the mind of duality, through the mechanization consciousness?"

Understanding the Alpha and the Omega of service

My beloved, if you will take a look at the world, you will see that there are many organizations in this world who are centered around giving service to those who have some kind of lack. Take for example the Red Cross, which goes out to disasters or wars and administers medical aid to those in need. Now, I am not saying that there is anything wrong with doing this. When there is a need, someone must fulfill that need and this is indeed the Omega expression of service. What I want to draw to your attention here is that if service is centered only on the Omega – only on the love that becomes passive, always adapting to situations in the world – then that service is not ultimate service. It will not change conditions in the world.

Surely, it is a worthy goal to give humanitarian aid when there is a war, but if you do nothing to change the collective consciousness to avoid future wars, then you have only given a half service. I can tell you exactly what will happen as a result of this kind of service. The Red Cross might be a world-wide organization that has great resources, but I can assure you that if humankind does not make a serious effort in the coming decade to overcome the consciousness of war, then you will see so many conflicts and so many wars that no organization – including the Red Cross, including all the rich nations in the world – can administer humanitarian aid to the different crises that will spring up around the world.

Service that is focused on the Omega aspect – and passively adapts to the conditions in the world – has become a closed system. It will become subject to the second law of thermodynamics that will cause that system to break down. This will precipitate so many of the situations that the service is meant to administer onto that there is not enough resources to do the work. Why is this so? It is so precisely because those people who are involved with humanitarian aid, such as the Red Cross, have lulled themselves to sleep. They are thinking that by doing this humanitarian service, they are doing enough, they are doing their share for humankind and thus they do not need to do any more. I come to speak to all people on this planet who are involved in any kind of charitable work. I come to bring them the light of the Great Central sun to challenge you to step up to a higher view of service where you realize that giving this kind of service simply is not enough.

We want earth to rise above conflicts and disasters

We of the ascended masters do not desire to see this planet continue on its current track where you have more and more conflicts, more and more natural disasters. We desire to see this planet accelerate beyond those disasters and those conflicts.

11 | True Service Means Acceleration into Unity

This can only happen when there is an acceleration in consciousness. As we have said over and over again, that acceleration in consciousness must start with the top 10 percent of the most spiritually aware people.

The top 10 percent are often the people who are involved in some kind of humanitarian service. They have the higher awareness, they have accelerated their vision (as I spoke about in my last discourse) to look beyond the separate self, to see the need to do something for others, to see the need do something for the world. They have not stepped up to the ultimate view of service. They think it is enough to simply administer onto the needs and the problems you see in the world—without doing something to change those problems by changing the consciousness that precipitates the same problems over and over again.

If these people are not willing to listen to Divine direction – coming from spiritual teachings or from their own higher selves – then they must simply enter the School of Hard Knocks. They must see that the problems they are trying to administer onto will accelerate to the point where they do not have the resources. Therefore, they will finally break down and say: "There must be a different way, we must do something more, we must change our approach." This is again the School of Hard Knocks, as opposed to the School of Divine Direction. I wish that all those who are in the top 10 percent – all those people out there who are very loving, who are very kind, who have a good understanding of the need to serve others – would simply accelerate, would simply step up and realize that more is needed.

It is essential – absolutely essential – for the bringing in of the Golden Age that the top 10 percent begin to realize that giving service to life does not mean that you give service according to the current need. If you do this, you can spend your life energy for the rest of this lifetime – and for an indefinite number of future lifetimes, however many you have left before the clock runs out – giving service without changing anything and without actually bringing the Golden Age closer to manifestation.

Service is the foundation for the Golden Age

For the Golden Age to be brought into manifestation, a critical mass among humankind must step up and realize the need to give service to life, to give service to a greater cause than their own personal comfortability or goals—or the need for recognition, money, fame, fortune or whatever it may be. If they do not recognize the higher need, then the Golden Age will not be manifest, no matter how much service they give, my beloved.

What I am trying to tell you here is that service has two aspects, as it is outpictured in the cross, which has a vertical bar and a horizontal bar. The kind of service that goes out and caters to people's needs is the horizontal or the Omega aspect of service. It is necessary to have this kind of service. I am not saying that this kind of service needs to be stopped. I will tell you that there are many people who need to engage in this kind of service in order to balance the karma they have with others. Even in giving horizontal service, they are balancing karma.

You who are the spiritual people should realize that you are not here to make karma and balance it. You are here to bring God's kingdom to earth and bring the Golden Age into manifestation. In order to do this, you need to step up to the vertical way of giving service. You realize that you are here to accelerate this planet beyond the current conditions by bringing the light of God, by bringing the power, wisdom, love, purity, vision, service and, ultimately, freedom of God. Most of the people in this world who give service, do so in a mechanical manner. Their concept of service, their approach to service, is based on the mechanization consciousness. It says that this world is a limited place, this world has certain problems. "We are probably never going to overcome war, famine or poverty so we must just do whatever we can to administer to those who are poor, those who have been ravaged by war or natural disasters."

This is a mechanistic approach that (as I spoke about yesterday) has been put upon the spiritual people, just as the mechanical approach to salvation and spirituality was put upon them in the form of the outer path. People who are spiritual, well-meaning and loving people have been seduced into believing that giving this outer, horizontal service is enough. Thereby, they will do what God requires of them, perhaps make their personal ascension or perhaps even contribute to – some time in the distant future – overcoming war, famine or poverty.

I tell you, my beloved, it will not happen. It will happen only when you lock in to the reality of vertical service, of creative service, that goes beyond the horizontal, mechanical approach. You realize that the only way to change conditions on this planet is to raise the consciousness of humankind. This must be done through understanding, by you speaking out against what is not right, thereby addressing the conditions that keep creating crisis after crisis. The other aspect is that you reach up for the light of God, bring that light, bring that power, bring that love, wisdom and so on. You bring them into manifestation so that, as Mother Mary explains in her book, you increase the amount of abundance that is manifest physically on this planet, and therefore you can overcome poverty.

Service and the removal of poverty

You cannot overcome poverty, my beloved, by re-distributing the amount of wealth that is already in the world, as the socialists believe. You can overcome poverty only by increasing the amount of wealth available in this world so that there is enough for everyone and so that the power elite cannot continue to monopolize it—there is simply too much for them to control. Because you have spoken out and awakened the people to the existence of the power elite, they will not allow them to continue their monopolization of the wealth, their creation of wars or their sustaining the consciousness that precipitates natural disasters.

Creative service is the need of the hour, if we are going to have the Golden Age on this planet in the foreseeable future. That is why I, Saint Germain, use this opportunity – having set the foundation in my previous five discourses – to send forth the call into the mass consciousness to all those who are a part of the top 10 percent, all those who are engaged in some form of service to others. I say to you now: "I Saint Germain, who is your sponsor, I call you to step up your vision, your approach, your attitude to service where you realize that there is more to service!"

What is the goal of life? It is to accelerate this planet until it outpictures the Kingdom of God, and this can be done only when people are willing to become more. You do not give service to life if you administer to some earthly need but basically leave the persons in the same state of consciousness in which you found them. You give service to life only when you demonstrate – clearly and unequivocally – that there is more to life. You do whatever is necessary by allowing yourself to be the open door for the light of God to accelerate those persons so that they are shaken out – or inspired out – of their old limited state of consciousness and realize there is more to life, there is something to reach for, there is a goal.

You know that Jesus has been working on the Sixth Ray and used to be the main master, what we call the Chohan, for the Sixth Ray. My beloved, look at the life of Jesus 2,000 years ago. Did he give passive service to life? No, he did not! Although he healed the sick and raised the dead, he did so in order to produce the miracles that would shake people out of the mechanization consciousness. He challenged the belief that there are certain things that cannot be brought forth on earth according to the laws of nature. This was not leaving people in the same state of consciousness in which he found them. It was doing as much as could possibly be done – according to the Law of Free Will – to accelerate them out of their limited state of consciousness.

The Golden Age requires acceleration

If you want an example of how to give service to life, then look at Jesus, look at my past life. Did I simply sit there passively and watch my current age pass by as Francis Bacon? No, I tuned in to the need of the hour and said: "People are so trapped in superstition, religious superstition, that they need some way out of it." I devised the foundation for the scientific method of comparing our belief to actual experimentation so that we can shake ourselves out of the superstition that springs from the mind that has become a closed system.

The method of scientific experimentation was a way to reach beyond the closed system of the medieval mind. It was so closed because of its belief in the infallibility of Catholic doctrine. I am not thereby saying that the scientific method is the ultimate way to reach beyond the closed system of the human mind. You know well that materialism has turned the scientific process into a closed system by saying: "We don't need to use the scientific method to investigate anything beyond the material universe or even investigate the human mind, the frontiers of the mind and what the mind can really do."

My beloved, you see that giving ultimate service to life is not a matter of bringing forth the magical formula that will bring the Kingdom of God to earth forever. It is a matter of realizing that the Kingdom of God or a Golden Age is not a static society. It is one that is accelerating constantly and is growing faster than the current society you see on earth. The Golden Age will be sustained only as long as that acceleration continues because people do not become complacent, they do not become comfortable, they do not become seduced by the consciousness that says: "Oh the service that you have given to life is enough."

Some spiritual people believe that they are the most advanced spiritual people on the planet because they have a certain teaching or guru. They have come to believe that it is the highest teaching on the planet and even the highest teaching that could ever be given. What has happened precisely to many of these people? They have been seduced by the mechanization consciousness into believing that doing what they have been doing for 10, 20 or 30 years is enough to fulfill the requirements for service, to be an ascended master student and to make your ascension.

This is an outright lie that springs from the consciousness of anti-christ. It has no reality to it, and those people who continue to believe it will *not* make their ascension at the end of this life, even if they have balanced the 51% of the karma that they have with others. They will not have balanced the 49% of the karma they have with themselves. What is the karma you have with yourself, beloved? It is not only the karma of putting yourself down by limiting yourself—it is actually the karma you have by not accelerating your service. You are not being all you can be. You do not fulfill the highest potential for your Divine plan, the one you planned along with us before you took embodiment. You are not living up to your full potential and giving your fullness to bringing forth the Golden Age of Saint Germain in this age.

If you have a realistic potential and you only fulfill 10, 20, 30, 50 or even 80 percent of that potential, then you have not given ultimate service to life. You will be limiting yourself, and thereby you will be making karma with yourself that has to be balanced before you can take your ascension. It is that simple. You can fool yourself, you can fool all other people on this planet, but you cannot fool God, you cannot fool the ascended masters. We see with the clarity of the Christ mind, which means that we do not condemn you, we do not judge you. On the other hand, we do not make excuses for you either. We see the reality of where you are at in consciousness and where you are at in fulfilling your highest potential.

We come not only with power, we come with love, we come with wisdom, we come with purity, vision, service and freedom. We are willing to work with you in giving you whatever you need, whatever assistance you need in order to raise your level of service to a higher level. We are always bound by the Law of Free Will and your willingness to look at yourself and say: "I may have done all these outer things, I may have done this outer service for 30 years, I may have studied certain teachings, and I may have blabbed about the importance of those teachings to any number of people. But I am willing to admit that I could do more, I could *be* more, I could accelerate my service and step it up to a higher level."

"I am willing to call out to my personal master and my own higher self and say: 'Strip me of that complacency, strip me of that blindness! Use the sword of truth to cut through my blindness and help me see where there is a part of my ego that is hiding behind some lie, even the lie that my current level of service is enough.'" If you will honestly do this, I can assure you, that the assistance will be forthcoming. If you will use the dictations I have given here, study them, listen to them, listen beyond the words to the vibration itself and absorb those dictations, absorb my vibration, then I can assure you that you can – in a very short time – step up to a higher level of service. In order to assist you with this, we will bring forth a series of invocations that will be designed especially to challenge, expose and help you rise above the mechanization consciousness on all of the seven rays so that you can fulfill the requirements to be more on the seven rays. [These are the invocations included in this book.]

The essential requirement for true service

I have through this discourse – I trust – demonstrated to you the essential requirement of service, namely that you do not meet people where they are and leave them where they are. You give service, ultimate service, only when you add some element of light or understanding so that you accelerate people beyond their current state of consciousness, as they are willing according to their free will. Obviously, you do not give service to life either by going to the opposite extreme of seeking to force people to change. That is not what we of the ascended masters are about.

We are about accelerating people beyond the dualistic consciousness so that they can see that there is an alternative to their current misery and that they can do something about it themselves. They do not do this by waiting for you to give them a hand-out, but by accelerating their understanding, their sense of identity, to where they realize they are co-creators with God. They can use their own built-in co-creative efforts to change their situation or their society, even the entire planet.

This, my beloved, is service. You accelerate people, you do not leave them where they are. I am not saying this always has to be done with the fire and determination you see in my voice right now. It needs to be done with a clear attitude that you are willing to be an instrument for accelerating other people or accelerating your society by doing whatever is necessary – according to your inner direction – to accelerate current conditions and help them become more, help all people become more.

This is true service! Heed my words! Heed my vibration! Absorb the words, absorb the vibration, absorb the service that I am, my beloved. I am determined to be of ultimate service to humankind by embodying the Flame of Freedom for planet earth, the Flame of Freedom that will always – always, always – seek to accelerate people so they can become free of whatever limitations they are trapped in. Eventually, they accelerate all the way to where they attain full Christ consciousness, full God consciousness, and where the Kingdom of God and the Golden Age of Saint Germain – which are one and the same – are manifest on this planet in full physical manifestation.

I thank you for your willingness to serve. I seal you in that flame of accelerated service. I want you from now on to look at the Sixth Ray not as the ray of ministration and service, but as the ray of acceleration into unity. Your efforts, your service, is directed at accelerating people beyond the mechanization consciousness, beyond the sense that they are separated from each other and separated from God. They see that they can come into unity with God and unity with each other, and *that* is how the Golden Age will be manifest on earth.

My beloved, I leave you with this concept that the Sixth Ray truly is the ray of acceleration into unity, as you saw with Jesus when he said: "I and my Father are one." And: "Inasmuch as ye have done it onto the least of my brethren, ye have done it onto me." This is true service—that sense of unity where you seek to raise up all life to be more, to be all it can be, to be here below all that it is Above. I seal this dictation, I seal your hearts in the flame of accelerated service, my beloved. And I thank you!

12 | INVOKING AN ACCELERATION OF SERVICE

In the name of the I AM THAT I AM, Jesus Christ, I call upon Saint Germain and Jesus for the transformation of the consciousness of poverty on earth. Awaken people to the reality that we are spiritual beings and that we can co-create a new future by working with the ascended masters. I especially call for …

[Make your own calls here.]

Part 1

1. Saint Germain, give people your fire and determination, give them a quickening, an acceleration that goes beyond intellectual understanding.

O Saint Germain, you do inspire,
my vision raised forever higher,
with you I form a figure-eight,
your Golden Age I co-create.

**O Saint Germain, what love you bring,
it truly makes all matter sing,
your violet flame does all restore,
with you we are becoming more.**

2. Saint Germain, help people see that if the intellect itself could raise the world into the Kingdom of God, then surely this would already have happened—considering the amount of intellectual people that have had positions in society.

O Saint Germain, what Freedom Flame,
released when we recite your name,
acceleration is your gift,
our planet it will surely lift.

**O Saint Germain, what love you bring,
it truly makes all matter sing,
your violet flame does all restore,
with you we are becoming more.**

3. Saint Germain, give people a higher understanding of what it means to give service to life, an understanding that is beyond the mechanization consciousness.

O Saint Germain, in love we claim,
our right to bring your violet flame,
from you Above, to us below,
it is an all-transforming flow.

> O Saint Germain, what love you bring,
> it truly makes all matter sing,
> your violet flame does all restore,
> with you we are becoming more.

4. Saint Germain, help people see that there is more to service than being passive and helping people according to their physical needs.

> O Saint Germain, I love you so,
> my aura filled with violet glow,
> my chakras filled with violet fire,
> I am your cosmic amplifier.

> O Saint Germain, what love you bring,
> it truly makes all matter sing,
> your violet flame does all restore,
> with you we are becoming more.

5. Saint Germain, help people see that their true needs are not human, bodily or worldly. The true need is to have an acceleration so that they are awakened and can see beyond the separate self and its worldly needs.

> O Saint Germain, I am now free,
> your violet flame is therapy,
> transform all hang-ups in my mind,
> as inner peace I surely find.

> O Saint Germain, what love you bring,
> it truly makes all matter sing,
> your violet flame does all restore,
> with you we are becoming more.

6. Saint Germain, help people see that there is worldly service, mechanical service, and there is spiritual service, creative service.

> O Saint Germain, my body pure,
> your violet flame for all is cure,
> consume the cause of all disease,
> and therefore I am all at ease.
>
> **O Saint Germain, what love you bring,**
> **it truly makes all matter sing,**
> **your violet flame does all restore,**
> **with you we are becoming more.**

7. Saint Germain, help people see that we will not serve life in an ultimate capacity by fulfilling people's outer needs through mechanical means.

> O Saint Germain, I'm karma-free,
> the past no longer burdens me,
> a brand new opportunity,
> I am in Christic unity.
>
> **O Saint Germain, what love you bring,**
> **it truly makes all matter sing,**
> **your violet flame does all restore,**
> **with you we are becoming more.**

8. Saint Germain, help people see that we will give ultimate service to life only if we step up our vision of service and realize that we need to accelerate people beyond their current needs—instead of seeking to fulfill those needs.

O Saint Germain, we are now one,
I am for you a violet sun,
as we transform this planet earth,
your Golden Age is given birth.

**O Saint Germain, what love you bring,
it truly makes all matter sing,
your violet flame does all restore,
with you we are becoming more.**

9. Saint Germain, help people see that when we seek to fulfill people's needs, even the needs of the poor, the infirm or the sick, we are enabling them to stay in the consciousness that has precipitated their physical condition.

O Saint Germain, the earth is free,
from burden of duality,
in oneness we bring what is best,
your Golden Age is manifest.

**O Saint Germain, what love you bring,
it truly makes all matter sing,
your violet flame does all restore,
with you we are becoming more.**

Part 2

1. Saint Germain, help people come to this essential realization, and step up to a higher vision of service, a higher love, a higher power.

> O Jesus, blessed brother mine,
> I walk the path that you outline,
> a great example to us all,
> I follow now your inner call.
>
> **O Jesus, let the Fire of Joy,
> consume the devil's subtle ploy,
> transfigured is our planet earth,
> the golden age is given birth.**

2. Saint Germain, help people realize that in order to give true service, we must have a balance of love and power so we do not go out and serve with a passivity of human love.

> O Jesus, open inner sight,
> the ego wants to prove it's right,
> but this I will no longer do,
> I want to be all one with you.
>
> **O Jesus, let the Fire of Joy,
> consume the devil's subtle ploy,
> transfigured is our planet earth,
> the golden age is given birth.**

3. Saint Germain, help people see that we need to go out with the power of God and say: "What is the situation here, what is the spiritual, psychological cause of it?"

> O Jesus, I now clearly see,
> the Key of Knowledge given me,
> my Christ self I hereby embrace,
> as you fill up my inner space.

**O Jesus, let the Fire of Joy,
consume the devil's subtle ploy,
transfigured is our planet earth,
the golden age is given birth.**

4. Saint Germain, help people see the need to say: "What needs to be done to accelerate these people out of their current limitations, out of their current state of consciousness, so that they can begin to co-create a better situation through the mind of Christ?"

O Jesus, show me serpent's lie,
expose the beam in my own eye,
as Christ discernment you me give,
in oneness I forever live.

**O Jesus, let the Fire of Joy,
consume the devil's subtle ploy,
transfigured is our planet earth,
the golden age is given birth.**

5. Saint Germain, help people see how to avoid being stuck in the current situation they have co-created through the mind of anti-Christ, through the mind of duality, through the mechanization consciousness.

O Jesus, I am truly meek,
and thus I turn the other cheek,
when the accuser attacks me,
I go within and merge with thee.

**O Jesus, let the Fire of Joy,
consume the devil's subtle ploy,
transfigured is our planet earth,
the golden age is given birth.**

6. Saint Germain, help people see that the organizations who are centered around giving service to those who have some kind of lack are fulfilling the Omega expression of service.

O Jesus, ego I let die,
surrender ev'ry earthly tie,
the dead can bury what is dead,
I choose to walk with you instead.

**O Jesus, let the Fire of Joy,
consume the devil's subtle ploy,
transfigured is our planet earth,
the golden age is given birth.**

7. Saint Germain, help people see that if service is centered only on the Omega – only on the love that becomes passive, always adapting to situations in the world – then that service is not ultimate service. It will not change conditions in the world.

O Jesus, help me rise above,
the devil's test through higher love,
show me separate self unreal,
my formless self you do reveal.

**O Jesus, let the Fire of Joy,
consume the devil's subtle ploy,
transfigured is our planet earth,
the golden age is given birth.**

12 | *Invoking an Acceleration of Service*

8. Saint Germain, help people see that although it is a worthy goal to give humanitarian aid when there is a war, if we do nothing to change the collective consciousness to avoid future wars, then we have only given a half service.

> O Jesus, what is that to me,
> I just let go and follow thee,
> with this I do pass ev'ry test,
> to find with you eternal rest.
>
> **O Jesus, let the Fire of Joy,**
> **consume the devil's subtle ploy,**
> **transfigured is our planet earth,**
> **the golden age is given birth.**

9. Saint Germain, help people see what will happen as a result of this kind of service. If humankind does not make a serious effort to overcome the consciousness of war, then there will be so many conflicts and wars that no organization can administer humanitarian aid to all in need.

> O Jesus, fiery master mine,
> my heart now melting into thine,
> I love with heart and mind and soul,
> the God who is my highest goal.
>
> **O Jesus, let the Fire of Joy,**
> **consume the devil's subtle ploy,**
> **transfigured is our planet earth,**
> **the golden age is given birth.**

Part 3

1. Saint Germain, help people see that service that is focused on the Omega aspect – and passively adapts to the conditions in the world – has become a closed system.

> O Saint Germain, you do inspire,
> my vision raised forever higher,
> with you I form a figure-eight,
> your Golden Age I co-create.
>
> **O Saint Germain, what love you bring,**
> **it truly makes all matter sing,**
> **your violet flame does all restore,**
> **with you we are becoming more.**

2. Saint Germain, help people see that passive service will become subject to the second law of thermodynamics that will cause the system to break down. This will precipitate so many crises that there is not enough resources to do the work.

> O Saint Germain, what Freedom Flame,
> released when we recite your name,
> acceleration is your gift,
> our planet it will surely lift.
>
> **O Saint Germain, what love you bring,**
> **it truly makes all matter sing,**
> **your violet flame does all restore,**
> **with you we are becoming more.**

3. Saint Germain, help people see that those who are involved with humanitarian aid have lulled themselves to sleep. They are thinking that by doing humanitarian service, they are doing enough, they are doing their share for humankind and thus they do not need to do any more.

> O Saint Germain, in love we claim,
> our right to bring your violet flame,
> from you Above, to us below,
> it is an all-transforming flow.
>
> **O Saint Germain, what love you bring,**
> **it truly makes all matter sing,**
> **your violet flame does all restore,**
> **with you we are becoming more.**

4. Saint Germain, challenge all people who are involved in charitable work to step up to a higher view of service where we realize that giving this kind of service simply is not enough.

> O Saint Germain, I love you so,
> my aura filled with violet glow,
> my chakras filled with violet fire,
> I am your cosmic amplifier.
>
> **O Saint Germain, what love you bring,**
> **it truly makes all matter sing,**
> **your violet flame does all restore,**
> **with you we are becoming more.**

5. Saint Germain, help people see that the ascended masters do not desire to see this planet continue on its current track where we have more and more conflicts, more and more natural disasters.

> O Saint Germain, I am now free,
> your violet flame is therapy,
> transform all hang-ups in my mind,
> as inner peace I surely find.
>
> **O Saint Germain, what love you bring,**
> **it truly makes all matter sing,**
> **your violet flame does all restore,**
> **with you we are becoming more.**

6. Saint Germain, help people see that you desire to accelerate earth beyond those disasters and conflicts. This can only happen when there is an acceleration in consciousness.

> O Saint Germain, my body pure,
> your violet flame for all is cure,
> consume the cause of all disease,
> and therefore I am all at ease.
>
> **O Saint Germain, what love you bring,**
> **it truly makes all matter sing,**
> **your violet flame does all restore,**
> **with you we are becoming more.**

7. Saint Germain, help the top 10 percent of the most spiritually aware people see that the acceleration in consciousness must start with them.

> O Saint Germain, I'm karma-free,
> the past no longer burdens me,
> a brand new opportunity,
> I am in Christic unity.
>
> **O Saint Germain, what love you bring,**
> **it truly makes all matter sing,**
> **your violet flame does all restore,**
> **with you we are becoming more.**

8. Saint Germain, help the top 10 percent see that although we are often involved in some kind of humanitarian service, we have not stepped up to the ultimate view of service.

> O Saint Germain, we are now one,
> I am for you a violet sun,
> as we transform this planet earth,
> your Golden Age is given birth.
>
> **O Saint Germain, what love you bring,**
> **it truly makes all matter sing,**
> **your violet flame does all restore,**
> **with you we are becoming more.**

9. Saint Germain, help the top 10 percent see how we often think it is enough to administer onto the needs and the problems we see in the world. We really need to change the consciousness that precipitates the same problems over and over again.

O Saint Germain, the earth is free,
from burden of duality,
in oneness we bring what is best,
your Golden Age is manifest.

**O Saint Germain, what love you bring,
it truly makes all matter sing,
your violet flame does all restore,
with you we are becoming more.**

Part 4

1. Saint Germain, help the top 10 percent see that if we are not willing to listen to Divine direction, then we must enter the School of Hard Knocks. The problems we are trying to administer onto will accelerate to the point where we do not have enough resources.

O Jesus, blessed brother mine,
I walk the path that you outline,
a great example to us all,
I follow now your inner call.

**O Jesus, let the Fire of Joy,
consume the devil's subtle ploy,
transfigured is our planet earth,
the golden age is given birth.**

2. Saint Germain, help the top 10 percent see the need to say: "There must be a different way, we must do something more, we must change our approach."

O Jesus, open inner sight,
the ego wants to prove it's right,
but this I will no longer do,
I want to be all one with you.

**O Jesus, let the Fire of Joy,
consume the devil's subtle ploy,
transfigured is our planet earth,
the golden age is given birth.**

3. Saint Germain, help the top 10 percent see the need to accelerate, to step up and realize that more is needed.

O Jesus, I now clearly see,
the Key of Knowledge given me,
my Christ self I hereby embrace,
as you fill up my inner space.

**O Jesus, let the Fire of Joy,
consume the devil's subtle ploy,
transfigured is our planet earth,
the golden age is given birth.**

4. Saint Germain, help the top 10 percent see that it is essential for the bringing in of the Golden Age that we realize that giving service to life does not mean that we give service according to the current need.

O Jesus, show me serpent's lie,
expose the beam in my own eye,
as Christ discernment you me give,
in oneness I forever live.

**O Jesus, let the Fire of Joy,
consume the devil's subtle ploy,
transfigured is our planet earth,
the golden age is given birth.**

5. Saint Germain, help the top 10 percent see that if we do this, we can spend the rest of this lifetime giving service without changing anything and without bringing the Golden Age closer to manifestation.

O Jesus, I am truly meek,
and thus I turn the other cheek,
when the accuser attacks me,
I go within and merge with thee.

**O Jesus, let the Fire of Joy,
consume the devil's subtle ploy,
transfigured is our planet earth,
the golden age is given birth.**

6. Saint Germain, help people see that for the Golden Age to be brought into manifestation, a critical mass must step up and realize the need to give service to life, to give service to a greater cause than our own personal comfortability or goals—or the need for recognition, money, fame or fortune.

O Jesus, ego I let die,
surrender ev'ry earthly tie,
the dead can bury what is dead,
I choose to walk with you instead.

**O Jesus, let the Fire of Joy,
consume the devil's subtle ploy,
transfigured is our planet earth,
the golden age is given birth.**

7. Saint Germain, help the top 10 percent see that if we do not recognize the higher need, then the Golden Age will not be manifest, no matter how much service we give.

O Jesus, help me rise above,
the devil's test through higher love,
show me separate self unreal,
my formless self you do reveal.

**O Jesus, let the Fire of Joy,
consume the devil's subtle ploy,
transfigured is our planet earth,
the golden age is given birth.**

8. Saint Germain, help the top 10 percent see that service has two aspects. The kind of service that goes out and caters to people's needs is the horizontal or the Omega aspect of service.

O Jesus, what is that to me,
I just let go and follow thee,
with this I do pass ev'ry test,
to find with you eternal rest.

**O Jesus, let the Fire of Joy,
consume the devil's subtle ploy,
transfigured is our planet earth,
the golden age is given birth.**

9. Saint Germain, help the top 10 percent see that this form of service is necessary for many people in order for them to balance their karma.

> O Jesus, fiery master mine,
> my heart now melting into thine,
> I love with heart and mind and soul,
> the God who is my highest goal.
>
> **O Jesus, let the Fire of Joy,**
> **consume the devil's subtle ploy,**
> **transfigured is our planet earth,**
> **the golden age is given birth.**

Part 5

1. Saint Germain, help the top 10 percent see that we are not here to make karma and balance it. We are here to bring the Golden Age into manifestation.

> O Saint Germain, you do inspire,
> my vision raised forever higher,
> with you I form a figure-eight,
> your Golden Age I co-create.
>
> **O Saint Germain, what love you bring,**
> **it truly makes all matter sing,**
> **your violet flame does all restore,**
> **with you we are becoming more.**

2. Saint Germain, help the top 10 percent see that in order to do this, we need to step up to the vertical way of giving service. We are here to accelerate this planet beyond current conditions by bringing the power, wisdom, love, purity, vision, service and freedom of God.

> O Saint Germain, what Freedom Flame,
> released when we recite your name,
> acceleration is your gift,
> our planet it will surely lift.

> **O Saint Germain, what love you bring,**
> **it truly makes all matter sing,**
> **your violet flame does all restore,**
> **with you we are becoming more.**

3. Saint Germain, help the top 10 percent see that most of the people who give service do so in a mechanical manner. Their concept of service, their approach to service, is based on the mechanization consciousness.

> O Saint Germain, in love we claim,
> our right to bring your violet flame,
> from you Above, to us below,
> it is an all-transforming flow.

> **O Saint Germain, what love you bring,**
> **it truly makes all matter sing,**
> **your violet flame does all restore,**
> **with you we are becoming more.**

4. Saint Germain, help the top 10 percent see that a mechanical approach to service says that this world is a limited place. We are probably never going to overcome war, famine or poverty so we must do what we can to help those who are affected by these conditions.

> O Saint Germain, I love you so,
> my aura filled with violet glow,
> my chakras filled with violet fire,
> I am your cosmic amplifier.

> **O Saint Germain, what love you bring,**
> **it truly makes all matter sing,**
> **your violet flame does all restore,**
> **with you we are becoming more.**

5. Saint Germain, help the top 10 percent see that people who are spiritual, well-meaning and loving people have been seduced into believing that giving this outer, horizontal service is enough.

> O Saint Germain, I am now free,
> your violet flame is therapy,
> transform all hang-ups in my mind,
> as inner peace I surely find.

> **O Saint Germain, what love you bring,**
> **it truly makes all matter sing,**
> **your violet flame does all restore,**
> **with you we are becoming more.**

6. Saint Germain, help the top 10 percent see that we will overcome war, famine or poverty only when we lock in to the vertical service, creative service, that goes beyond the horizontal, mechanical approach.

> O Saint Germain, my body pure,
> your violet flame for all is cure,
> consume the cause of all disease,
> and therefore I am all at ease.
>
> **O Saint Germain, what love you bring,
> it truly makes all matter sing,
> your violet flame does all restore,
> with you we are becoming more.**

7. Saint Germain, help the top 10 percent see that the only way to change conditions on this planet is to raise the consciousness of humankind. This must be done through understanding, by us speaking out against what is not right, thereby addressing the conditions that keep creating crisis after crisis.

> O Saint Germain, I'm karma-free,
> the past no longer burdens me,
> a brand new opportunity,
> I am in Christic unity.
>
> **O Saint Germain, what love you bring,
> it truly makes all matter sing,
> your violet flame does all restore,
> with you we are becoming more.**

8. Saint Germain, help the top 10 percent see that we also need to reach up for the light of God and bring it into manifestation, so that we increase the amount of abundance that is manifest physically on this planet and thereby overcome poverty.

> O Saint Germain, we are now one,
> I am for you a violet sun,
> as we transform this planet earth,
> your Golden Age is given birth.
>
> **O Saint Germain, what love you bring,**
> **it truly makes all matter sing,**
> **your violet flame does all restore,**
> **with you we are becoming more.**

9. Saint Germain, help the top 10 percent see that we cannot overcome poverty by re-distributing the amount of wealth that is already in the world. We can overcome poverty only by increasing the amount of wealth available so that there is enough for everyone.

> O Saint Germain, the earth is free,
> from burden of duality,
> in oneness we bring what is best,
> your Golden Age is manifest.
>
> **O Saint Germain, what love you bring,**
> **it truly makes all matter sing,**
> **your violet flame does all restore,**
> **with you we are becoming more.**

Part 6

1. Saint Germain, help the top 10 percent see the need to increase the amount of wealth so that the power elite cannot continue to monopolize it. There is simply too much for them to control.

> O Jesus, blessed brother mine,
> I walk the path that you outline,
> a great example to us all,
> I follow now your inner call.
>
> **O Jesus, let the Fire of Joy,**
> **consume the devil's subtle ploy,**
> **transfigured is our planet earth,**
> **the golden age is given birth.**

2. Saint Germain, help the top 10 percent see that when we speak out and awaken the people to the existence of the power elite, they will not allow them to continue their monopolization of wealth, their creation of wars or the consciousness that precipitates natural disasters.

> O Jesus, open inner sight,
> the ego wants to prove it's right,
> but this I will no longer do,
> I want to be all one with you.
>
> **O Jesus, let the Fire of Joy,**
> **consume the devil's subtle ploy,**
> **transfigured is our planet earth,**
> **the golden age is given birth.**

3. Saint Germain, help the top 10 percent see that creative service is the need of the hour for the Golden Age to be manifest on this planet.

> O Jesus, I now clearly see,
> the Key of Knowledge given me,
> my Christ self I hereby embrace,
> as you fill up my inner space.
>
> **O Jesus, let the Fire of Joy,**
> **consume the devil's subtle ploy,**
> **transfigured is our planet earth,**
> **the golden age is given birth.**

4. Saint Germain, I reinforce the call you are sending into the mass consciousness: "I Saint Germain, who is your sponsor, I call you to step up your vision, your approach, your attitude to service where you realize that there is more to service!"

> O Jesus, show me serpent's lie,
> expose the beam in my own eye,
> as Christ discernment you me give,
> in oneness I forever live.
>
> **O Jesus, let the Fire of Joy,**
> **consume the devil's subtle ploy,**
> **transfigured is our planet earth,**
> **the golden age is given birth.**

5. Saint Germain, help the top 10 percent see that the goal of life is to accelerate this planet until it outpictures the Kingdom of God. This can be done only when people are willing to become more.

12 | Invoking an Acceleration of Service

> O Jesus, I am truly meek,
> and thus I turn the other cheek,
> when the accuser attacks me,
> I go within and merge with thee.
>
> **O Jesus, let the Fire of Joy,**
> **consume the devil's subtle ploy,**
> **transfigured is our planet earth,**
> **the golden age is given birth.**

6. Saint Germain, help the top 10 percent see that we do not give service to life if we administer to some earthly need but leave the persons in the same state of consciousness in which we found them.

> O Jesus, ego I let die,
> surrender ev'ry earthly tie,
> the dead can bury what is dead,
> I choose to walk with you instead.
>
> **O Jesus, let the Fire of Joy,**
> **consume the devil's subtle ploy,**
> **transfigured is our planet earth,**
> **the golden age is given birth.**

7. Saint Germain, help the top 10 percent see that we give service to life only when we demonstrate that there is more to life. We allow ourselves to be the open door for the light of God to accelerate people so they are inspired out of their old state of consciousness.

> O Jesus, help me rise above,
> the devil's test through higher love,
> show me separate self unreal,
> my formless self you do reveal.
>
> **O Jesus, let the Fire of Joy,**
> **consume the devil's subtle ploy,**
> **transfigured is our planet earth,**
> **the golden age is given birth.**

8. Saint Germain, help the top 10 percent see that Jesus did not give passive service to life. He challenged the belief that there are certain things that cannot be brought forth on earth according to the laws of nature.

> O Jesus, what is that to me,
> I just let go and follow thee,
> with this I do pass ev'ry test,
> to find with you eternal rest.
>
> **O Jesus, let the Fire of Joy,**
> **consume the devil's subtle ploy,**
> **transfigured is our planet earth,**
> **the golden age is given birth.**

9. Saint Germain, help the top 10 percent see that Jesus did not leave people in the same state of consciousness in which he found them. He did everything possible to accelerate them out of their limited state of consciousness.

12 | Invoking an Acceleration of Service

> O Jesus, fiery master mine,
> my heart now melting into thine,
> I love with heart and mind and soul,
> the God who is my highest goal.
>
> **O Jesus, let the Fire of Joy,**
> **consume the devil's subtle ploy,**
> **transfigured is our planet earth,**
> **the golden age is given birth.**

Part 7

1. Saint Germain, help the top 10 percent see that as Francis Bacon you tuned in to the need of the hour and said: "People are so trapped in religious superstition that they need some way out of it."

> O Saint Germain, you do inspire,
> my vision raised forever higher,
> with you I form a figure-eight,
> your Golden Age I co-create.
>
> **O Saint Germain, what love you bring,**
> **it truly makes all matter sing,**
> **your violet flame does all restore,**
> **with you we are becoming more.**

2. Saint Germain, help the top 10 percent see that you devised the foundation for the scientific method of comparing our belief to actual experimentation so that we can shake ourselves out of the superstition that springs from a closed mind.

O Saint Germain, what Freedom Flame,
released when we recite your name,
acceleration is your gift,
our planet it will surely lift.

O Saint Germain, what love you bring,
it truly makes all matter sing,
your violet flame does all restore,
with you we are becoming more.

3. Saint Germain, help the top 10 percent see that the method of scientific experimentation was a way to reach beyond the closed system of the medieval mind.

O Saint Germain, in love we claim,
our right to bring your violet flame,
from you Above, to us below,
it is an all-transforming flow.

O Saint Germain, what love you bring,
it truly makes all matter sing,
your violet flame does all restore,
with you we are becoming more.

4. Saint Germain, help the top 10 percent see that the scientific method is not the ultimate way to reach beyond the closed system of the human mind.

O Saint Germain, I love you so,
my aura filled with violet glow,
my chakras filled with violet fire,
I am your cosmic amplifier.

**O Saint Germain, what love you bring,
it truly makes all matter sing,
your violet flame does all restore,
with you we are becoming more.**

5. Saint Germain, help the top 10 percent see that materialism has turned the scientific process into a closed system by saying that we don't need to use the scientific method to investigate anything beyond the material universe or even investigate the human mind.

> O Saint Germain, I am now free,
> your violet flame is therapy,
> transform all hang-ups in my mind,
> as inner peace I surely find.

**O Saint Germain, what love you bring,
it truly makes all matter sing,
your violet flame does all restore,
with you we are becoming more.**

6. Saint Germain, help the top 10 percent see that giving ultimate service to life is not a matter of bringing forth the magical formula that will bring the Kingdom of God to earth forever. It is a matter of realizing that the Kingdom of God or a Golden Age is not a static society.

> O Saint Germain, my body pure,
> your violet flame for all is cure,
> consume the cause of all disease,
> and therefore I am all at ease.

> O Saint Germain, what love you bring,
> it truly makes all matter sing,
> your violet flame does all restore,
> with you we are becoming more.

7. Saint Germain, help the top 10 percent see that a golden age society is accelerating constantly and is growing faster than the current society we see on earth.

> O Saint Germain, I'm karma-free,
> the past no longer burdens me,
> a brand new opportunity,
> I am in Christic unity.

> O Saint Germain, what love you bring,
> it truly makes all matter sing,
> your violet flame does all restore,
> with you we are becoming more.

8. Saint Germain, help the top 10 percent see that the Golden Age will be sustained only as long as that acceleration continues because people do not become complacent and think the service they have given to life is enough.

> O Saint Germain, we are now one,
> I am for you a violet sun,
> as we transform this planet earth,
> your Golden Age is given birth.

> O Saint Germain, what love you bring,
> it truly makes all matter sing,
> your violet flame does all restore,
> with you we are becoming more.

9. Saint Germain, help the top 10 percent see that some people believe they are the most advanced spiritual people or have the highest teaching or guru.

> O Saint Germain, the earth is free,
> from burden of duality,
> in oneness we bring what is best,
> your Golden Age is manifest.
>
> **O Saint Germain, what love you bring,**
> **it truly makes all matter sing,**
> **your violet flame does all restore,**
> **with you we are becoming more.**

Part 8

1. Saint Germain, help the top 10 percent see that some spiritual people have been seduced by the mechanization consciousness into believing that doing what they have been doing for many years is enough to fulfill the requirements for service or for making our ascension.

> O Jesus, blessed brother mine,
> I walk the path that you outline,
> a great example to us all,
> I follow now your inner call.
>
> **O Jesus, let the Fire of Joy,**
> **consume the devil's subtle ploy,**
> **transfigured is our planet earth,**
> **the golden age is given birth.**

2. Saint Germain, help the top 10 percent see that this is an outright lie that springs from the consciousness of anti-christ and such people will not make their ascensions.

> O Jesus, open inner sight,
> the ego wants to prove it's right,
> but this I will no longer do,
> I want to be all one with you.
>
> **O Jesus, let the Fire of Joy,**
> **consume the devil's subtle ploy,**
> **transfigured is our planet earth,**
> **the golden age is given birth.**

3. Saint Germain, help the top 10 percent see that we make karma by putting ourselves down, by limiting ourselves. We also make karma by not accelerating our service and being all we can be.

> O Jesus, I now clearly see,
> the Key of Knowledge given me,
> my Christ self I hereby embrace,
> as you fill up my inner space.
>
> **O Jesus, let the Fire of Joy,**
> **consume the devil's subtle ploy,**
> **transfigured is our planet earth,**
> **the golden age is given birth.**

4. Saint Germain, help the top 10 percent see how to fulfill the highest potential for our Divine plans, the ones we planned before we took embodiment. Help us live up to our full potential for bringing forth the Golden Age of Saint Germain in this age.

> O Jesus, show me serpent's lie,
> expose the beam in my own eye,
> as Christ discernment you me give,
> in oneness I forever live.
>
> **O Jesus, let the Fire of Joy,**
> **consume the devil's subtle ploy,**
> **transfigured is our planet earth,**
> **the golden age is given birth.**

5. Saint Germain, I am willing to work with you, and I ask you to give me the assistance I need in order to raise my level of service. I am willing to do more, I am willing be more, to accelerate my service and step it up to a higher level.

> O Jesus, I am truly meek,
> and thus I turn the other cheek,
> when the accuser attacks me,
> I go within and merge with thee.
>
> **O Jesus, let the Fire of Joy,**
> **consume the devil's subtle ploy,**
> **transfigured is our planet earth,**
> **the golden age is given birth.**

6. Saint Germain, I call out to you and my own higher self and say: "Strip me of that complacency, strip me of that blindness! Use the sword of truth to cut through my blindness and help me see where there is a part of my ego that is hiding behind some lie, even the lie that my current level of service is enough."

> O Jesus, ego I let die,
> surrender ev'ry earthly tie,
> the dead can bury what is dead,
> I choose to walk with you instead.
>
> **O Jesus, let the Fire of Joy,**
> **consume the devil's subtle ploy,**
> **transfigured is our planet earth,**
> **the golden age is given birth.**

7. Saint Germain, help me serve with a clear attitude that I am willing to be an instrument for accelerating other people or accelerating society by accelerating current conditions and helping them become more, helping all people become more.

> O Jesus, help me rise above,
> the devil's test through higher love,
> show me separate self unreal,
> my formless self you do reveal.
>
> **O Jesus, let the Fire of Joy,**
> **consume the devil's subtle ploy,**
> **transfigured is our planet earth,**
> **the golden age is given birth.**

8. Saint Germain, I will absorb the words, absorb the vibration, absorb the service that you are so that I can help bring your Golden Age into manifestation.

> O Jesus, what is that to me,
> I just let go and follow thee,
> with this I do pass ev'ry test,
> to find with you eternal rest.

> **O Jesus, let the Fire of Joy,**
> **consume the devil's subtle ploy,**
> **transfigured is our planet earth,**
> **the golden age is given birth.**

9. Saint Germain, I am determined to be of ultimate service to humankind by embodying the Sixth Ray as the ray of acceleration into unity.

> O Jesus, fiery master mine,
> my heart now melting into thine,
> I love with heart and mind and soul,
> the God who is my highest goal.

> **O Jesus, let the Fire of Joy,**
> **consume the devil's subtle ploy,**
> **transfigured is our planet earth,**
> **the golden age is given birth.**

Sealing

In the name of the I AM THAT I AM, I accept that Archangel Michael, Astrea and Shiva form an impenetrable shield around myself and all constructive people, sealing us from all fear-based energies in all four octaves. I accept that the Light of God is consuming and transforming all fear-based energies that make up the forces behind war!

13 | FREEDOM MEANS SURRENDER INTO ONENESS

My beloved hearts, you have heard various variations of the joke: "How many electricians does it take to change a light bulb? How many politicians does it take to change a light bulb?" I, Saint Germain, want to present you with a new thought: "How many ascended master students does it take to change a planet?" [Pause] I am waiting for your answer, my beloved. Audience: "One!"

Right the first time! It takes one. There is immense value in one person making up his or her mind that this or that manifestation of imperfection is no longer allowed on my planet.

From the cradle to the grave, human beings are bombarded with energies and ideas that are designed for one purpose only. That is to prevent you from exercising your co-creative powers in making this planet a more godly place to live. You are being programmed to be passive, to live like all other people, to think that one person cannot make a difference, that you do not have the power to change your society – even on the small level – and certainly not the power on a planetary level. I tell you, we have explained, over and over again, that everything on this planet is determined by the free will of human beings in embodiment.

One person *can* make a difference by making up his or her mind with absolute total unwavering determination. This is something that is not actually an act of will, as you normally conceive will. It is an act of *being*, of being who you *are*, being in contact with a higher part of your being so that the light from your higher being shines through the lower mind. You can come to a determination that is not the outer will – that can easily be shifted by this or that impulse from without – but is an inner determination. It is an inner knowing that this is the new reality on your planet because you are being that change. You are willing to *be* the change in the world by holding the spiritual balance for that change. You hold the vision – unwavering – that this or that manifestation will not come to be on this planet.

Understanding the power of "One"

Many years ago, this messenger was very concerned – at a young age – about nuclear war. He went deep into meditation one night and cried out to God, feeling a greater degree of oneness with God on the issue of nuclear war. He cried out to stop this, and he felt a return current, a reassurance that there would not be a nuclear war, at least a large-scale nuclear war, on this planet. This was because – unbeknownst to his outer mind – he had vowed to play a part in holding the balance so that there would not be such a war. One person cannot necessarily hold a balance if millions of people pull in the other direction. Again, the Law of Free Will must outplay itself in giving people the lessons they need in order to change their consciousness. While there is value in one person shifting his or her consciousness, there is in most issues a certain critical mass that must be reached so that there is a counter-balance between those who are willing to raise their consciousness and those who are not, including those who are simply indifferent without knowing better.

When I say that it only takes one ascended master student to change a planet, this is true, in the sense that one person making up his or her mind will shift the collective consciousness. It takes a certain critical mass of individuals to prevent certain outer manifestations. If one person, or just a few, could remove some ungodly condition from this planet, how would the majority learn the lesson and come to the point where they have decided that they too have had enough of this or that manifestation?

The power of one must be understood at different levels of consciousness. There is value in *you* making up your mind, but it is also necessary to realize that you are not a separate individual living in a world with six billion other separate individuals. It is necessary that you contact the oneness in your own being, which gives you the sense of oneness with your own I AM Presence. It also takes you to the next step of realizing your oneness with all other people. You realize, my beloved, that it is not always enough for you to come to an inner determination based on oneness with your own higher being. It is also necessary for you to fulfill the Omega requirement and go out and seek to awaken others so that they can come into oneness with their own higher beings. Eventually, a critical mass of people can come together in oneness on a particular issue and can therefore shift the collective consciousness

The critical mass

What is the percentage? What is the critical mass? With the abolishment of slavery, there came a shift in the collective consciousness of humankind where it became obvious to many people that it was not acceptable any longer that people could be owned as property. That shift occurred when the top 10 percent had come to that realization. The magical number, in terms of truly shifting the collective consciousness, is ten percent.

If the lower 10 percent are in agreement that a certain manifestation is acceptable to them – and this is what they want out of their own self-interest – then if there is not a counter-balance of the top 10 percent saying: "No, we will not allow this on our planet," then according to the Law of Free Will, the lower 10 percent will pull the population down. When the top 10 percent come into alignment, come into agreement, then they will pull the population up, and a positive shift will occur. Then – suddenly – many among the population can now see what they could not see before because they were blinded by the duality consciousness, by the mass consciousness.

Even many of those who had experienced slavery themselves did not have enough awareness to speak out and say: "This is not right, this is not acceptable." Right up until the shift had occurred, the majority of the population simply could not see what seems obvious to most people today, namely that human beings are not things that can be bought and sold in the marketplace. When the top 10 percent had shifted, all of a sudden many among the population – without being consciously aware of the shift – realized: "Oh yes, this is obvious!" Now they supported the outer change.

Again, everything begins with one person, but there is great strength in numbers. If two people in two different parts of the world – with no outer connection between them – reach the same determination, then it will count. If those two people establish some sense of oneness between them with their outer minds, then it will count exponentially more. The whole is more than the sum of the parts.

New ideas are released by the ascended masters

Every positive change that has happened on this planet started with an idea released from the realm of the ascended masters, which then descended through the four levels of the material universe—the identity, mental, emotional and physical realms. We are constantly releasing such ideas, but they will not have an effect in the physical until one or more people grasp that ascended master idea with their outer awareness. They either start expressing it as an idea of what needs to change or they start expressing it as a practical innovation, as a practical invention, that suddenly brings forth a technology that revolutionizes some aspect of society.

What we are looking for is, of course, that more and more people will be able to tune in to the ideas we are releasing. As Jesus said 2,000 years ago: "Fear not little flock, for it is the Father's good pleasure to give you the kingdom." The Father's good pleasure is executed by the ascended masters who are working with humankind on earth. I can assure you that we of the ascended masters have solutions to every problem you find on planet earth. The catch is, my beloved, that those solutions cannot be given unless people are willing to change their consciousness. As we have said before, you cannot solve a problem with the same state of consciousness that created or precipitated the problem. This is simply not possible, and that is why it is essential that the consciousness shifts so that people can reach beyond the old way of looking at a particular problem and be open to receiving the solution.

What you have seen in the past is that typically one person was able to raise his or her consciousness, tune in to the ascended masters and receive an idea—whether it be a political or spiritual idea, or a practical idea about a particular invention. You have also seen a few instances where two people independently of each other made the same discovery or came forth with the same invention. What we are looking for is a situation where many people are open and attuned to the ascended masters so that many people at the same time – all across the planet – will tune in to a particular idea. This, of course, is especially important when it comes to ideas about political changes or spiritual changes. Here, it is not enough that one person brings forth a technical invention, but many people need to catch on to an idea before it will begin to have an impact on society.

The Golden Age is an age of community

It was a Piscean-age phenomenon that you had one Christed being, one person, who would stand up and claim to be the Son of God and speak out for a higher understanding. In the Aquarian age, it is not the matrix that there should be one person who stands out above all other people. As you saw with Jesus, when one person brings forth a new idea, either that person will be killed or that person will be idolized. Either way, there is a limitation put on how the idea can spread to the population so that people can internalize it and make it their own.

In the Aquarian age, we need thousands, tens of thousands and millions of people to be so attuned with the new ideas we are releasing that many of the people catch that idea as soon as it is released and immediately start speaking about it. All around the world there is a mushrooming in the awareness that something has changed or something needs to change. There is a new awareness and a new determination that these old problems are no longer acceptable to us. We want a change and we want it *now*. Not because somebody says so, but because *we* say so. We know in our hearts that this is true, that this is right, that this is necessary.

We are not looking at the Aquarian age as an age in which we have a few remarkable leaders, but where we have millions of remarkable people who dare to stand up and speak the truth that they know in their hearts. Even if they cannot argue for it in rational, analytical terms, or by pointing to any outer authority, they are speaking out from their hearts.

Speaking from the heart

My beloved, surely you can look at the world today and say that if one person starts speaking from his or her heart, it will have little impact on society. I can assure you that if more and more people start speaking from their hearts – simply stating the truth and stating the need for change – then it *will* begin to have an impact on society. You will see a shift beyond what most people can even imagine. Part of the programming that I spoke about in the beginning is precisely this idea that change is brought by the powerful people, by those who are in positions of authority, be it in church, the government or science. Any new change in society must come from that realm, and only what is approved by the elite will actually be carried out in society. So they say.

The true positive changes that have happened on this planet have always happened because a number of so-called ordinary people embraced the idea. If George Washington, Thomas Jefferson or any single person had signed the declaration of independence, it would have gone nowhere, I can assure you. Because 50 people were willing to sign it and risk their lives, it created a chain reaction. Because many more people were willing to support it, even to the point of being willing to risk their lives to do so, then it created the momentum that became the United States of America. This was the first country in the world to truly be based on the concept that human beings have rights that are not defined by any authority on earth – be it the king, the emperor or the Pope – but are defined by a higher authority that no government on earth has the right to override.

Closing the figure-eight flow

What I come to give you in this release is the continuation of the six discourses I gave in South America. In this release I especially talk about how poverty and the poverty consciousness relates to the Seventh Ray. There is a reason I am giving this dictation here in North America, here in California. It is precisely that North America in general has a higher degree of the Freedom Flame than is yet manifest in South America. There, people are still too burdened by the old world views, especially coming from the Catholic Church or the influence of socialism—where both world views deny – precisely – the power of the individual.

In North America, especially in the United States, you find much more of an individual freedom flame where people believe that they can, if not make a difference on a planetary level, then certainly create a better world for themselves. They are more innovative, more open to new ideas. This, of course, is especially true in the state of California where there is a great potential that the shift in consciousness that we are talking about can start here and create a momentum that can roll throughout the other 49 states and eventually throughout the world.

This is an appropriate place to close the figure-eight flow between North and South America so that we can hopefully get the energies moving that will eventually clear up this entire hemisphere. Then we can have the power of all seven rays flowing through the people and bringing about a shift in awareness.

I give you this piece of information to encourage those who are in a position to do so to bring Mother Mary's invocations to Central America. There are many wonderful hearts in that part of the world, but I must tell you that some of those hearts have become somewhat complacent. They have come to feel that the level of service they have been giving for a number of years is sufficient.

Saint Germain moves on

I come to tell you that if you think the God of Freedom can be limited to any organization or any teaching, then you have lost attunement with my heart. I move on, my beloved. When the need is there, then I move on to wherever there can be the greatest expression of the Freedom Flame and the ideas and energies that I desire to bring to this planet.

I would like to give you the realistic assessment, my beloved, that surely you cannot imagine that I, Saint Germain – having the responsibility to bring forth the Golden Age on planet earth – would let that Golden Age wait on a limited number of ascended master students in a particular teaching or organization? If you – even for a split second – imagine that this is the case, I must tell you that you have lost the connection to my heart. I encourage you greatly to reestablish that connection by tuning in to your own hearts and realizing that I, Saint Germain, do not stand still, never have stood still, never will stand still and never will let any organization, person or movement on earth limit me, box me in.

I AM the God of Freedom, my beloved, and I will not be slowed down by anyone. I move on—simply leaving those behind who are not willing to move on with me. This does not mean that I do not care for those I leave behind. It does mean that I care more for the greater cause of freedom, of building the Golden Age, which is a cause that is far greater than any organization or any individual, my beloved.

This is what you will see also when I was the Wonderman of Europe, traveling around, seeking to work with the crowned heads of Europe who thought – each one of them – that they were the most important king on earth. They wanted me to treat them according to that self-assessment, which of course sprang entirely from the ego. In some cases there were kings that would not work with me because I would not treat them as if they were the most important king. I saw the bigger picture and the need for a unification of Europe—that surely went beyond what any single king could grasp at the time.

You who claim to be ascended master students should be smarter than this. You should be able to see beyond your own ego and its need to feel that you are more important than any other spiritual people on this planet. My beloved, we need to move beyond the relative, dualistic game of comparison, of thinking that one teaching, one organization, one guru, one messenger is more important than anyone else. What is most important on earth is all of the people who have some attunement to the ascended masters. We are beyond the age of exclusivity. The idea that there could be one Christ, one king, one emperor or one inventor was a test that humankind faced during the Piscean age—and needed to pass during that age. Most people have not done so. Surely, the ascended master students should be able to pass this test and realize that no one person is more important than anyone else. You all have the potential to be part of the movement of the ascended masters, part of bringing the Golden Age—if you are willing to tune in to the Kingdom of God within you and find that kingdom each one of you—instead of looking for it outside of yourselves.

An Aquarian age organization must not cause you to look to an outer teaching, outer messengers or gurus. It is designed for one purpose only, and that is to help you find God within yourselves. If you do that, you are fulfilling the purpose for this movement. If you turn it into another exclusivist teaching or organization, then you are just following the same path that you have been following for lifetimes—and it is time to wake up from it, my beloved.

Receive a higher teaching on freedom

Why is this so important? How does this relate to freedom, how does it relate to overcoming the poverty consciousness? What is the essence of poverty? It is that you are separated from God's abundance. The essence of poverty is separation. Well, what is the essence of anti-freedom? It is that you are separated from God, you are separated from oneness with God. Out of that illusion of separation spring countless other illusions that keep you trapped in a mental box where you define borders around yourselves and say: "I am inside this mental box. All other people are outside that mental box. God is somewhere way beyond that mental box." This, my beloved, is anti-freedom.

I know that in the past I and other masters have spoken about freedom and the Flame of Freedom. What we could give at that time was what the people were ready for. I come now to give you a higher teaching on freedom. As I gave a higher teaching on service, saying that most of you had a limited view of service, I can assure you that most of you also have a limited view of freedom.

What exactly does it mean to be free, my beloved? The separate mind, the ego, defines freedom as the ability to do whatever it wants, to have whatever it wants, to have all of its needs fulfilled. Indeed, in human society, even in spiritual and religious movements, a certain attitude has developed that if we can do whatever we want, then we are free. This means, to some degree, that if we can escape the consequences of our actions, then we are free.

You see many spiritual people who have attempted to walk the spiritual path for the purpose of learning some magical formula, finding some philosopher's stone, that will allow them to do whatever they want and escape the return current of the consequences of their actions. They believe this is freedom. I tell you, my beloved, this is a completely perverted concept of freedom that springs from the consciousness of those who have fallen into duality and thus have left off from oneness with God. It is freedom only for the separate self, but that is not true freedom. The separate self has no reality, no existence in God—and thus, how could it ever be free?

You see, one separate self can gain freedom only by taking freedom from one or more other separate selves. This is why you saw – during the feudal societies – that one landlord had great freedom, materially speaking, but he had taken freedom from thousands of peasants who lived on his land and whom he treated as property. This, of course, cannot be true freedom. When you look at this – even with the logical, linear mind

– you realize that you could not possibly have all people on earth be landlords or emperors. Who is going to be the slaves that keep the emperors in power and in comfort?

This, of course, is not logically possible so you need to rethink what it means to be free. You need to realize that true freedom does not mean to escape the consequences of your actions. It means to acknowledge the reality that the physical universe is the cosmic mirror that sends back to you what you send out.

The separate self can never be free

If you free your mind from the illusion of separation and the entire consciousness of seeking to gain something for the ego, for the separate self – if you free your mind from the illusions that spring from the consciousness of separation and lack – then you will begin to project into the cosmic mirror images and ideas that do not seek to raise up the separate self. They seek to raise up other people to do something for humankind. You develop a global awareness where you seek to raise the all, rather than the separate self. When you do this, the cosmic mirror will gladly and lovingly – as cycles go through the four levels of the material universe – reflect back to you exactly what you are sending out.

You will escape the limitations that are created by the separate self and its belief that, in order to gain for itself, it must take from others. This is the belief that there is not enough wealth and abundance in the material world to go around for everyone. If you will begin to shift your thinking and take a look at this – even with the outer logical mind – you can begin to see that what takes away your freedom is the illusion that it is possible to gain something by taking it through force. Instead, you can seek to do what Jesus meant when he said: "Seek ye first the Kingdom of God and his righteousness, and all these things will be added onto you."

The Kingdom of God is within you, so you seek first that inner oneness with your own higher being. When you attain oneness with your own higher being, you begin to see that as you are connected to God, so are all other beings connected to God through their higher selves. You see that if you work to set other people free, then God will give you the multiplication of your efforts. This is beyond anything you could possibly attain by taking it through force in the material realm. Literally, my beloved, the message that Jesus brought was the message that God is ready to give you infinite abundance—if you are willing to share that abundance with everyone else, instead of seeking to hoard it for the pleasure, the sense of security or power of the ego, the separate self.

What you realize when you begin to contemplate these concepts is precisely that there can be no true freedom in separation. Why is this so? Where is freedom meant to be found? Freedom can be found in only one place and that is in oneness—oneness with your higher being, oneness with your fellow beings, oneness with your source, oneness with the Infinite as we call it in the new book [*The Art of Non-War*]. Only when you are one with the Infinite, can you have infinite freedom. Only when freedom is infinite, can it be truly free. The concept of freedom that most people have on earth is a dualistic concept where freedom is always seen as being in opposition to bondage or anti-freedom. There are many people on earth who are not able to even grasp the concept of infinite, non-dualistic freedom, meaning freedom that has no opposite for it needs no opposite.

Understanding infinite freedom

I can tell you that some of you – and many spiritual people around the planet – have had glimpses of experiencing true non-dualistic freedom. You have not been able to fully acknowledge or understand it with your outer minds. Your minds are still so focused on the dualistic polarity where you think that in order to be truly happy, you have to know what it means to be truly unhappy. You think you can experience freedom only when you have experienced bondage because you need the contrast in order to know what it really means to be free or happy.

I tell you, my beloved, beyond this dualistic interplay of light and darkness, there is the reality of God. We have often called it bliss because once you start putting words on it, you limit it. People immediately start projecting their dualistic concepts and images on it, yet, true freedom is true bliss that has no opposite.

When you first experience it, you might not know what to do with that experience. It literally takes some adjustment, especially of overcoming the linear thinking of the outer mind, before you realize that this is a state of freedom that is truly free because it can never have an opposite. You can never be anti-free when you are in that state of being, that state of flowing with the River of Life, what we call the flow of the is. What we desire all of you to have – all of you who are ascended master students, all of those who are in the top 10 percent among humanity – is that awareness, that experience, of the reality of God that is beyond the dualistic extremes. Therefore, you no longer look at the world through the filter of duality.

Why ignorance is not really bliss

There is the old saying that: "Ignorance is bliss." There is some truth to it, in the sense that as long as people believe in the programming they have been told since childhood, they do not realize how many problems there are in the world. They do not realize that there are forces who are working against freedom, who are working against positive change, who are always seeking to pull this world into conflict.

These people are blissfully ignorant of these problems that could at any moment wipe out their jobs, wipe out their lives to a war or some other calamity. What you see in most people is that they go through an awakening in their lives where they on one hand become more aware of the spiritual side of life, but they also become more aware of the problems on this planet and the need to do something about them. Obviously, there are so many problems in the world that if you focus your attention upon them, you can never really feel at peace. How can you when at any moment something somewhere could blow up and create a major conflict or war?

It is unavoidable, at the present level of consciousness, that when people awaken to the spiritual side of life, they are awakened to a greater awareness of both light and darkness. It is almost unavoidable that most students go through a period of focusing on the problems, not only the problems in themselves but also the problems in the world. What I desire you to understand is that we of the ascended masters have no desire to see our most devoted students live for 20, 30, 40 years or longer being focused on that duality between light and darkness, never feeling at peace, never feeling that they can truly enjoy life. They think there is always more work to be done, more prayers to be said, more decrees or rosaries to be given. They feel like they are always behind, they are always running after the carrot that is dangling in front of their nose. The carrot keeps moving and the harder they push, the faster the carrot keeps moving away.

We of the ascended masters know that in order to awaken people from the common indifference, they need to be shaken out of their comfortability. We have a desire to see people awakened from that state—what Jesus called the consciousness of death. We do not desire people to stay in that sense of duality, of being so aware of the light and darkness, always doubting whether the light will win out over the darkness or whether some calamity will happen, some earth-change or some man-made conflict.

Save the world by saving yourself

My beloved, what we desire you to see is that there comes a point where focusing on the problems and the negatives actually becomes an excuse. The ego will use it to get ascended master students to focus so much on changing world conditions that you simply say, whether subconsciously or consciously: "I do not have time to work on my personal psychology, for I have to save the world for Saint Germain."

How do you save the world for Saint Germain? You do so precisely by starting with yourself, by overcoming your own ego so that you come into that oneness with your own higher being. Instead of running around doing, doing, doing, you are centered in the peace, the higher bliss, of being.

You are the open door which no human can shut because you have decided not to allow your ego to shut the door that is your connection to your higher self. The light of that higher self, the Being of that higher self, can radiate through your lower form and anchor its light, its vibration, here in the physical octave. This has a far greater impact than anything else you can do, including any amount of violet flame decrees or invocations. This is not to say that you do not need to take outer actions. We desire to bring you to the point where your outer actions do not spring from the outer mind, the outer will and the outer determination. They spring from the inner reality of who you are so your outer actions are based on being. You are being as you are doing. *That* will have the maximum impact on this planet!

The peace that passes understanding

At the same time, it will also give you that deeper sense of peace that passes understanding. Think about this expression from the Bible, the "peace that passes understanding." What does it mean, my beloved? What is understanding? It is the outer mind, the logical mind, the intellect. The intellect is an analytical faculty that always operates with two dualities, two polarities. Peace that can be understood by the linear, analytical mind must have an opposite in the form of anti-peace. This is why many, many people – even many intelligent people – currently believe, even at subconscious levels, that there is no way to eradicate war on this planet. It simply is not possible to be free of the ghost of war that will always haunt humankind.

I tell you, it is entirely possible to remove war from this planet. It is a completely realistic and attainable goal. [See the book: *Help the Ascended Masters Stop War*.] Humankind is actually much closer than you would think by looking at the headlines here or there around the world. As happened with slavery, there is a potential and a momentum built that could very quickly break through. Then, a majority of the people suddenly come to see that war is not necessary, that war can be

13 | Freedom Means Surrender into Oneness

avoided and that it is time for them to stand up and demand an end to war. They will no longer allow themselves or their children to become cannon fodder for the endless ongoing struggle, precipitated by a small elite who are absolutely dedicated to destroying this planet and the Golden Age I have planned for earth.

We desire you, who are ascended master students, to rise above that dualistic consciousness. Not that you isolate yourself from the world and suddenly no longer pay attention to the news. We desire you to know what is going on, but we desire you to be in a state where what is happening in the world would not disturb your inner peace, your inner connection to your higher being. No matter what might happen, no matter what conflict there might be, you can *be* in that situation. You can be the anchor for the spiritual light, that will prevent a situation from escalating into a more widespread conflict.

You will have a situation where the power elite have planned a conflict, and they have set all of the people in motion to blow up this or that, to create this or that conflict. They start executing their plan, but suddenly – to their surprise – the ball stops rolling, so to speak. The people who should have been drawn into the conflict refuse to be pulled into the vortex of negativity and conflict. Instead, they stand back and say: "We will no longer engage in these energies."

The carefully orchestrated plans of the power elite come to naught. They just die out. The members of the power elite stand there and cannot understand how this could happen: "Why did our plans not work, as they have worked so many times in the past? We just needed to create a tension and then provide the one little spark that lit the powder keg, and everything would blow up and people would be killing each other in the streets. Now they are not doing this." My beloved, it can very well be because one person – in a state of being, in a state of oneness – is holding the balance for tens of thousands or millions of people. They are not drawn into a conflict, but they finally stand back and say: "No, we have to find a higher way, a higher approach to problems. We have to find a non-violent solution to our problems."

It is time to contemplate the River of Life

This is what I desire to see for you, who are ascended master students. I desire you to be truly free by rising above the duality that takes away your freedom. You can never truly be at peace by seeing how the world is being pulled from one extreme to the other. You can come to a state of consciousness where you are so centered within that you know that even though there may be conflicts here or there on this planet, the world is moving forward as it has been moving forward throughout recorded history, but even beyond.

Even though we have told you of past golden ages that came to an end, I desire you to lock in to the fact that beyond the cycle of ups and downs there is a greater movement, which is what we have called the River of Life. It is a movement that cannot be stopped by any force on earth, not even the collective consciousness of all human beings in embodiment. The River of Life flows directly from the Creator's Being, through all levels of the higher spiritual realms, through all beings who are one with the Creator and who are one with each other in that River of Life.

We are many. We are such a multitude that you could scarcely understand the numbers with your outer minds. We have come into oneness, and as Jesus said: "I, if I be lifted up, will draw all men onto me." We have become one and we see the underlying oneness of all life. We refuse to let any dualistic consciousness pull us into denying that oneness. We are providing the force, the unstoppable force of the River of Life, that is bringing the earth and humankind forward. Even though we sometimes have to drag humankind kicking and screaming to do what is best for themselves.

It is time that you, who are the spiritual people, truly begin to contemplate that River of Life and place yourself in that river, becoming one with us. You are free from the dualistic pull of ups and downs, of fears and hopes, that are always somewhat preventing you from feeling at peace, from enjoying life. We are certainly not encouraging you to stand still and become comfortable. We *are* encouraging you to come to that point where – no matter what is happening on earth – you can find some enjoyment, some gratitude, some appreciation. Even the appreciation for the sun rising every morning, no matter what is happening on the earth, appreciation for the change of the seasons, the beauty of nature, the sun sparkling on the river, the flowers unfolding, the birds singing, human beings being kind to each other, the beauty of a child who innocently enjoys life.

All of these things, you can enjoy. We desire you, who are our most dedicated students, to enjoy life, enjoy the time you have left on this planet, by not being in the dualistic state of enjoyment that is always tied to the negative. You are locking in to that greater joy, the state of being, the state of flowing with the River of Life. This, of course, is something that can happen to large numbers of people only in a part of the world where physical, material life is not as difficult as it is in the countries that are still trapped in materialistic poverty.

Again, this is why this dictation is given in North America where many people have a greater state of material abundance that gives them free time and attention to focus on the spiritual side of life. I hope you realize, my beloved, that the fact that you have been able to follow the spiritual path is caused by the very condition that you do not have to toil every day just to make a living, to get food on the table, so that you have no energy or attention left over to speculate about the purpose of life, or the purpose of your own existence.

What does it really mean to be free?

As the conclusion of this release, let me give you a concept to ponder about freedom. Freedom is a word that has been so misused on this planet that it almost has lost its meaning. As I did with the Sixth Ray, I desire to give you a different concept to ponder.

What does it really mean to be free? What is the meaning of freedom? The true meaning of freedom is surrender into oneness—the surrender of the separate self, the illusion of separation, the illusion of lack. You surrender your conscious being, your conscious self, into oneness with the River of Life so that you begin to flow with the River of Life.

Even though you are in physical embodiment and you see the imperfections on earth, you are locked in to that greater force behind all outer appearances—the River of Life itself. You know that as long as you stay centered in that peace, you will be the open door whereby the River of Life can bring humanity and the earth forward, towards greater states of abundance and peace. Even what might seem to be a backwards step or a negative experience (such as some conflict around the world), is actually – through you holding the vision and the balance – turned into a positive learning experience where the people finally wake up and say: "We have had enough of this conflict, we want positive change!" The negative is turned into a positive because it helps people rise above the dualistic state of consciousness that will inevitably create an endless string of conflicts until people abandon that state of consciousness.

Tell the story of your awakening to the spiritual path

Many spiritual people knew from an early age that there was more to life, there was something you had to find. There are literally many millions of people on this planet who are at that level but have not quite realized consciously, as you did, that there is more—more to know, more to understand. Some of you did not realize this, did not have this breakthrough, until late in life.

I tell you, there is immense value in you formulating your stories of how you received your own awakening. This is why we encourage you to tell your story today. We encourage you to do even more, to find ways to bring out your stories. It can be through books, it can be through recordings and videos, it can be through social networking sites on the internet, or any of the many other tools for communication you have available to you.

You might sometimes feel apprehensive about going out and tackling the beast of politics and speaking out against world conditions. None of you should feel apprehensive about telling your personal story of how you found the spiritual path and realized there was more to life so that you might inspire someone else to go through that same transformation. This should be something that is natural to you. If you have benefited from finding the path and the teachings of the ascended masters, then why would you not want to share that with others?

If you feel some apprehension against doing this, be willing to look in the mirror. Be willing to look at yourself and say: "Why do I feel apprehensive towards sharing my personal story?" What you will find – if you look honestly – is that behind that apprehension, some aspect of your ego is still hiding. It is making you feel whatever you feel that holds you back from freely sharing your story. You have not quite depersonalized your path. You have not quite surrendered into oneness with your own higher being and oneness with other parts of life. You are still trapped in some illusion of the separate self, and you feel whatever you feel that keeps you from freely sharing.

I encourage you to take a look at this. Be honest, be willing to work on yourself until you come to the point where you have depersonalized your life and you say: "This is not *my* life. It is not reserved for me. I have walked this path because I volunteered to be one of the forerunners with Saint Germain who took on a particular aspect of the mass consciousness. By working through this myself, I might make it easier for others by carving a path through the jungle of the collective consciousness. I can also go out and share the process with others so that they might be inspired by it." They also might realize the truth that we of the ascended masters have preached for a long time—that what one has done, all can do.

While there is value in you overcoming – personally – a certain element of the mass consciousness, this is only the Alpha aspect. The Omega aspect is that you go out and share that process with others. Each one of you comes from a particular background, each one of you has faced certain problems. Do you really believe that you went through those problems only as a result of your own karma or your own psychology? If you believe this, I can assure you that if that was the case, you would not be listening to this message. If you are open to direct communication from the ascended masters, that openness is due to the fact that in past lives you attained a certain mastery over self. In this lifetime, all of your problems were not exclusively due to your own karma or your own psychology.

13 | Freedom Means Surrender into Oneness

You have carried part of this for the mass consciousness. You volunteered to take this on so that you could help others.

That is why you are in a unique position to reach out to those who are still trapped in the problems that you have experienced yourself. You can share with them how you came to some insight or awakening that helped you rise above the consciousness that used to blind you. Now that you see more clearly, you see how to solve the problems that seemed insurmountable back then.

The key to solving any human problem is a shift in consciousness. As I said earlier, you cannot solve a problem with the same state of consciousness that created the problem. The key to solving any problem is to shift your consciousness so you see beyond the consciousness that created the problem—whereby the solution begins to become obvious. Without having to argue this or that, without having to have outer proof, you change your life because you know from within that this is right, this is the obvious thing to do.

Share your experiences, my beloved. You are not your own. You were bought with a price, as Jesus said. If you are the spiritual people that are open to direct communication from this strange being called Saint Germain, then I had to buy you with a price. I had to sponsor your embodiment. I had to, at critical moments, give part of my life and momentum to help you rise above the problems you were facing. Realize that I did this partly because I love you personally, but also because I love all of humankind. I desire you to fulfill your potential to become the examples and the forerunners who can stand up and witness to the fact that change is possible, that there are solutions to all human problems and that we can overcome whatever limitations we face. You can do this even when the experts in church and state and elsewhere claim they are insurmountable obstacles to progress. I have bought you with a price because I saw your potential. I saw your desire to play a part in the awakening that is necessary before the Golden Age can begin to manifest. Once again, I remind you lovingly of this. As I said in South America, I would rather jolt you out of your comfortability in order to awaken you than have to meet you after you leave embodiment and see you go through the regret of realizing that you did not live up to your full potential because you did not share with others what you had learned and experienced on the path of overcoming.

Contemplate surrender into oneness

My beloved, be willing to work on this issue, the surrender into oneness. If you feel you cannot surrender, then be willing to acknowledge that it is because there is still a part of the separate self that you have not seen for what it is. Be willing to look at it until you see it. You see its unreality, you see how it is limiting yourself and taking your outer peace. You see how it is preventing you from fulfilling your reason for being, your Divine plan, preventing you from making the contribution that you are meant to make in bringing forth my Golden Age.

Find the greater love that you all have in your beings. It can be a greater love for yourself, for other people, for the earth, for Saint Germain or another ascended being. Find that love so you are willing to look in the mirror and say: "What is keeping me from fulfilling my Divine plan? What is keeping me from being free to be here below all that I AM above so that I can play an active part, so that the earth can be here below all that it is above." Meaning, all that it is above in the mind of Saint Germain where I hold that vision for the Golden Age to be manifest. My beloved, I seal you for now in the Flame of Freedom, the freedom that has no opposite but is the

13 | *Freedom Means Surrender into Oneness*

surrender into oneness with all life, oneness with the River of Life. Be at peace, be sealed in that freedom until I shall address you again. I have indeed more to say about what comes after the Seventh Ray. We shall reveal what we used to call the secret rays, but it shall no longer be secret for I shall expose to you what it truly means. Be sealed, my beloved—and my gratitude for your being here.

Added by Saint Germain for this book:

I want to summarize the connection between freedom and poverty. The equation is simple: The more poor people are, the fewer choices they have, the fewer options they have from which to choose. One can say that poverty takes away people's freedom.

It is obvious, I trust, that the fallen beings, the power elite, have deliberately created a situation of lack that keeps the majority of the population in poverty. They do this for various reasons. One is that they desperately want to feel that they are above the people of earth because it gives them a sense of self-importance. Another is that they want to control people, and keeping them in poverty is one way to do this. One can therefore say that poverty is used deliberately as a very efficient weapon for controlling people, meaning that the fallen beings want to keep people in poverty. There is, of course, a need to call for the judgment of the fallen beings who have engineered this and for the binding and consuming of the demons that uphold it.

That being said, everything on earth is subject to the Law of Free Will. Even the fallen beings are subject to this, although they would be very reluctant to admit it. Some of them even believe they are not subject to this law because they are so good at manipulating people. In reality, no one can manipulate you against your will. The catch is that in order to exercise your will, you have to know what is going on so you can make a conscious choice. The fallen beings are, of course, experts at keeping people in total or partial ignorance that paralyzes them because they do not know what to do.

Nevertheless, no one can keep you in ignorance against your will. The law states that when the student is ready – and *willing* – a teacher *must* appear that can give the student the knowledge that will take him or her to the next level of evolution. It must therefore be recognized that the fallen beings can manipulate people only by taking advantage of some mechanism in their psychology that causes them to ignore or reject the teacher. It is true that the fallen beings have often inserted such mechanisms into people's minds in past lives. Yet even this happened only because people allowed it, and it can only be upheld because people continue to allow it.

The brutal fact, that will be denied by many, is that the poor people are poor because there is a choice they have not made. They have chosen not to know better, and they have done this because they do not want to do better. Why is this so? To understand such questions, you need to recognize that people are not stupid. At some level of people's consciousness (for many in the subconscious mind) there is an evaluation of what gives people the biggest advantage. People are asking: "What can I gain from this and what is the risk?"

This is not an objective evaluation, such as you can perform in between embodiments when you formulate your Divine plan. It is a subjective evaluation based on what people see and don't see while in embodiment, looking through the density of their four lower bodies. Naturally, this is a limited perspective, and I am not here seeking to blame anyone. What I seek to point out is that whatever people do, there is an evaluation of

13 | Freedom Means Surrender into Oneness

risk versus reward. If people feel that the risk outweighs the reward, they will choose to do nothing, or to not do the thing that could move them to a higher level of life, either in consciousness or in their physical situation. When people do not take a step to free themselves from, for example, poverty, it is because there is something they are afraid of.

Again, I am not here denying that there are conditions on earth that keep billions of people in poverty, and thus physical changes need to happen. I am pointing out that those physical changes cannot happen until there is a shift, or rather many shifts, in the collective and individual consciousness. This starts by recognizing that in people's consciousness, poverty gives them an advantage that right now seems to offer them something. What it seems to offer them is relief from something they consider a big risk. They perceive that poverty gives them the advantage of protecting them from what they fear.

What is it they are so afraid of that they would rather stay in poverty than face their fear and move through it? They are afraid of freedom, the freedom to make choices, the freedom to have many options from which to choose, the freedom to be able to define themselves.

If you think this sounds hard to believe, look at yourselves as the spiritual people. You all have a fear of freedom, of being in a situation where all options are open to you so you are free to choose to be anything you want to be. How can I say this? Well, my beloved, you are in embodiment on earth, are you not? You have not yet chosen to be an ascended master. Therefore, you still have some fear of total freedom, and you actually want something that you can project is an external condition that limits you, that limits your options, that boxes you in, that defines you. Again, I am not blaming you. I am pointing out that those of you who have the potential to make your ascensions in this lifetime will do so only when you face your fear of total freedom and consciously choose freedom over choices. You consciously choose that you are willing to define yourself, rather than wanting conditions in the material universe to define you.

The poor people on earth are poor because sometime in their past, they chose that they did not want to co-create their circumstances in the material world. They wanted conditions in the material world to define them. They did this by projecting that there are external conditions over which they have no power, and these conditions are defining what choices they have. In reality, the only condition that is defining what choices you have is the condition in your own psyche. When you will not acknowledge this and act on the inescapable consequence, you must project that external conditions determine your station in life.

You therefore need to make calls to free people from this denial of responsibility and for them to overcome their fear of making choices. You also need to demonstrate that you are willing to do the same in your own life, and that is why you need to tell your story. The fallen beings will say that once people have chosen to submit themselves to them, neither ascended masters nor people in embodiment have the right to interfere with people's choices. The reality is that we do have a right to demonstrate to people that there is another choice than the one they have made. This is not interfering with people's choices (as the fallen beings are doing), it is showing people the full range of their choices.

Again, start with yourself and consider why you are afraid of freedom. Then face your fear and walk through it so you can get on with doing what you came here to do, namely demonstrate to others what you can do when you are no longer afraid of making choices and when you no longer allow material conditions to define you.

This is what Jesus did when he was in embodiment. This is what I did when I was in embodiment. This is what Master MORE did when he was in embodiment. This is what Mother Mary did when she was in embodiment. This is what all of us have done and what you can do also.

Truly, those who believe on me, the works that I do shall ye do also, nay greater works than these shall ye do. The world has moved on and greater works are possible today than were possible yesterday.

14 | INVOKING FREEDOM FROM THE FEAR OF MAKING CHOICES

In the name of the I AM THAT I AM, Jesus Christ, I call upon Saint Germain and Lord Maitreya for the transformation of the consciousness of poverty on earth. Awaken people to the reality that we are spiritual beings and that we can co-create a new future by working with the ascended masters. I especially call for …

[Make your own calls here.]

Part 1

1. Saint Germain, help the top 10 percent make up our minds that poverty is no longer allowed on this planet.

> O Saint Germain, you do inspire,
> my vision raised forever higher,
> with you I form a figure-eight,
> your Golden Age I co-create.
>
> **O Saint Germain, what love you bring,**
> **it truly makes all matter sing,**
> **your violet flame does all restore,**
> **with you we are becoming more.**

2. Saint Germain, help the top 10 percent see that we are being programmed to be passive, to live like all other people, to think that one person cannot make a difference, that we do not have the power to change society or the planet.

> O Saint Germain, what Freedom Flame,
> released when we recite your name,
> acceleration is your gift,
> our planet it will surely lift.
>
> **O Saint Germain, what love you bring,**
> **it truly makes all matter sing,**
> **your violet flame does all restore,**
> **with you we are becoming more.**

3. Saint Germain, help the top 10 percent see that everything on earth is determined by the free will of human beings in embodiment. One person can make a difference by making up his or her mind with unwavering determination.

14 | Invoking Freedom from the Fear of Making Choices

O Saint Germain, in love we claim,
our right to bring your violet flame,
from you Above, to us below,
it is an all-transforming flow.

**O Saint Germain, what love you bring,
it truly makes all matter sing,
your violet flame does all restore,
with you we are becoming more.**

4. Saint Germain, help the top 10 percent come to a determination that is beyond the outer will. Help us reach an inner determination, an inner knowing, that there is a new reality on our planet because we are being the change.

O Saint Germain, I love you so,
my aura filled with violet glow,
my chakras filled with violet fire,
I am your cosmic amplifier.

**O Saint Germain, what love you bring,
it truly makes all matter sing,
your violet flame does all restore,
with you we are becoming more.**

5. Saint Germain, I am willing to be the change in the world by holding the spiritual balance for that change. I hold the vision that abundance is a manifest reality on this planet.

O Saint Germain, I am now free,
your violet flame is therapy,
transform all hang-ups in my mind,
as inner peace I surely find.

**O Saint Germain, what love you bring,
it truly makes all matter sing,
your violet flame does all restore,
with you we are becoming more.**

6. Saint Germain, help the top 10 percent see that while there is value in one person shifting his or her consciousness, a critical mass must be reached so that there is a counter-balance between those who are willing to raise their consciousness and those who are not.

O Saint Germain, my body pure,
your violet flame for all is cure,
consume the cause of all disease,
and therefore I am all at ease.

**O Saint Germain, what love you bring,
it truly makes all matter sing,
your violet flame does all restore,
with you we are becoming more.**

7. Saint Germain, help the top 10 percent see that one person making up his or her mind will shift the collective consciousness. Yet it takes a critical mass of individuals to prevent certain outer manifestations.

O Saint Germain, I'm karma-free,
the past no longer burdens me,
a brand new opportunity,
I am in Christic unity.

**O Saint Germain, what love you bring,
it truly makes all matter sing,
your violet flame does all restore,
with you we are becoming more.**

8. Saint Germain, help the top 10 percent see that if one person could remove some ungodly condition from this planet, the majority would not come to the point where they have decided that they too have had enough of this manifestation.

O Saint Germain, we are now one,
I am for you a violet sun,
as we transform this planet earth,
your Golden Age is given birth.

**O Saint Germain, what love you bring,
it truly makes all matter sing,
your violet flame does all restore,
with you we are becoming more.**

9. Saint Germain, help the top 10 percent see that it is not always enough to come to an inner determination based on oneness with our own higher being. We also need to go out and seek to awaken others so that a critical mass of people can shift the collective consciousness.

O Saint Germain, the earth is free,
from burden of duality,
in oneness we bring what is best,
your Golden Age is manifest.

**O Saint Germain, what love you bring,
it truly makes all matter sing,
your violet flame does all restore,
with you we are becoming more.**

Part 2

1. Saint Germain, help the top 10 percent see that the critical mass is reached when the top 10 percent come to the realization that poverty is no longer acceptable.

> Maitreya, I am truly meek,
> your counsel wise I humbly seek,
> your vision I so want to see,
> with you in Eden I will be.

> **Maitreya, kindness is the cure,
> in fires of kindness I am pure.
> Maitreya, now release the fire,
> that raises me forever higher.**

2. Saint Germain, help the top 10 percent see that the lower 10 percent will pull the population down until the top 10 percent come into agreement and pull the population up.

> Maitreya, help me to return,
> to learn from you, I truly yearn,
> as oneness is all I desire
> I feel initiation's fire.

**Maitreya, kindness is the cure,
in fires of kindness I am pure.
Maitreya, now release the fire,
that raises me forever higher.**

3. Saint Germain, help the top 10 percent see that when we are in agreement, many among the population can now see what they could not see before because they were blinded by the duality consciousness.

Maitreya, I hereby decide,
from you I will no longer hide,
expose to me the very lie
that caused edenic self to die.

**Maitreya, kindness is the cure,
in fires of kindness I am pure.
Maitreya, now release the fire,
that raises me forever higher.**

4. Saint Germain, help the top 10 percent see that there is great strength in numbers. If two people in different parts of the world reach the same determination, then it will count. The whole is more than the sum of the parts.

Maitreya, blessed Guru mine,
my heart of hearts forever thine,
I vow that I will listen well,
so we can break the serpent's spell.

> Maitreya, kindness is the cure,
> in fires of kindness I am pure.
> Maitreya, now release the fire,
> that raises me forever higher.

5. Saint Germain, help the top 10 percent see that the ascended masters are constantly releasing new ideas, but they will not have an effect in the physical until one or more people grasp an idea with the outer awareness.

> Maitreya, help me see the lie
> whereby the serpent broke the tie,
> the serpent now has naught in me,
> in oneness I am truly free.

> Maitreya, kindness is the cure,
> in fires of kindness I am pure.
> Maitreya, now release the fire,
> that raises me forever higher.

6. Saint Germain, help the top 10 percent see that the ascended masters have solutions to every problem on earth. Yet those solutions cannot be given unless people are willing to change their consciousness.

> Maitreya, truth does set me free
> from falsehoods of duality,
> the fruit of knowledge I let go,
> so your true spirit I do know.

**Maitreya, kindness is the cure,
in fires of kindness I am pure.
Maitreya, now release the fire,
that raises me forever higher.**

7. Saint Germain, help the top 10 percent see that we cannot solve a problem with the same state of consciousness that created or precipitated the problem. It is essential that the consciousness shifts so that people can reach beyond the old way of looking at a particular problem and be open to receiving the solution.

> Maitreya, I submit to you,
> intentions pure, my heart is true,
> from ego I am truly free,
> as I am now all one with thee.

**Maitreya, kindness is the cure,
in fires of kindness I am pure.
Maitreya, now release the fire,
that raises me forever higher.**

8. Saint Germain, help the top 10 percent see that the ascended masters want a situation where many people are open and attuned to you so that many people at the same time will tune in to a particular idea.

> Maitreya, kindness is the key,
> all shades of kindness teach to me,
> for I am now the open door,
> the Art of Kindness to restore.

> Maitreya, kindness is the cure,
> in fires of kindness I am pure.
> Maitreya, now release the fire,
> that raises me forever higher.

9. Saint Germain, help the top 10 percent see that in the Aquarian age, you need millions of people to be so attuned to the new ideas you are releasing that many people catch an idea as soon as it is released and immediately start speaking about it.

> Maitreya, oh sweet mystery,
> immersed in your reality,
> the myst'ry school will now return,
> for this, my heart does truly burn.

> Maitreya, kindness is the cure,
> in fires of kindness I am pure.
> Maitreya, now release the fire,
> that raises me forever higher.

Part 3

1. Saint Germain, help the top 10 percent see that you are not looking at the Aquarian age as an age in which there are a few remarkable leaders, but where millions of remarkable people dare to stand up and speak the truth that they know in their hearts.

14 | *Invoking Freedom from the Fear of Making Choices*

> O Saint Germain, you do inspire,
> my vision raised forever higher,
> with you I form a figure-eight,
> your Golden Age I co-create.
>
> **O Saint Germain, what love you bring,**
> **it truly makes all matter sing,**
> **your violet flame does all restore,**
> **with you we are becoming more.**

2. Saint Germain, help the top 10 percent see that if more and more people start speaking from their hearts, stating the truth and stating the need for change, then it will begin to have an impact on society.

> O Saint Germain, what Freedom Flame,
> released when we recite your name,
> acceleration is your gift,
> our planet it will surely lift.
>
> **O Saint Germain, what love you bring,**
> **it truly makes all matter sing,**
> **your violet flame does all restore,**
> **with you we are becoming more.**

3. Saint Germain, help the top 10 percent see beyond the programming that change is brought by the powerful people and that any change in society must come from the elite.

> O Saint Germain, in love we claim,
> our right to bring your violet flame,
> from you Above, to us below,
> it is an all-transforming flow.

**O Saint Germain, what love you bring,
it truly makes all matter sing,
your violet flame does all restore,
with you we are becoming more.**

4. Saint Germain, help the top 10 percent see that the true positive changes that have happened on this planet, have always happened because a number of so-called ordinary people embraced the idea.

O Saint Germain, I love you so,
my aura filled with violet glow,
my chakras filled with violet fire,
I am your cosmic amplifier.

**O Saint Germain, what love you bring,
it truly makes all matter sing,
your violet flame does all restore,
with you we are becoming more.**

5. Saint Germain, help the top 10 percent see that no one person is more important than anyone else. We all have the potential to be part of the movement of the ascended masters, part of bringing the Golden Age.

O Saint Germain, I am now free,
your violet flame is therapy,
transform all hang-ups in my mind,
as inner peace I surely find.

> **O Saint Germain, what love you bring,**
> **it truly makes all matter sing,**
> **your violet flame does all restore,**
> **with you we are becoming more.**

6. Saint Germain, help the top 10 percent see that a true Aquarian age organization is designed to help us find God within ourselves, and we must not turn it into another exclusivist teaching or organization.

> O Saint Germain, my body pure,
> your violet flame for all is cure,
> consume the cause of all disease,
> and therefore I am all at ease.

> **O Saint Germain, what love you bring,**
> **it truly makes all matter sing,**
> **your violet flame does all restore,**
> **with you we are becoming more.**

7. Saint Germain, help the top 10 percent see that the essence of poverty is that we are separated from God's abundance. The essence of poverty is separation.

> O Saint Germain, I'm karma-free,
> the past no longer burdens me,
> a brand new opportunity,
> I am in Christic unity.

> **O Saint Germain, what love you bring,**
> **it truly makes all matter sing,**
> **your violet flame does all restore,**
> **with you we are becoming more.**

8. Saint Germain, help the top 10 percent see that the essence of anti-freedom is that we are separated from God, we are separated from oneness with God. Out of that illusion of separation spring countless other illusions.

> O Saint Germain, we are now one,
> I am for you a violet sun,
> as we transform this planet earth,
> your Golden Age is given birth.
>
> **O Saint Germain, what love you bring,**
> **it truly makes all matter sing,**
> **your violet flame does all restore,**
> **with you we are becoming more.**

9. Saint Germain, help the top 10 percent see through the illusions that keep us trapped in a mental box where we define borders around ourselves. We think we are inside the box and other people and God are outside the box.

> O Saint Germain, the earth is free,
> from burden of duality,
> in oneness we bring what is best,
> your Golden Age is manifest.
>
> **O Saint Germain, what love you bring,**
> **it truly makes all matter sing,**
> **your violet flame does all restore,**
> **with you we are becoming more.**

Part 4

1. Saint Germain, help the top 10 percent see that the separate mind, the ego, defines freedom as the ability to do whatever it wants, to have whatever it wants, to have all of its needs fulfilled.

> Maitreya, I am truly meek,
> your counsel wise I humbly seek,
> your vision I so want to see,
> with you in Eden I will be.
>
> **Maitreya, kindness is the cure,**
> **in fires of kindness I am pure.**
> **Maitreya, now release the fire,**
> **that raises me forever higher.**

2. Saint Germain, help the top 10 percent see that in human society, even in spiritual and religious movements, a certain attitude has developed that if we can do whatever we want and escape the consequences of our actions, then we are free.

> Maitreya, help me to return,
> to learn from you, I truly yearn,
> as oneness is all I desire
> I feel initiation's fire.
>
> **Maitreya, kindness is the cure,**
> **in fires of kindness I am pure.**
> **Maitreya, now release the fire,**
> **that raises me forever higher.**

3. Saint Germain, help the top 10 percent see that this is a perverted concept of freedom. The separate self has no reality, no existence in God—and thus it can never be free.

> Maitreya, I hereby decide,
> from you I will no longer hide,
> expose to me the very lie
> that caused edenic self to die.

> **Maitreya, kindness is the cure,**
> **in fires of kindness I am pure.**
> **Maitreya, now release the fire,**
> **that raises me forever higher.**

4. Saint Germain, help the top 10 percent see that the separate self can gain freedom only by taking freedom from one or more other separate selves.

> Maitreya, blessed Guru mine,
> my heart of hearts forever thine,
> I vow that I will listen well,
> so we can break the serpent's spell.

> **Maitreya, kindness is the cure,**
> **in fires of kindness I am pure.**
> **Maitreya, now release the fire,**
> **that raises me forever higher.**

5. Saint Germain, help the top 10 percent see that true freedom does not mean to escape the consequences of our actions. It means to acknowledge the reality that the physical universe is the cosmic mirror that sends back to us what we send out.

14 | Invoking Freedom from the Fear of Making Choices

> Maitreya, help me see the lie
> whereby the serpent broke the tie,
> the serpent now has naught in me,
> in oneness I am truly free.
>
> **Maitreya, kindness is the cure,**
> **in fires of kindness I am pure.**
> **Maitreya, now release the fire,**
> **that raises me forever higher.**

6. Saint Germain, help the top 10 percent see the need to develop a global awareness where we seek to raise the All, rather than the separate self.

> Maitreya, truth does set me free
> from falsehoods of duality,
> the fruit of knowledge I let go,
> so your true spirit I do know.
>
> **Maitreya, kindness is the cure,**
> **in fires of kindness I am pure.**
> **Maitreya, now release the fire,**
> **that raises me forever higher.**

7. Saint Germain, help the top 10 percent see that when we do this, the cosmic mirror will gladly reflect back to us exactly what we are sending out.

> Maitreya, I submit to you,
> intentions pure, my heart is true,
> from ego I am truly free,
> as I am now all one with thee.

> Maitreya, kindness is the cure,
> in fires of kindness I am pure.
> Maitreya, now release the fire,
> that raises me forever higher.

8. Saint Germain, help the top 10 percent escape the limitations that are created by the separate self and its belief that, in order to gain for itself, it must take from others. This is the belief that there is not enough wealth and abundance in the material world to go around for everyone.

> Maitreya, kindness is the key,
> all shades of kindness teach to me,
> for I am now the open door,
> the Art of Kindness to restore.

> **Maitreya, kindness is the cure,**
> **in fires of kindness I am pure.**
> **Maitreya, now release the fire,**
> **that raises me forever higher.**

9. Saint Germain, help the top 10 percent see that what takes away our freedom is the illusion that it is possible to gain something by taking it through force.

> Maitreya, oh sweet mystery,
> immersed in your reality,
> the myst'ry school will now return,
> for this, my heart does truly burn.

14 | Invoking Freedom from the Fear of Making Choices

> Maitreya, kindness is the cure,
> in fires of kindness I am pure.
> Maitreya, now release the fire,
> that raises me forever higher.

Part 5

1. Saint Germain, help the top 10 percent see that Jesus brought the message that God is ready to give us infinite abundance—if we are willing to share that abundance with everyone else, instead of seeking to hoard it for the pleasure, the sense of security or the power of the separate self.

> O Saint Germain, you do inspire,
> my vision raised forever higher,
> with you I form a figure-eight,
> your Golden Age I co-create.

> **O Saint Germain, what love you bring,**
> **it truly makes all matter sing,**
> **your violet flame does all restore,**
> **with you we are becoming more.**

2. Saint Germain, help the top 10 percent see that there can be no true freedom in separation. Freedom is found only in oneness with our higher being, oneness with our fellow beings, oneness with our source.

O Saint Germain, what Freedom Flame,
released when we recite your name,
acceleration is your gift,
our planet it will surely lift.

**O Saint Germain, what love you bring,
it truly makes all matter sing,
your violet flame does all restore,
with you we are becoming more.**

3. Saint Germain, help the top 10 percent overcome the illusion that in order to be truly happy, we have to know what it means to be truly unhappy, the illusion that we can experience freedom only when we have experienced bondage because we need the contrast.

O Saint Germain, in love we claim,
our right to bring your violet flame,
from you Above, to us below,
it is an all-transforming flow.

**O Saint Germain, what love you bring,
it truly makes all matter sing,
your violet flame does all restore,
with you we are becoming more.**

4. Saint Germain, help the top 10 percent see that the ascended masters desire all of us to have the awareness, the experience, of the reality of God that is beyond the dualistic extremes. Therefore, we no longer look at the world through the filter of duality.

> O Saint Germain, I love you so,
> my aura filled with violet glow,
> my chakras filled with violet fire,
> I am your cosmic amplifier.

> **O Saint Germain, what love you bring,**
> **it truly makes all matter sing,**
> **your violet flame does all restore,**
> **with you we are becoming more.**

5. Saint Germain, help the top 10 percent see that it is unavoidable that when people awaken to the spiritual side of life, they are awakened to a greater awareness of both light and darkness, causing them to focus on the problems in the world.

> O Saint Germain, I am now free,
> your violet flame is therapy,
> transform all hang-ups in my mind,
> as inner peace I surely find.

> **O Saint Germain, what love you bring,**
> **it truly makes all matter sing,**
> **your violet flame does all restore,**
> **with you we are becoming more.**

6. Saint Germain, help the top 10 percent see that the ascended masters do not desire people to stay in that sense of duality, of being so aware of the light and darkness, always doubting whether the light will win out over the darkness or whether some calamity will happen.

> O Saint Germain, my body pure,
> your violet flame for all is cure,
> consume the cause of all disease,
> and therefore I am all at ease.
>
> **O Saint Germain, what love you bring,
> it truly makes all matter sing,
> your violet flame does all restore,
> with you we are becoming more.**

7. Saint Germain, help the top 10 percent see that there comes a point where focusing on the problems and the negatives becomes an excuse. The ego will use it to get us to focus so much on changing the world that we do not have time to work on our personal psychology.

> O Saint Germain, I'm karma-free,
> the past no longer burdens me,
> a brand new opportunity,
> I am in Christic unity.
>
> **O Saint Germain, what love you bring,
> it truly makes all matter sing,
> your violet flame does all restore,
> with you we are becoming more.**

8. Saint Germain, help the top 10 percent see that we change the world by overcoming our own egos so that the light of our higher selves can radiate through us and anchor itself in the physical octave.

O Saint Germain, we are now one,
I am for you a violet sun,
as we transform this planet earth,
your Golden Age is given birth.

**O Saint Germain, what love you bring,
it truly makes all matter sing,
your violet flame does all restore,
with you we are becoming more.**

9. Saint Germain, help the top 10 percent come to the point where our outer actions do not spring from the outer mind. They spring from the inner reality of who we are, so our outer actions are based on being. We are being as we are doing.

O Saint Germain, the earth is free,
from burden of duality,
in oneness we bring what is best,
your Golden Age is manifest.

**O Saint Germain, what love you bring,
it truly makes all matter sing,
your violet flame does all restore,
with you we are becoming more.**

Part 6

1. Saint Germain, help the top 10 percent have the deeper sense of peace that passes understanding. We do not isolate ourselves from the world, but what is happening in the world does not disturb our inner peace.

> Maitreya, I am truly meek,
> your counsel wise I humbly seek,
> your vision I so want to see,
> with you in Eden I will be.
>
> **Maitreya, kindness is the cure,
> in fires of kindness I am pure.
> Maitreya, now release the fire,
> that raises me forever higher.**

2. Saint Germain, help the top 10 percent maintain our inner connections to our higher beings, so that no matter what might happen, we can anchor the spiritual light that will prevent a situation from escalating.

> Maitreya, help me to return,
> to learn from you, I truly yearn,
> as oneness is all I desire
> I feel initiation's fire.
>
> **Maitreya, kindness is the cure,
> in fires of kindness I am pure.
> Maitreya, now release the fire,
> that raises me forever higher.**

3. Saint Germain, help the top 10 percent see how we can derail the plans of the power elite by getting people to refuse to be pulled into the vortex of negativity and conflict.

> Maitreya, I hereby decide,
> from you I will no longer hide,
> expose to me the very lie
> that caused edenic self to die.

**Maitreya, kindness is the cure,
in fires of kindness I am pure.
Maitreya, now release the fire,
that raises me forever higher.**

4. Saint Germain, help the top 10 percent come to a state of consciousness where we are so centered within that we know that even though there may be conflicts here or there, this planet is moving forward as it has been moving forward throughout recorded history.

Maitreya, blessed Guru mine,
my heart of hearts forever thine,
I vow that I will listen well,
so we can break the serpent's spell.

**Maitreya, kindness is the cure,
in fires of kindness I am pure.
Maitreya, now release the fire,
that raises me forever higher.**

5. Saint Germain, help the top 10 percent see that beyond the cycle of ups and downs there is a greater movement, which is the River of Life. It is a movement that cannot be stopped by any force on earth, not even the collective consciousness of all human beings in embodiment.

Maitreya, help me see the lie
whereby the serpent broke the tie,
the serpent now has naught in me,
in oneness I am truly free.

**Maitreya, kindness is the cure,
in fires of kindness I am pure.
Maitreya, now release the fire,
that raises me forever higher.**

6. Saint Germain, help the top 10 percent see that the River of Life flows directly from the Creator's Being, through all levels of the higher spiritual realms, through all beings who are one with the Creator and who are one with each other in that River of Life.

Maitreya, truth does set me free
from falsehoods of duality,
the fruit of knowledge I let go,
so your true spirit I do know.

**Maitreya, kindness is the cure,
in fires of kindness I am pure.
Maitreya, now release the fire,
that raises me forever higher.**

7. Saint Germain, help the top 10 percent see that the ascended masters are providing the unstoppable force of the River of Life that is bringing the earth and humankind forward.

Maitreya, I submit to you,
intentions pure, my heart is true,
from ego I am truly free,
as I am now all one with thee.

**Maitreya, kindness is the cure,
in fires of kindness I am pure.
Maitreya, now release the fire,
that raises me forever higher.**

8. Saint Germain, help the top 10 percent begin to contemplate the River of Life and place ourselves in that river, becoming one with the ascended masters.

Maitreya, kindness is the key,
all shades of kindness teach to me,
for I am now the open door,
the Art of Kindness to restore.

**Maitreya, kindness is the cure,
in fires of kindness I am pure.
Maitreya, now release the fire,
that raises me forever higher.**

9. Saint Germain, help the top 10 percent lock in to the greater joy, the state of being, the state of flowing with the River of Life.

Maitreya, oh sweet mystery,
immersed in your reality,
the myst'ry school will now return,
for this, my heart does truly burn.

**Maitreya, kindness is the cure,
in fires of kindness I am pure.
Maitreya, now release the fire,
that raises me forever higher.**

Part 7

1. Saint Germain, help the top 10 percent see that the more poor people are, the fewer choices they have, the fewer options they have from which to choose. Poverty takes away people's freedom.

> O Saint Germain, you do inspire,
> my vision raised forever higher,
> with you I form a figure-eight,
> your Golden Age I co-create.
>
> **O Saint Germain, what love you bring,**
> **it truly makes all matter sing,**
> **your violet flame does all restore,**
> **with you we are becoming more.**

2. Saint Germain, I call forth the judgment of Christ upon the fallen beings, the power elite, who have deliberately created a situation of lack that keeps the majority of the population in poverty.

> O Saint Germain, what Freedom Flame,
> released when we recite your name,
> acceleration is your gift,
> our planet it will surely lift.
>
> **O Saint Germain, what love you bring,**
> **it truly makes all matter sing,**
> **your violet flame does all restore,**
> **with you we are becoming more.**

14 | Invoking Freedom from the Fear of Making Choices

3. Saint Germain, I call forth the judgment of Christ upon the fallen beings who desperately want to feel that they are above the people of earth because it gives them a sense of self-importance.

> O Saint Germain, in love we claim,
> our right to bring your violet flame,
> from you Above, to us below,
> it is an all-transforming flow.
>
> **O Saint Germain, what love you bring,**
> **it truly makes all matter sing,**
> **your violet flame does all restore,**
> **with you we are becoming more.**

4. Saint Germain, I call forth the judgment of Christ upon the fallen beings who are deliberately using poverty as a very efficient weapon for controlling people.

> O Saint Germain, I love you so,
> my aura filled with violet glow,
> my chakras filled with violet fire,
> I am your cosmic amplifier.
>
> **O Saint Germain, what love you bring,**
> **it truly makes all matter sing,**
> **your violet flame does all restore,**
> **with you we are becoming more.**

5. Saint Germain, I call forth the judgment of Christ upon the fallen beings who have engineered poverty and want to keep people in poverty. I call for the binding and consuming of the demons that uphold poverty.

O Saint Germain, I am now free,
your violet flame is therapy,
transform all hang-ups in my mind,
as inner peace I surely find.

**O Saint Germain, what love you bring,
it truly makes all matter sing,
your violet flame does all restore,
with you we are becoming more.**

6. Saint Germain, I call forth the judgment of Christ upon the fallen beings who believe they are not subject to the Law of Free Will because they are so good at manipulating people.

O Saint Germain, my body pure,
your violet flame for all is cure,
consume the cause of all disease,
and therefore I am all at ease.

**O Saint Germain, what love you bring,
it truly makes all matter sing,
your violet flame does all restore,
with you we are becoming more.**

7. Saint Germain, I call forth the judgment of Christ upon the fallen beings who are experts at keeping people in total or partial ignorance that paralyzes them because they do not know what to do.

O Saint Germain, I'm karma-free,
the past no longer burdens me,
a brand new opportunity,
I am in Christic unity.

14 | Invoking Freedom from the Fear of Making Choices

**O Saint Germain, what love you bring,
it truly makes all matter sing,
your violet flame does all restore,
with you we are becoming more.**

8. Saint Germain, help the top 10 percent see that the fallen beings can manipulate us only by taking advantage of some mechanism in our psychology that causes us to ignore or reject the teacher.

O Saint Germain, we are now one,
I am for you a violet sun,
as we transform this planet earth,
your Golden Age is given birth.

**O Saint Germain, what love you bring,
it truly makes all matter sing,
your violet flame does all restore,
with you we are becoming more.**

9. Saint Germain, help people acknowledge the brutal fact that the poor people are poor because there is a choice they have not made. They have chosen not to know better, and they have done this because they do not want to do better.

O Saint Germain, the earth is free,
from burden of duality,
in oneness we bring what is best,
your Golden Age is manifest.

**O Saint Germain, what love you bring,
it truly makes all matter sing,
your violet flame does all restore,
with you we are becoming more.**

Part 8

1. Saint Germain, help people see that whatever we do, there is an evaluation of risk versus reward. When people do not take a step to free themselves from poverty, it is because there is something they are afraid of.

Maitreya, I am truly meek,
your counsel wise I humbly seek,
your vision I so want to see,
with you in Eden I will be.

**Maitreya, kindness is the cure,
in fires of kindness I am pure.
Maitreya, now release the fire,
that raises me forever higher.**

2. Saint Germain, help people see that although the conditions that keep people in poverty need to change, this cannot happen until there are many shifts in the collective and individual consciousness.

Maitreya, help me to return,
to learn from you, I truly yearn,
as oneness is all I desire
I feel initiation's fire.

**Maitreya, kindness is the cure,
in fires of kindness I am pure.
Maitreya, now release the fire,
that raises me forever higher.**

3. Saint Germain, help people see that poor people have a subtle belief that poverty gives them an advantage that seems to offer them relief from something they consider a big risk. They perceive that poverty gives them the advantage of protecting them from what they fear.

Maitreya, I hereby decide,
from you I will no longer hide,
expose to me the very lie
that caused edenic self to die.

**Maitreya, kindness is the cure,
in fires of kindness I am pure.
Maitreya, now release the fire,
that raises me forever higher.**

4. Saint Germain, help people see that they are afraid of freedom, the freedom to make choices, the freedom to have many options from which to choose, the freedom to be able to define themselves.

Maitreya, blessed Guru mine,
my heart of hearts forever thine,
I vow that I will listen well,
so we can break the serpent's spell.

**Maitreya, kindness is the cure,
in fires of kindness I am pure.
Maitreya, now release the fire,
that raises me forever higher.**

5. Saint Germain, help people see that in order to overcome the poverty consciousness, we must consciously choose that we are willing to define ourselves, rather than wanting conditions in the material universe to define us.

Maitreya, help me see the lie
whereby the serpent broke the tie,
the serpent now has naught in me,
in oneness I am truly free.

**Maitreya, kindness is the cure,
in fires of kindness I am pure.
Maitreya, now release the fire,
that raises me forever higher.**

6. Saint Germain, help people see that the poor people on earth are poor because sometime in their past, they chose that they did not want to co-create their circumstances in the material world. They wanted conditions in the material world to define them.

Maitreya, truth does set me free
from falsehoods of duality,
the fruit of knowledge I let go,
so your true spirit I do know.

14 | Invoking Freedom from the Fear of Making Choices

**Maitreya, kindness is the cure,
in fires of kindness I am pure.
Maitreya, now release the fire,
that raises me forever higher.**

7. Saint Germain, help people see that they did this by projecting that there are external conditions over which they have no power, and these conditions are defining what choices they have.

Maitreya, I submit to you,
intentions pure, my heart is true,
from ego I am truly free,
as I am now all one with thee.

**Maitreya, kindness is the cure,
in fires of kindness I am pure.
Maitreya, now release the fire,
that raises me forever higher.**

8. Saint Germain, help people see that the only condition that is defining what choices we have is a condition in our own psyches. When we will not acknowledge this and act on the inescapable consequence, we must project that external conditions determine our station in life.

Maitreya, kindness is the key,
all shades of kindness teach to me,
for I am now the open door,
the Art of Kindness to restore.

**Maitreya, kindness is the cure,
in fires of kindness I am pure.
Maitreya, now release the fire,
that raises me forever higher.**

9. Saint Germain, free people from this denial of responsibility and help them overcome their fear of making choices, so that a critical mass of us can co-create a more abundant state in which no one lives in poverty.

Maitreya, oh sweet mystery,
immersed in your reality,
the myst'ry school will now return,
for this, my heart does truly burn.

**Maitreya, kindness is the cure,
in fires of kindness I am pure.
Maitreya, now release the fire,
that raises me forever higher.**

Sealing

In the name of the I AM THAT I AM, I accept that Archangel Michael, Astrea and Shiva form an impenetrable shield around myself and all constructive people, sealing us from all fear-based energies in all four octaves. I accept that the Light of God is consuming and transforming all fear-based energies that make up the forces behind war!

15 | PROTECTING YOURSELF FROM THE FALLEN BEINGS

The Ascended Master Mother Mary: I know very well that our teachings can encourage some students to become unbalanced. You become so fired up, so to speak, about doing what you came here to do. Some people feel that they have wasted a big part of their lives by not having found the teachings. When they finally find the teachings, they want to compensate for this by throwing themselves at it and making calls all day and neglecting other parts of life. I am not asking you to do this.

I know that poverty is an extreme condition on earth. I know that when you are a soldier in war, you are in a very extreme state. I am not asking you, as an ascended master student, to go into a warlike mindset and put other aspects of your life aside and think that now you have to live some unbalanced, extreme lifestyle in order to bring the judgment of the fallen beings. I am asking you to live a balanced spiritual life, but to still find time to make the calls and give us the authority and the energy to multiply so that we can do our work.

Yes, poverty is an extreme condition. Yes, it needs to be removed, but do you not see that what the fallen beings are doing by creating poverty and war is that they are forcing human beings in embodiment to go towards greater and greater extremes to defeat the enemy?

Do you not also see that for everything that happens in the physical, there is a parallel in consciousness? When you see people take extreme physical actions, you know that they have gone into a parallel extreme in their emotional, mental and identity bodies. Do you not also see that it is this unbalance in the three higher bodies that leads to the imbalance at the physical level? Why would you think that you going into an imbalanced state would help remove poverty from the earth?

You would actually contribute to the imbalance on earth, even though you are a spiritual student following a spiritual teaching. There are ascended master students who have found our teachings, given in past dispensations, and who have used them to become so unbalanced that they have actually contributed to the survival of war and poverty on earth through their imbalance. They have also become so angry with the fallen beings, or with certain human beings from another political system, that they have contributed to the misqualified energy that feeds the entire machine. This I am asking you to *not* do.

I am asking you to take our teachings, and the many other teachings we have given about balance, and to walk a balanced path, to live a balanced life. I am not asking you to go to war against poverty. I am asking you to fight poverty by finding your own personal inner balance, by finding your personal inner peace and, from that state of peace, making the calls that give us the authority to go in and do the dirty work, so to speak, of cleaning up the astral pit and the mental and identity realms.

This is *our* job. This is *our* task. This is *our* joy. We are perfectly capable of doing this without going into a state of imbalance. Archangel Michael is absolutely unbending when he is dealing with the fallen beings, but he is not angry with them. He is not in his mind fighting a battle against them. He is simply doing his work, being completely centered in the peace of God.

For you to be most efficient in making the calls for the removing of the forces of poverty, you need to transcend the consciousness that you want to see removed. This we have given you the tools to do, both in this book and in our other books. I would consider it important for those who are using this book in order to make the calls that you also study the book *Warrior of Peace* and other of our books that talk about the duality consciousness. Certainly, you should be familiar with the teachings given by Maitreya, and you may find them in a concentrated form in the book *Cosmology of Evil*.

If a critical mass of people take this book, take the tools and teachings, and make use of them, then we can make an incredibly significant step towards removing poverty from this planet. If a critical mass of people took and used the tools and teachings Saint Germain has given in this book, then we could start a process that would quickly become irreversible and would lead to the complete removal of poverty from planet earth.

It is possible that, within a few decades, people would look back and would scarcely be able to understand that such dramatic changes could happen in such a short time. They would look at the specter of poverty as it has been hanging over humankind for thousands of years and they would say: "How could it disappear so quickly?" Probably, official society would never recognize the importance of spiritual people making the calls. If a critical mass of people would embrace the teachings and tools in this book, then I can assure you that poverty could become an impossibility in the lifetimes of many of you. Would this not be a great joy to your heart? Would it not give you a sense that you have fulfilled an important part of your purpose for coming to this planet? Would it not make you feel that it was worthwhile, even though this is such a difficult and dense planet upon which to embody?

I know many of you have gone through many hardships, many sufferings, but if you could feel that you had made an important contribution to the removal of poverty, would it not all have been worth it? Would you not feel this connection to the River of Life and a sense that, even though one human lifetime may seem insignificant, it can still be part of the cosmic purpose, the cosmic upward movement that is the River of Life?

Overcoming the recoil from the fallen beings

I know that if you start making the calls on poverty, you will go through a period where you will feel very burdened by the energies you are dealing with. You should be able to realize by now that, when you start using the tools in this book, the fallen beings will throw everything they have at you in all four levels. They will attempt to manipulate you. They will attempt to burden you in all ways. They might even attempt to do this with the people in your circle of influence. That is why you need to make the calls for the protection not only of yourself but of all people around you.

Again, I am not asking you to go into a state of fear or a sense of being at war or fighting the fallen beings. I am just asking you to make the calls so that we can do the work of

15 | Protecting Yourself from the Fallen Beings

protecting you. I am also asking you to be aware that when you feel burdened, when you feel you are under attack, it is because there is something, some illusion, in your consciousness that the fallen beings are using to burden you. I am asking you to look at that beam in your own eye and to use our teachings and tools to remove it so that you can transcend it and become even more efficient.

What I am telling you here is this: If you make the decision to seriously start using the tools and teachings in this book, you will go through an initial period where you will feel, perhaps, even more burdened than you feel today. You will feel you are being attacked. You should know that this is the fallen beings throwing everything at you in order to discourage you from doing the work that will lead to their removal from the earth. You should not be surprised that they would do this. They will do absolutely anything they can to prevent anyone from using the teachings and tools of the ascended masters because it will lead to their own removal from the earth. For them, it is seen as a life-and-death battle.

I am asking you to *not* see it this way but to simply be aware of what is happening and what will be happening. Then make the calls for it. Then look at yourself and overcome the illusion that gives them an inroad into your consciousness. If you do this knowingly, you will be surprised at how quickly you can work through this period. You will come out the other side feeling that you have now raised yourself to a point where the fallen beings cannot reach you as they used to be able to do. You have accelerated yourself. You have accelerated your consciousness beyond the reach of those fallen beings who were attacking you in the past. This is a great sense of freedom, a great sense of inner knowing.

You cannot awaken by remaining blind

My beloved, do you begin to see here that even though they say "ignorance is bliss," ignorance is *not* bliss? There are spiritual people who feel that all they need to do is to be positive and send out positive vibrations. There are those who say that you should not put your mind on anything dark or evil because even by making the calls or the invocations we are giving you, you are, they say, giving your energy to the dark forces. I can assure you that these invocations are designed in such a way that they will not give your energy to the dark forces, unless you give them from a state of extreme imbalance. If you give them with non-attachment, centered in peace, knowing that *we* will do the work, then you will not give your energies to the dark forces.

What I am pointing out to you is that the spiritual path is a path of awakening. You do not awaken by remaining blind. There are spiritual people who refuse to look at the existence of dark forces, and they think they can still walk the spiritual path, but you cannot walk the path beyond a certain level. The real path is that, as you begin to awaken yourself, you must look at the planet you are on. You must look at what is going on here. You must acknowledge the presence of fallen beings because they are such an intricate part of planet earth and have been for so long. You cannot walk the spiritual path on a planet like earth without becoming aware of the fallen beings. I am not asking you to fight them or give them energy. I am not asking you to be afraid of them. I am asking you to be aware.

Do you understand what I am saying? You cannot walk the spiritual path towards a higher state of consciousness by remaining unaware. You cannot walk the path by refusing to look at something just because it is inconvenient or unpleasant to you. You walk the path by being willing to look at *everything*.

First, you must look at the fallen beings. Then you will be disturbed when you begin to acknowledge the things Saint Germain talks about in this book. As you keep rising, you will come to a point where you have now transcended the fallen beings. Now you can look at them and acknowledge their existence with complete non-attachment and inner peace.

Looking at darkness while maintaining harmony

Some spiritual students think that it is so important to be at peace and maintain their inner harmony that they will not look at anything that might disturb that harmony. As long as there is *anything* that can disturb your inner harmony, you have not reached a high level of spiritual attainment. You have only created the outer impression of having spiritual attainment because you are supposedly always able to maintain this state of inner harmony and balance. This is not true spiritual attainment. This is not mastery.

The Buddha did not enter nirvana by ignoring the demons of Mara. The last test he faced was that he had to look at all the demons of Mara, and he had to allow them to do anything and everything they could think of to get him to react. He had to sit there and see it all and remain non-attached so that he did not react. *Then,* he could enter nirvana. You cannot enter your own personal nirvana until you are able and willing to look at everything the fallen beings can throw at you and simply look at it all and say: "I am not this."

You cannot walk the spiritual path by being unaware of what is happening on the planet where you have taken embodiment. You must see everything, and then you must see beyond it. You see that, behind all the demons of Mara, everything is still the Buddha nature. Everything is still one. You look at everything here on earth and you say: "I am not this." Then, you look at the oneness of the spiritual realm and you say: "I AM this. I am that 'I AM' up there, not the separate 'I am' down here." Then you can enter nirvana.

Be here Below all that You are Above

I will be the first to greet you. I am asking you to consider that your goal for taking embodiment on earth in this lifetime was not primarily to enter nirvana. It was to do some work while you are in embodiment on this planet. You came here to make a difference because you saw how critical this time is for the evolution of the earth. You set aside your personal entering of nirvana in order to do the work of raising the earth and setting free the billions of lifestreams that embody upon it.

With this, I simply want to welcome you into the ranks of those who consider themselves not only ascended master students but who are also beginning to consider themselves the extensions of the ascended masters on earth.

You are among those who are beginning to realize that the highest potential of earth is to be "as Above, so below." This will happen only when you become as Above, so below. Will you become here below all that you already are Above? I AM Mother Mary Above. Will *you* be Mother Mary below?

16 | PROTECTION FROM DARK FORCES

In the name of the I AM THAT I AM, Jesus Christ, I call upon Mother Mary, Archangel Michael, Astrea and Saint Germain to help us accelerate ourselves beyond the reach of the dark forces. Awaken people to the reality that we are spiritual beings and that we can co-create a new future by working with the ascended masters. I especially call for …

[Make your own calls here.]

Part 1

1. Archangel Michael, I accept your total protection for myself and all people in my circle of influence from any backlash from the fallen beings in the form of physical accidents, mishaps or acts of violence.

Archangel Michael, light so blue,
my heart has room for only you.
My mind is one, no longer two,
your love for me is ever true.

**Archangel Michael, you are here,
your light consumes all doubt and fear.
Your Presence is forever near,
you are to me so very dear.**

2. Archangel Michael, I accept your total protection for myself and all people in my circle of influence from any backlash from the fallen beings in the form of disease or problems with the physical body.

Archangel Michael, I will be,
all one with your reality.
No fear can hold me as I see,
this world no power has o'er me.

**Archangel Michael, you are here,
your light consumes all doubt and fear.
Your Presence is forever near,
you are to me so very dear.**

3. Archangel Michael, I accept your total protection for myself and all people in my circle of influence from any backlash from the fallen beings in the form of emotional projections causing erratic or insane behavior.

Archangel Michael, hold me tight,
shatter now the darkest night.
Clear my chakras with your light,
restore to me my inner sight.

**Archangel Michael, you are here,
your light consumes all doubt and fear.
Your Presence is forever near,
you are to me so very dear.**

4. Archangel Michael, I accept your total protection for myself and all people in my circle of influence from any backlash from the fallen beings in the form of emotional projections causing depression or a sense of discouragement.

Archangel Michael, now I stand,
with you the light I do command.
My heart I ever will expand,
till highest truth I understand.

**Archangel Michael, you are here,
your light consumes all doubt and fear.
Your Presence is forever near,
you are to me so very dear.**

5. Archangel Michael, I accept your total protection for myself and all people in my circle of influence from any backlash from the fallen beings in the form of mental projections causing confusion or mental instability.

> Archangel Michael, in my heart,
> from me you never will depart.
> Of hierarchy I am a part,
> I now accept a fresh new start.
>
> **Archangel Michael, you are here,**
> **your light consumes all doubt and fear.**
> **Your Presence is forever near,**
> **you are to me so very dear.**

6. Archangel Michael, I accept your total protection for myself and all people in my circle of influence from any backlash from the fallen beings in the form of mental projections causing fanaticism or closed-mindedness.

> Archangel Michael, sword of blue,
> all darkness you are cutting through.
> My Christhood I do now pursue,
> discernment shows me what is true.
>
> **Archangel Michael, you are here,**
> **your light consumes all doubt and fear.**
> **Your Presence is forever near,**
> **you are to me so very dear.**

7. Archangel Michael, I accept your total protection for myself and all people in my circle of influence from any backlash from the fallen beings in the form of identity projections causing attachments to certain belief systems.

Archangel Michael, in your wings,
I now let go of lesser things.
God's homing call in my heart rings,
my heart with yours forever sings.

**Archangel Michael, you are here,
your light consumes all doubt and fear.
Your Presence is forever near,
you are to me so very dear.**

8. Archangel Michael, I accept your total protection for myself and all people in my circle of influence from any backlash from the fallen beings in the form of identity projections causing an identity crisis or fanaticism.

Archangel Michael, take me home,
in higher spheres I want to roam.
I am reborn from cosmic foam,
my life is now a sacred poem.

**Archangel Michael, you are here,
your light consumes all doubt and fear.
Your Presence is forever near,
you are to me so very dear.**

9. Archangel Michael, I accept your total protection for myself and all people in my circle of influence from any backlash from the fallen beings in the form of any opposition to our spiritual growth.

Archangel Michael, light you are,
shining like the bluest star.
You are a cosmic avatar,
with you I will go very far.

**Archangel Michael, you are here,
your light consumes all doubt and fear.
Your Presence is forever near,
you are to me so very dear.**

Part 2

1. Beloved Astrea, I accept that you are cutting free myself and all people in my circle of influence from any fallen beings in embodiment or any people controlled by fallen beings in the three higher octaves.

Astrea, loving Being white,
your Presence is my pure delight,
your sword and circle white and blue,
the astral plane is cutting through.

**Astrea, come accelerate,
with purity I do vibrate,
release the fire so blue and white,
my aura filled with vibrant light.**

2. Beloved Astrea, I accept that you are cutting free myself and all people in my circle of influence from any fallen beings, demons or entities in the astral plane.

Astrea, calm the raging storm,
so purity will be the norm,
my aura filled with blue and white,
with shining armor, like a knight.

**Astrea, come accelerate,
with purity I do vibrate,
release the fire so blue and white,
my aura filled with vibrant light.**

3. Beloved Astrea, I accept that you are cutting free myself and all people in my circle of influence from any fallen beings or demons in the mental realm.

Astrea, come and cut me free,
from every binding entity,
let astral forces all be bound,
true freedom I have surely found.

**Astrea, come accelerate,
with purity I do vibrate,
release the fire so blue and white,
my aura filled with vibrant light.**

4. Beloved Astrea, I accept that you are cutting free myself and all people in my circle of influence from any fallen beings or demons in the identity octave.

Astrea, I sincerely urge,
from demons all, do me purge,
consume them all and take me higher,
I will endure your cleansing fire.

> Astrea, come accelerate,
> with purity I do vibrate,
> release the fire so blue and white,
> my aura filled with vibrant light.

5. Beloved Astrea, I accept that you are binding and consuming the demons and fallen beings in the astral plane who are attacking myself or any people in my circle of influence as an act of revenge for me making the calls for putting a stop to their activities.

> Astrea, do all spirits bind,
> so that I am no longer blind,
> I see the spirit and its twin,
> the victory of Christ I win.

> **Astrea, come accelerate,
> with purity I do vibrate,
> release the fire so blue and white,
> my aura filled with vibrant light.**

6. Beloved Astrea, I accept that you are binding and consuming the demons and fallen beings in the mental realm who are attacking myself or any people in my circle of influence as an act of revenge for me making the calls for putting a stop to their activities.

> Astrea, clear my every cell,
> from energies of death and hell,
> my body is now free to grow,
> each cell emits an inner glow.

**Astrea, come accelerate,
with purity I do vibrate,
release the fire so blue and white,
my aura filled with vibrant light.**

7. Beloved Astrea, I accept that you are binding and consuming the demons and fallen beings in the identity realm who are attacking myself or any people in my circle of influence as an act of revenge for me making the calls for putting a stop to their activities.

Astrea, clear my feeling mind,
in purity my peace I find,
with higher feeling you release,
I co-create in perfect peace.

**Astrea, come accelerate,
with purity I do vibrate,
release the fire so blue and white,
my aura filled with vibrant light.**

8. Beloved Astrea, I accept that you are binding and consuming the demons and fallen beings who are aggressively seeking to discourage me from doing the work that will lead to their removal from the earth.

Astrea, clear my mental realm,
my Christ self always at the helm,
I see now how to manifest,
the matrix that for all is best.

> Astrea, come accelerate,
> with purity I do vibrate,
> release the fire so blue and white,
> my aura filled with vibrant light.

9. Beloved Astrea, I accept that you are binding and consuming the demons and fallen beings who are seeking to prevent anyone from using the teachings and tools of the ascended masters that will lead to their removal from the earth.

> Astrea, with great clarity,
> I claim a new identity,
> etheric blueprint I now see,
> I co-create more consciously.

> Astrea, come accelerate,
> with purity I do vibrate,
> release the fire so blue and white,
> my aura filled with vibrant light.

Part 3

1. Mother Mary, I accept that you are helping myself and all people in my circle of influence see and transcend all physical habits that are making us vulnerable to the attacks of the demons and fallen beings in all for octaves.

> O blessed Mary, Mother mine,
> there is no greater love than thine,
> as we are one in heart and mind,
> my place in hierarchy I find.

**O Mother Mary, generate,
the song that does accelerate,
the earth into a higher state,
all matter does now scintillate.**

2. Mother Mary, I accept that you are helping myself and all people in my circle of influence see and transcend all emotional patterns that are making us vulnerable to the attacks of the demons and fallen beings in all for octaves.

I came to earth from heaven sent,
as I am in embodiment,
I use Divine authority,
commanding you to set earth free.

**O Mother Mary, generate,
the song that does accelerate,
the earth into a higher state,
all matter does now scintillate.**

3. Mother Mary, I accept that you are helping myself and all people in my circle of influence see and transcend all mental illusions that are making us vulnerable to the attacks of the demons and fallen beings in all for octaves.

I call now in God's sacred name,
for you to use your Mother Flame,
to burn all fear-based energy,
restoring sacred harmony.

**O Mother Mary, generate,
the song that does accelerate,
the earth into a higher state,
all matter does now scintillate.**

4. Mother Mary, I accept that you are helping myself and all people in my circle of influence see and transcend all false sense of identity that is making us vulnerable to the attacks of the demons and fallen beings in all for octaves.

Your sacred name I hereby praise,
collective consciousness you raise,
no more of fear and doubt and shame,
consume it with your Mother Flame.

**O Mother Mary, generate,
the song that does accelerate,
the earth into a higher state,
all matter does now scintillate.**

5. Mother Mary, I accept that you are helping myself and all people in my circle of influence see and transcend any tendency to think we are in opposition to the fallen beings or other people.

All darkness from the earth you purge,
your light moves as a mighty surge,
no force of darkness can now stop,
the spiral that goes only up.

> **O Mother Mary, generate,**
> **the song that does accelerate,**
> **the earth into a higher state,**
> **all matter does now scintillate.**

6. Mother Mary, I accept that you are helping myself and all people in my circle of influence see and transcend any tendency to think we have to live an extremist or unbalanced lifestyle in order to fulfill our Divine plans.

> All elemental life you bless,
> removing from them man-made stress,
> the nature spirits are now free,
> outpicturing Divine decree.

> **O Mother Mary, generate,**
> **the song that does accelerate,**
> **the earth into a higher state,**
> **all matter does now scintillate.**

7. Mother Mary, I accept that you are helping myself and all people in my circle of influence see and transcend any tendency to go into a mindset where we produce inharmonious energies that actually feed the dark forces.

> I raise my voice and take my stand,
> a stop to war I do command,
> no more shall warring scar the earth,
> a golden age is given birth.

> **O Mother Mary, generate,
> the song that does accelerate,
> the earth into a higher state,
> all matter does now scintillate.**

8. Mother Mary, I accept that you are helping myself and all people in my circle of influence see and transcend the intent of the fallen beings to force us to go towards greater and greater extremes in order to defeat an enemy.

> As Mother Earth is free at last,
> disasters belong to the past,
> your Mother Light is so intense,
> that matter is now far less dense.

> **O Mother Mary, generate,
> the song that does accelerate,
> the earth into a higher state,
> all matter does now scintillate.**

9. Mother Mary, I accept that you are helping myself and all people in my circle of influence see and transcend any imbalance in the three higher bodies that leads to imbalances at the physical level.

> In Mother Light the earth is pure,
> the upward spiral will endure,
> prosperity is now the norm,
> God's vision manifest as form.

> O Mother Mary, generate,
> the song that does accelerate,
> the earth into a higher state,
> all matter does now scintillate.

Part 4

1. Saint Germain, send oceans of violet flame into the lives of myself and all people in my circle of influence. Transmute any karmic vulnerability to physical accidents, mishaps or other events that block our Divine plans.

> O Saint Germain, you do inspire,
> my vision raised forever higher,
> with you I form a figure-eight,
> your Golden Age I co-create.

> **O Saint Germain, what love you bring,**
> **it truly makes all matter sing,**
> **your violet flame does all restore,**
> **with you we are becoming more.**

2. Saint Germain, send oceans of violet flame into the physical bodies of myself and all people in my circle of influence. Transmute any karmic vulnerability to physical diseases or bodily imbalances that block our Divine plans.

> O Saint Germain, what Freedom Flame,
> released when we recite your name,
> acceleration is your gift,
> our planet it will surely lift.

**O Saint Germain, what love you bring,
it truly makes all matter sing,
your violet flame does all restore,
with you we are becoming more.**

3. Saint Germain, send oceans of violet flame into the emotional bodies of myself and all people in my circle of influence. Transmute any karmic ties to any beings in the emotional octave and any tendency for depression or emotional instability.

O Saint Germain, in love we claim,
our right to bring your violet flame,
from you Above, to us below,
it is an all-transforming flow.

**O Saint Germain, what love you bring,
it truly makes all matter sing,
your violet flame does all restore,
with you we are becoming more.**

4. Saint Germain, send oceans of violet flame into the mental bodies of myself and all people in my circle of influence. Transmute any karmic ties to any beings in the mental octave and any tendency for confusion or lack of clarity.

O Saint Germain, I love you so,
my aura filled with violet glow,
my chakras filled with violet fire,
I am your cosmic amplifier.

**O Saint Germain, what love you bring,
it truly makes all matter sing,
your violet flame does all restore,
with you we are becoming more.**

5. Saint Germain, send oceans of violet flame into the identity bodies of myself and all people in my circle of influence. Transmute any karmic ties to any beings in the identity octave and any tendency for fanaticism or closed-mindedness.

O Saint Germain, I am now free,
your violet flame is therapy,
transform all hang-ups in my mind,
as inner peace I surely find.

**O Saint Germain, what love you bring,
it truly makes all matter sing,
your violet flame does all restore,
with you we are becoming more.**

6. Saint Germain, send oceans of violet flame into the lives of myself and all people in my circle of influence. Transmute any karmic vulnerability that prevents us from walking a balanced path and living a balanced life.

O Saint Germain, my body pure,
your violet flame for all is cure,
consume the cause of all disease,
and therefore I am all at ease.

**O Saint Germain, what love you bring,
it truly makes all matter sing,
your violet flame does all restore,
with you we are becoming more.**

7. Saint Germain, send oceans of violet flame into the lives of myself and all people in my circle of influence. Transmute any karmic vulnerability that prevents us from finding the personal inner balance that allows us to make the calls that give the ascended masters the authority to remove the dark forces from the earth.

O Saint Germain, I'm karma-free,
the past no longer burdens me,
a brand new opportunity,
I am in Christic unity.

**O Saint Germain, what love you bring,
it truly makes all matter sing,
your violet flame does all restore,
with you we are becoming more.**

8. Saint Germain, send oceans of violet flame into the lives of myself and all people in my circle of influence. Transmute any illusion in our own consciousness that makes us vulnerable to the energies and attacks from the dark forces.

O Saint Germain, we are now one,
I am for you a violet sun,
as we transform this planet earth,
your Golden Age is given birth.

> O Saint Germain, what love you bring,
> it truly makes all matter sing,
> your violet flame does all restore,
> with you we are becoming more.

9. Saint Germain, send oceans of violet flame into the lives of myself and all people in my circle of influence. Transmute any karmic vulnerability and energies so that the fallen beings can no longer hurt us because we have accelerated our consciousness beyond their reach.

> O Saint Germain, the earth is free,
> from burden of duality,
> in oneness we bring what is best,
> your Golden Age is manifest.

> O Saint Germain, what love you bring,
> it truly makes all matter sing,
> your violet flame does all restore,
> with you we are becoming more.

Sealing

In the name of the I AM THAT I AM, I accept that Archangel Michael, Astrea and Shiva form an impenetrable shield around myself and all constructive people, sealing us from all fear-based energies in all four octaves. I accept that the Light of God is consuming and transforming all fear-based energies that make up the dark forces!

www.ingramcontent.com/pod-product-compliance
Lightning Source LLC
Chambersburg PA
CBHW031843220426
43663CB00006B/481